Introducing Aesthetics and the Philosophy of Art

Introducing Aesthetics and the Philosophy of Art

Darren Hudson Hick

BLOOMSBURY ACADEMIC
LONDON • NEW YORK • OXFORD • NEW DELHI • SYDNEY

BLOOMSBURY ACADEMIC
Bloomsbury Publishing Plc
50 Bedford Square, London, WC1B 3DP, UK
1385 Broadway, New York, NY 10018, USA

BLOOMSBURY, BLOOMSBURY ACADEMIC and the Diana logo are trademarks of
Bloomsbury Publishing Plc

First published 2017
Reprinted 2019

A catalogue record for this book is available from the British Library.

Library of Congress Cataloging-In-Publication Data
Names: Hick, Darren Hudson, author.
Title: Introducing aesthetics and the philosophy of art / Darren Hudson Hick.
Description: New York : Bloomsbury Academic, An Imprint of Bloomsbury
Publishing Plc, 2017. | Includes bibliographical references and index.
Identifiers: LCCN 2016058156| ISBN 9781350006898 (hb) | ISBN 9781350006928 (epdf)
Subjects: LCSH: Aesthetics. | Art–Philosophy.
Classification: LCC BH201 .H53 2017 | DDC 111/.85–dc23
LC record available at https://lccn.loc.gov/2016058156

ISBN: HB: 978-1-3500-0689-8
PB: 978-1-3500-0690-4
ePDF: 978-1-3500-0692-8
eBook: 978-1-3500-0691-1

Cover design: Avni Patel
Cover image: © Delaina Pearson, 2017

Typeset by Fakenham Prepress Solutions, Fakenham, Norfolk, NR21 8NN

To find out more about our authors and books visit www.bloomsbury.com
and sign up for our newsletters.

This book is dedicated to the memory of
R. A. Sharpe, who first introduced me to
aesthetics, and whose work and teaching continue
to guide me.

Contents

8 Aesthetics Without Art 217

Figures

Preface

You may be wondering: *Why is there a picture of plastic pink flamingos on the cover of this book? I thought this was a book about the philosophy of* art *– are those* art?

Good question.

The particular flamingos depicted on the cover are the pair designed by Don Featherstone back in 1957: they're the *original* plastic pink flamingos. (Well, not the *original* originals, but we'll get to that on page 123.) Featherstone created the first pink flamingos as part of his job with Union Products, an American manufacturer of plastic lawn ornaments, and they have since become a staple on American lawns – an icon of popular culture – spawning a number of knock-off flamingo species. Featherstone was trained as a sculptor at the school of the Worcester Art Museum, and legally speaking, at least, his pink flamingos are sculptures. Does *that* mean they're art?

Good question.

In 1996, the satirical science magazine *Annals of Improbable Research* awarded Featherstone the tongue-in-cheek Ig Nobel Prize in Art. If plastic pink flamingos *are* art – even if they're *bad* art – does that mean they *mean* something? If so, what? And how would we know? Would we need to ask Featherstone? If they *aren't* art, what standards should I judge them by?

The *New York Times* calls the Featherstone flamingo '[l]ess hideous than a garden gnome, more diplomatic than a lawn jockey'.[1] Calling garden gnomes 'hideous' seems a little harsh; calling lawn jockeys 'undiplomatic' seems more than a little charitable. Let's start with the gnomes: what *makes* them hideous, or at least *more hideous* than plastic pink flamingos? Is that just a matter of preference, or is there some fact of the matter of which is more hideous? Can I tell just by looking at a gnome or flamingo that one is more hideous than the other? Professor Robert Thomson once suggested: 'As iconic emblems of kitsch, there are two pillars of cheesy campiness in the American pantheon. One is the velvet Elvis. The other is the pink flamingo.'[2]

Is *kitschiness* a bad thing to have? What about *cheesiness*? For that matter, what about downright *ugliness*? As for lawn jockeys, would it be wrong to put one on your lawn? How about on the cover of your book? If lawn jockeys are immoral depictions of African Americans, does that make them bad art? Not art at all? Does morality have anything to do with aesthetics?

Featherstone's original pink flamingos were advertised with instructions 'Place in garden, lawn, to beautify landscape.' Thousands upon thousands of Americans seem to have followed those instructions. Indeed, the flamingos on the cover of this book now reside on my front lawn. What do you think the chances are that they have beautified my yard? My neighbourhood? Would my lawn be prettier if, instead, a pair of real pink flamingos had descended upon it?

Featherstone's pink flamingos are pink because they're made with plastic that has been dyed pink. *Real* pink flamingos – the kind that hatch from eggs – are pink because of all of the beta-carotene-loaded algae that they eat. Does knowing that make them more beautiful? Less beautiful? Does it matter at all? Would it matter to you if they were just dyed pink?

Although plastic pink flamingos don't tend to come up much in aesthetics and the philosophy of art, the questions they raise certainly do. None of these are easy questions, and I'm not going to tell you the answers. If philosophy came with easy answers, most philosophers probably wouldn't do it. I have views of my own on at least some of these questions, but I'm not going to tell you what those are either. That isn't what this book is about. Rather, this text is designed to introduce you to a number of the core issues in aesthetics and the philosophy of art, some of which have bothered thinkers since antiquity, and most of which still bother philosophers today. Other questions are quite new. We will consider an array of theories and arguments, both historical and contemporary, leaving it up to you to figure out which view, if any, is the best view. Perhaps they all miss the mark, and *you* have the best view – if so, all the better for aesthetics. Philosophy is a dialectical discipline – it grows through ongoing investigation, consideration and discussion. This book is written to give you the background and tools to engage in and contribute to that discussion.

Ultimately, aesthetics and the philosophy of art are *about* things in the world – things like the Featherstone pink flamingo. As much as the philosophers who ask them, it is things like these that raise philosophical questions and challenge philosophical theories. As such, I provide a variety of examples throughout the text to help raise, illustrate and – in some cases – complicate these issues. In particular, each chapter opens with an extended case to serve as a starting point to motivate the problems in the chapter, and to operate as a touchstone through the discussion. A number of these are new to this edition. Each chapter closes with a number of tools for readers, including a short chapter summary, a timeline of artworks and philosophical views discussed through the chapter, an index of key terms and concepts from the chapter, and a guide to further reading on the topics discussed. As well, regarding the idea that aesthetics and the philosophy of art *are* dialectical in nature, I have provided a list of three or four questions that have been left unresolved in each chapter. Some of these have been addressed elsewhere by philosophers, but most have not.

In addition to the eight chapters in this book, I have included an extended Introduction, meant to provide a historical grounding to the topics discussed in depth in the chapters. Much of the history of aesthetics and the philosophy of art tends to go overlooked by contemporary philosophers (with the exceptions of Plato, Aristotle, Hume and Kant). However, the history of philosophy is rich with discussion on issues fundamental to contemporary aesthetics. And so, while historical discussion is interwoven into each chapter, the Introduction provides a developmental overview of the discipline, from its beginnings in pre-Socratic thinking up to the nineteenth century, where the project of defining 'art' – the topic of Chapter 1 – begins in earnest.

I owe many thanks to my editor Colleen Coalter and designers [Cover Designer] and Fakenham Prepress Solutions [and anyone else at Bloomsbury who I haven't thought of] for their effort and encouragement throughout the creation of this edition. I want to thank my many friends and colleagues who have supported this book, particularly Craig Derksen, Cynthia Freeland, Sherri Irvin, Francesca di Poppa and Danny Nathan. I especially want to thank my wife, Delaina Pearson, who now probably knows far more about the ontology of art than most other soil scientists, and yet doesn't openly complain about this. Finally, I want to thank the two anonymous reviewers whose early feedback helped to shape the current edition of this text, and my many, many students who have helped to shape not only how I teach aesthetics and the philosophy of art, but how I think about them as well.

Introduction: Aesthetics and the Philosophy of Art, An Extremely Brief History

Chapter Outline

I. On art and beauty

Within philosophy, 'aesthetics' and 'the philosophy of art' are often treated as interchangeable terms, and indeed both tend to refer to the same body of interrelated questions in the field. The meaning of 'philosophy of art' is clear enough – it refers to those issues in philosophy that pertain to art: to painting and sculpture, to literature and theatre, and so on. 'Aesthetics', meanwhile, can be a trickier issue. The term itself was not coined until the eighteenth century, when it was used by the German philosopher Alexander Baumgarten to describe perception and judgement by means of the senses, as opposed to the intellect. Traditionally, however, talk of aesthetics is couched in terms of beauty, and such talk has a much longer history in philosophy. In contemporary discussion, a great many terms are likewise treated as aesthetic ones – elegance, gracefulness, sublimity, and certainly the opposite of beauty, ugliness; however, beauty tends to be regarded as the central concept upon which these others depend. The lumping together of 'aesthetics' and 'the philosophy of art' is, as such, perhaps not difficult to understand. Certainly, we judge artworks using aesthetic terms, and there seems no greater compliment for a work of art than to judge it beautiful. Yet, we also find beauty in nature, in the human form, and perhaps in everyday items, and these too concern aestheticians. Conversely, contemporary art seems less and less concerned with beauty, and more and more concerned with mankind, with society and with art itself. Nevertheless, throughout the history of Western philosophy, issues of beauty and issues of art have a habit of becoming intertwined, and it is the purpose of this introduction to highlight some of the central threads in this tradition before turning in the book to a selection of topics that preoccupy contemporary aesthetics.

Strictly speaking, this introduction is not necessary for an understanding of the chapters to follow. However, all too often it seems, contemporary philosophers of art tend to ignore the long history of aesthetics, a valuable foundation upon which to study today's central topics of discussion. That being said, it simply is not possible to give a full and comprehensive history of Western aesthetics in so small as space as this. Rather, I will focus here on only some of the central lines of thinking in the history of the philosophy of art, and on some of its central figures. Indeed, at several points, entire centuries will be skipped over and any number of important philosophers will be left out entirely. For a more complete history, I would recommend either Monroe C. Beardsley's *Aesthetics from Classical Greece to the Present* (University of Alabama Press, 1996) or the even more comprehensive *History of Aesthetics* in three volumes by Władysław Tatarkiewicz (Continuum, 2005).

II. The ancient period

The Pythagoreans and the Sophists

In the Western tradition, aesthetics and the philosophy of art find their origin where philosophy generally is born – in ancient Greece – and perhaps the first philosophical approach to beauty and the arts comes from the man credited with coining the term 'philosophy', Pythagoras. Although most of what we know of Pythagoras comes from references written long after he died, a number of views have been attributed to him and his followers. Pythagoras is perhaps best known for his Pythagorean theorem – the principle that the square of the length of the hypotenuse of a right-angled triangle is equal to the sum of the square of the lengths of the other two sides – though the theorem was only a small part of a much grander view of the universe. Pythagoras's followers, the Pythagoreans, and perhaps

Pythagoras himself, believed that underlying everything in the universe was mathematics – that the universe was *harmonious, ordered* and *regular*, and that such ordered regularity was a guarantee of beauty. On this basis, they believed that beauty itself was a quantifiable and objective principle of nature.

Pythagoras is credited with discovering the mathematical basis to musical intervals – that musical strings at fixed lengths relative to each other produce harmonious sounds, and that the relation between these is grounded in simple numeric ratios. Pythagoras was not interested in music as a distinct philosophical project, however, nor even as an artistic pursuit, but rather for the part it played in his larger philosophical framework. First, music offered insight into the laws of order, harmony and regularity of nature, and so knowledge of the universe itself. (As such, music was thought by the Pythagoreans to be a discovery, and not an invention, of mankind.) Second, because the soul too was thought by the Pythagoreans to have a mathematical basis, and to be harmoniously or inharmoniously proportioned, music was thought to have the power both to express and to purify the soul – to allow the soul temporary freedom from the body.

It is difficult to overestimate the importance of these Pythagorean views. Pythagoras's discovery of the mathematical nature of musical intervals is the fundamental basis to musical theory today. But more than this, the view that beauty has an objective, mathematical basis, and that music allows for a purging of the soul, would resonate both through the arts and philosophy in the centuries to come.

The view that beauty is grounded in mathematical principles had an enormous effect not only on music, but also on the plastic arts: architecture, sculpture and painting. On the notion that beauty followed discoverable laws, the classical Greek artists worked to develop principled, quantifiable rules of art. In music, these were called the *nomos* (or *law*); in the plastic arts, these were called the *canon* (or *measure*). The sculptor Polyclitus was perhaps the first – or at least the most famous – to set out a list of such rules in his *Canon*. Polyclitus's school lasted for three generations, but the effect of his *Canon* lasted much longer, and can be found throughout the sculpture and architecture of the ancient world and well beyond. Others wrote on rules of proportion in music, in song and in painting.

The Pythagorean views of beauty and the arts were not without their detractors, however. In particular, challenges came from the Sophists, another group of early Greek philosophers. To the notion that beauty is objective and quantifiable, the Sophists proposed the theory that beauty is relative to the appreciator – to the sort of thing that he is, to his own particular tastes and to his circumstances. Where the Pythagoreans were objectivists about beauty, the Sophists were firm subjectivists. And although the Sophist perspective did not have the immediate effect in the arts that the Pythagorean view did, this counterproposal to the Pythagorean view would continue to challenge thinking about the arts for centuries to come. To the Pythagorean view that music had the power to purify the soul, the Sophist Gorgias suggested that poetry – through words – moved audiences to terror, pity and sadness, allowing audience members to feel others' problems as their own. Gorgias compared the effect to that of drugs, 'poisoning' the soul. Theatre enchanted its audience and threw a spell over it, and so its effects could be as negative as they could be positive.

Socrates and Plato

Socrates is considered by many to be the father of Western philosophy. Because Socrates himself never wrote down any of his philosophy, what we know about his views we get primarily from the dialogues written by his pupils, Plato and Xenophon, in which the authors chronicle Socrates' encounters with various philosophers and public figures. However, because of this, it can be difficult at times to determine where Socrates ends and his students begin.

In Xenophon's dialogue, the *Memorabilia*, Socrates is challenged by the philosopher Aristippus about the nature of beauty. Socrates argues that a thing capable of being used by man is beautiful when it is well suited to its purpose. What is beautiful in wrestling may be ugly in running, and vice versa. In the wrong conditions, he suggests, a painting is more apt to take joy away than give it. Here, Socrates' notion of beauty seems largely synonymous with the 'good', and seems heavily influenced by the relativist views of the Sophists. Later in the *Memorabilia*, Socrates questions the painter Parrhasius and the sculptor Cleiton about the representational nature of the plastic arts. The artist, Socrates observes, does not merely represent the human form as it is found in any particular model, but takes the most beautiful aspects from many models and puts them together. At one and the same time, the artist imitates and idealizes – not only in the proportions of the body, but also in representing the soul through the expression depicted in the representation. Here, Socrates' thinking seems to draw on the Pythagorean view. In Xenophon's Socrates, then, we find the central clash in the ancient Greeks' central concepts of beauty.

In an early dialogue by Plato, *Hippias Major*, Socrates tackles the notion of beauty with the Sophist, Hippias. Socrates argues, contrary to the view expressed in the *Memorabilia*, that beauty cannot be equated with the good, nor with what is useful. Rather, Socrates suggests, we might think of beauty as that which makes us feel joy through sight and sound. However appealing, Socrates argues that such an understanding leaves out the beauty of noble deeds and laws, which are grounded neither in sight nor sound. Socrates struggles, but is unable to reach a satisfactory definition of beauty in the *Hippias Major*. In the later dialogues of the *Timaeus*, the *Philebus* and the *Sophist*, however, Plato's Socrates returns to a Pythagorean notion, suggesting that what is beautiful is proportionate, and what is disproportionate is always ugly.

In the *Ion*, Plato turns to Gorgias's suggestion that poets could enchant, and so poison, their listeners. Ion is a rhapsode, a dramatic reader of poetry – in particular, the works of Homer. When Socrates encounters him, Ion has just won first prize at the festival of Asclepius, the god of healing. Ion is understandably a bit high on his achievement. Socrates draws Ion into a discussion about where he gets his ability to so wonderfully interpret, embellish and deliver Homer's poetry. When Ion is unable to explain his ability, Socrates suggests that rather that being a skill, Ion's ability comes from divine inspiration. Where the poets are compelled by the gods, Socrates suggests, the rhapsode is in turn inspired by the poets. Ion admits that, when reciting Homer, he is often overcome with emotion, and Socrates points out that the same happens to audience members. In this way, Socrates contends, neither the poet, nor the rhapsode, nor the audience member is in his right mind when dealing with poetry. As the poet is overcome with a tragedy, so too is the rhapsode, and in turn the audience.

In the later Platonic dialogue, the *Republic*, Socrates suggests that while we praise the poet's ability to so affect us, this is at odds with our desire to keep our emotions in check. By the time Plato writes the *Republic*, it seems fairly clear that he is incorporating his own philosophies, and inserting them into the mouth of Socrates. Plato, through the character of Socrates, suggests that the poet uses *imitation* to appeal to the emotional part of the soul, which is ordinarily kept in check by the soul's rational aspect. With his rationality overwhelmed by his emotions, man is out of control, and imitation is to blame. The representational arts, Plato believed, had another failing as well: by giving us only a small part – an image – of the subject, they misrepresent reality. In depicting courage or honour or even man, the artist only gives us the *appearance* of what he imitates, and gives us no access to its true *form*. Being necessarily particular, any such representation cannot represent courage or honour or man per se, but only a shadow of these things, only the barest suggestion of what they are about. There is courage, and then there are Achilles' acts of courage, and then there is Homer's representation of Achilles' courageous acts in the *Iliad*. Rather than getting closer to the ideal – as Xenophon's Socrates contends – the artist's representation is far removed from the true form of courage. Neither Homer nor Ion know about courage – rather, only about its appearance – and it is this appearance, Plato contends, which so appeals to the soul's emotional aspect and overcomes our reason.

In his final dialogue, the *Laws*, Plato seems to have reached a conclusion on the matter of beauty and art. Here, through the character of the Athenian, Plato suggests that the sense of beauty – grounded in such formal matters as proportion, harmony and order – is a sense peculiar to man, and which connects him to the gods. It is the ideal arrangement of parts that makes these things beautiful, and not merely how they appear to the audience. He voices approval of those works which adhere to these proper qualities, and disapproval of those which abandon such forms and through imitation instead appeal to man's harmful, irrational pleasures.

Aristotle

Plato's pupil, Aristotle, wrote several treatises on aesthetics – substantially more than any before him – but only part of one survives – the *Poetics* – and this seems to be a collection of his lectures prepared by his students. Although originally covering theatrical tragedy and comedy, the section of the *Poetics* dealing with comedy has been lost. However, from what remains we can find much of Aristotle's thinking about the arts. Where Plato condemned the imitative arts for being far removed from the true forms of things, Aristotle praised the imitative arts for their imitation. Aristotle contends that all of us are born both with the instinct to imitate and the instinct to enjoy works of imitation. He notes that where the sight of something causes us pain, contemplating an image of that same thing may give us pleasure, and the arts allow us to exercise this uniquely human capacity. It is not *what* is imitated that gives us pleasure, Aristotle argues, but rather imitation *itself*.

Imitation, for Aristotle, is not simply slavish copying. The imitative arts – painting, sculpture, poetry, music – may represent things as they really are, as better than they are or as worse than they are. The artist may represent things as they are *said* or *thought* to be or as they *ought* to be. As such, he may embellish on reality, and so surpass it. Contrary to Plato's argument that the imitative arts are faulty in only giving us the particular and not what it really true, Aristotle suggests the opposite. Poetry, he says, is more profound than history: where history deals with particulars and so represents only some particular thing, poetry trades in what is universal to man, and allows us to present something *general*. The artist does not merely *imitate*; rather, in doing so, he *creates*.

Where Plato argued in the *Republic* that in appealing to the emotional part of us, poetry is to be condemned, Aristotle contends that the instinct to create and enjoy imitation is part of what makes us uniquely human. And where Plato's Socrates argues in the *Ion* that in being overcome by poetry, we descend into madness, Aristotle suggests that the emotional effect of poetry is therapeutic – it is *helpful* to the human condition, not *harmful*. Poetry, including theatre, allows us to vent and so purge our emotions of pity and fear, a phenomenon Aristotle called *catharsis*. Rather than *soothing* fears and anxieties, Aristotle suggests, theatre allows the audience to safely *engage* with them, and theatrical plots, he argues, should be designed to promote just this. Although spectacle can arouse our pity and fear, the best theatrical route to catharsis, Aristotle contends, is through the believable unfolding of action on stage. As such, for the sake of the plot and so catharsis, it is better to represent something impossible but believable than something actual but improbable.

As for beauty, Aristotle suggests it is grounded in size and order, and is a particular form of goodness and pleasure. As such, Aristotle follows the path set out by the Pythagoreans and developed by Socrates and Plato. However, Aristotle adds a new element to this perspective: moderation. If something – a person, an animal, a plot – is either too big or too small to be easily apprehended by the viewer, it cannot be beautiful. Rather, it must appear *unified* to its audience. Beauty, for Aristotle, is formal in nature. In Aristotle's terminology, it is a 'formal cause'.

The theories set out by the Pythagoreans, by the Sophists, and by Socrates, Plato, and Aristotle, have had an immeasurable effect on the philosophy to follow, and no less in aesthetics than in any other area of the discipline. In the centuries immediately following, their views dominated thinking about beauty and the arts, and were variously championed, challenged and dissected, but remained largely unchanged.

III. The Middle Ages

St Augustine and St Bonaventure

The Battle of Carthage in 146 BCE between the expanding Roman Republic and the Greek state of Carthage effectively brought an end to ancient Greece, and established the Greek peninsula as a domain of Roman rule. The Roman Republic became the Roman Empire, and as the Empire enveloped the Mediterranean and surrounding regions, the influence of Greek culture spread through the Empire. The Roman gods took on the traits of the Greek deities, and Roman artisans largely focused on copying and adapting the art and style of the ancient Greeks. However, about the middle of the third century CE, the Empire nearly collapsed under a series of military, political and economic crises, and shortly after this, Christianity began to gain a foothold. Late in the Roman Empire, Christianity had become so widespread that it gained not only tolerance but acceptance, and in 380 became the official religion of the Empire.

In 387, a young philosopher, Augustine of Hippo, was converted to Christianity, and within a decade became a bishop. Augustine had written his major treatise on beauty prior to his conversion, and sought later in his work to find a way to meld his classically influenced beliefs on beauty with his newfound religious beliefs. Augustine's basic aesthetic perspective was firmly rooted in classical principles. Sensuous beauty, for Augustine, consists in the harmony, order and unity of a thing's parts: the more harmonious, ordered and unified, the more beautiful. And what is beautiful, argues Augustine, gives pleasure. This early view of Augustine's is very much in line with the Pythagorean perspective: the world, Augustine suggested, is a 'beautiful poem'. However, Augustine would later contend, above the beauty sensible to the eyes and ears is spiritual beauty – the beauty of the soul – accessible not to the senses but to the intellect. In this, Augustine seems to be following a Platonic line of thinking – that there is, beyond this physical world, some true measure of things which is only dimly reflected in what we see. However, Augustine goes a step further, folding Plato's thinking into an explicitly Christian construction. Physical beauty, the late Augustine argues, is but a reflection of the highest beauty: the beauty of God.

Augustine's influence is perhaps due as much to circumstances of history as to the strength of his views. In the centuries following Augustine's writing, there was a widespread revolt in the West on all things pagan; as a result much of classical philosophy became inaccessible for centuries, and its direct influence quickly waned. However, perhaps because of its Christian trappings, Augustine's thinking was kept alive, and served to influence a number of philosophers who followed him, including the Carolingian philosophers in the eighth and ninth centuries, and thinkers in the Benedictine Order of Cistercians in the twelfth century. However, Augustine's influence is perhaps best seen in the thinking of St Bonaventure, a thirteenth-century Italian cardinal and scholastic philosopher.

The scholastics were interested in reconciling ancient Greek philosophy with Christian doctrines, and the period of high scholasticism in the thirteenth and fourteenth centuries was dominated by two groups: the Franciscans and the Dominicans. Bonaventure was a Franciscan. His views were decidedly Platonic in structure, and Augustine's influence is clear. Augustine had called the world a 'beautiful poem', and Bonaventure argues that, like a poem, the world's beauty can only be beheld when considered in its entirety. Like Augustine, Bonaventure argues that the world is beautiful because its creator, God, is the source of true beauty. The world's beauty, Bonaventure suggests, is based on proper proportion, this proportion on congruity, and this congruity on quantifiable equality. In the spiritual arena, Bonaventure suggested that beauty consists in ideas, while in the physical world, it consists in material parts and their relations.

It is through perception, Bonaventure contends, that we become aware of physical beauty. When the mind of the perceiver and the form of the perceived are in harmony, there is pleasure, and so the sensuous world penetrates to the human soul. Following Augustine, Bonaventure argues that this pleasure – and the beauty that causes it – can come in degrees, and is subject to fixed laws. In art, Bonaventure suggests, beauty consists both in the model – what is represented – and in the image itself. The task of the artist for Bonaventure is to create beautiful, useful and enduring works.

St Thomas Aquinas

A contemporary of Bonaventure's, but of the Dominican Order, was St Thomas Aquinas, perhaps the most influential philosopher of the medieval period. Where Bonaventure was decidedly Platonic in his influences, Aquinas was Aristotelian. Aquinas wrote little on aesthetics, and was concerned with its issues only insofar as they worked into his grander philosophical projects, but this does not diminish the influence of what he did have to say on the topic.

Knowledge, argues Aquinas, consists of understanding a thing's essential nature, and both seeing and knowing are cognitive acts. Beauty, Aquinas contends, is necessarily wrapped up in the pleasure that it provides, and where 'useful' things give pleasure distantly, beauty is *immediately* pleasurable. Where the 'good' is what we aspire to, beauty is what we contemplate, and our desire for beauty is immediately satisfied upon apprehending it. The pleasure of beauty is chiefly derived from sight, Aquinas argues, and so understanding a thing's beauty comes from sensorily apprehending its formal, essential nature, but 'seeing' for Aquinas was an essentially intellectual affair, and so applied not only to seeing *visually* but also *contemplatively*. Where, from a Platonic perspective, a thing's beauty is derived from some higher beauty which it reflects, on the Aristotelian view that Aquinas develops, a thing's beauty is known simply through its very apprehensible, formal nature. There is, for Aquinas, no single thing, *beauty*, which all beautiful things exhibit. Rather, there are all manner of qualities we call 'beauty', and the pleasure of beauty depends both on the perceiver and the perceived, the subject and the object.

A thing's beauty, Aquinas suggests, depends upon three conditions: its integrity or perfection; its proportion or harmony; and its brightness or clarity. Regarding the first condition, if something lacks something which it requires or has something which it should not, it lacks integrity or is imperfect, and so in this respect cannot be beautiful. A man with a missing limb and a play with a superfluous act would both lack integrity, and so beauty. The second condition is Pythagorean in conception, but Aquinas takes harmony to include not only the quantitative, but also the qualitative – for instance, in the relation between a thing and its soul, or in how well a representation aligns with what is represented. In discussing the third condition – brightness or clarity – Aquinas sometimes speaks literally, as in the vibrancy of colour, and sometimes figuratively, as in spiritual 'clarity' or 'clarity' of virtue. All of these conditions depend upon our apprehension of the object, and where all three conditions are fulfilled, we apprehend beauty. In line with Bonaventure, Aquinas suggests that the goal of art is to produce something beautiful, and that beauty may rest in the artwork itself or in its accomplishment as a representation.

IV. The modern period

Throughout the ancient period, art had focused almost exclusively on the gods and heroes of myth – first those of the Greeks, and then those of the

Romans modelled upon them. Most of the great works of ancient Greek architecture had been temples and monuments to the gods, and the Romans largely followed suit. With the Christianizing of the Roman Empire, however, the great works of architecture in Rome became basilicas and cathedrals, and both sculpture and painting shifted from representing the gods and heroes of the Greeks and Romans to representing public figures and then, largely, to biblical themes.

About the time of Europe's Black Death pandemic in the mid-fourteenth century, however, something happened: artists and writers began to look back upon the ancient period with a renewed fondness – not as a period of pagan worship, but as a period of learning and philosophy. Thus began the rise of *humanism*, and with it, the *Renaissance*. The influence of Christianity was by no means extinguished, but artists began to focus as much on man as on God. The study of poetry gained renewed life, and all manner of thinkers moved to weigh in on matters of art and beauty.

Ficino and Alberti

One of the most influential of the early humanists was Marsilio Ficino. A devotee of Plato, Ficino translated Plato's complete works into Latin, which had been revived by the humanists as a spoken language. However, Ficino attempted to temper Plato's theories with those of other classical thinkers, and as a result produced influential theories of his own. First, Ficino argued that beauty could be found not only in the relations between things – order, proportion and harmony – but also in their brilliance, an argument Ficino revived from the ancient Neoplatonist, Plotinus. Ficino departed from Plotinus, however, in arguing that beauty was not truly to be found in the things we perceive, but rather in our mental images of those things. Beauty, Ficino contended, is apprehended when what is perceived aligns with our innate perfect idea of that which is perceived. As such, in Ficino's view, it is only those who already have an idea of beauty that can perceive it. Similarly, Ficino argues, the artist begins with his ideas of beauty, and creates works from these. However, like Plato, Ficino contends that where the painter or sculptor uses skill to adhere to perfect forms of beauty, the poet relies on the madness that comes with divine inspiration.

Ficino finds his philosophical nemesis in his contemporary, Leon Battista Alberti. Ficino's thinking reflects the philosophical school of rationalism, believing that we are born with some innate ideas, while Alberti approaches art and beauty as an empiricist, believing that all of our ideas come from experience. The proverbial 'Renaissance Man', Alberti wrote literary works, painted, sculpted and produced architecture of renown. However, Alberti's importance to the history of art rests perhaps as much on his philosophy of art as on his art itself. Alberti authored three groundbreaking treatises: *On Painting*, *On Sculpture* and *On Architecture*. Where Ficino argued for a transcendent and innate notion of beauty, Alberti's approach was empirical and naturalistic. Judgements of beauty for Alberti were reasoned judgements, and no less objective than scientific ones, but ones that relied upon an innate *sense* of beauty in man – a natural ability to recognize it and a natural tendency to be pleased by it. Alberti revived the argument that beauty arises from the harmony – the conformity and interplay – of parts, as well as the Aristotelian notion that where a thing is lacking or has too much of something, that thing fails to be beautiful. Rather than being found in our own ideas, however, Alberti contends that beauty is found in nature, and thereafter becomes a goal for the artist. The artist's goal is not necessarily to represent nature, but to follow its laws, and so the artist can properly invent as well as imitate. As such, the artist, like the audience, relies upon his observation of the world and his rational judgement. Even in his attempts to arouse an emotional response in his audience, Alberti argues, the artist relies first on his own emotional experience.

The British Enlightenment

Following the path of inquiry established by Ficino and Alberti, a group of mostly British philosophers of the eighteenth century set out what would become known as the problem of taste. Anthony Ashley Cooper, 3rd Earl of Shaftesbury, notes that perceptions of beauty – grounded, he suggests, in harmony – are grasped immediately by the viewer, and immediately arouse the passions. Echoing Alberti, Shaftesbury suggests that a figurative 'inward eye' distinguishes without difficulty the harmonious from the disharmonious, the beautiful from the ugly. The same 'inward eye', contends Shaftesbury, also distinguishes agreeable from disagreeable human actions and dispositions, and so is central not only to aesthetic, but also to moral, judgement. However, echoing Ficino, Shaftesbury contends that the 'inward eye' distinguishes the beautiful from the ugly, the good from the bad, by pre-rationally comparing the object of perception with an innate concept had by the viewer. This human capacity to distinguish the beautiful from the ugly would come to be known as 'taste'. Although pleasurable by nature, prior as it is to any desire to possess the object of perception – whether art or nature – Shaftesbury suggests, the sense of beauty is distinct from any practical interest that might be had in its objects.

Shaftesbury is shortly followed in this line of inquiry by Francis Hutcheson. Picking up on an empirical argument recently set out by John Locke, Hutcheson notes that our sensations do not depend upon our will, but rather arise involuntarily with perception. Ideas of beauty, Hutcheson suggests, arise in us as a result of an 'internal sense' to be distinguished from our external senses of sight, hearing and the like. When this internal sense of beauty is particularly acute, says Hutcheson, we call it taste. Where external senses teach us measurement, anatomy and so on, our internal sense allows us aesthetic pleasure. And although we can sense both 'absolute' beauty (that which is perceived in an object in and of itself) and 'comparative' beauty (the beauty perceived in an object as a representation or imitation), this is not, he says, as a result of some knowledge (or principles or proportions) of beauty, but rather arises from its immediate sensation. As with our external senses, Hutcheson notes, the *sense* of beauty is not a matter of our will, and cannot be affected by it, as our *desire* for beauty can.

Hutcheson contends that what our internal sense picks up on is 'uniformity amidst variety', and that we are naturally disposed to find such sensations pleasurable. We find uniformity amidst variety in nature, in art and in the proportions of people, Hutcheson notes, but we also find it in theorems – in geometry, in natural laws, in philosophy – as when a given theory gives rise to all manner of corollaries deducible from it. However, while he argues that all that is needed to show the truth of his theory is that mankind universally prefers uniformity amidst variety to its absence, and that the sense of beauty precedes all custom or education, Hutcheson rejects the notion that any of this depends upon mankind having innate ideas of beauty. Rather, he suggests, the internal sense operates very much as external senses do, which likewise require no innate ideas in man.

Hutcheson's inquiry into taste would provoke theories by a great number of thinkers, but none more famously than the Scottish empirical philosopher, David Hume. Hume wonders why it is that where people have a natural capacity for taste, taste varies so significantly between them, even those of roughly the same background and prejudices. As a matter of sentiment, taste does not seem open to dispute – it is like simple sense data or pain, and simply cannot be wrong. As a matter of judgement, however, taste seems a reasonable issue for disagreement. What one person calls beautiful, another may as easily call ugly. Hume argues that beauty does not truly exist in those objects we call 'beautiful', but rather exists only in the mind of the perceiver, though not in the sense of there being some innate ideas of beauty. So how are we to seek a 'standard of taste'? Is it a hopeless project? Hume's suggestion is that despite all the variety of tastes, there appear certain observable, general principles of beauty. The problem is that not everyone is an ideal judge of beauty: some have defective organs of sense, and others are simply indelicate in their discrimination. While the former may be irresolvable, the latter is not. Rather, Hume suggests, the faculty of taste can be improved by practice, observation and contemplation. The observer must seek to free his mind from all prejudices and observe only the object, to become as much as possible a 'man in general'. Although ideal judges are relatively few and far between, Hume suggests that the endurance of great works of art comes about as a result of surviving the peculiar sentiments of given individuals and the peculiar trends of any given age or culture.

Kant and the German idealists

Toward the end of the eighteenth century, the German philosopher Immanuel Kant turned his eye towards the issues of aesthetics raised by the British. Kant hoped to work the peculiar problems of aesthetics into his much larger philosophical programme, which he had already begun in *The Critique of Pure Reason* and *The Critique of Practical Reason*. With these as his conceptual backdrop, Kant took up aesthetic problems in the third and final book in the series, *The Critique of Judgment*. Kant's view, it must be said, is extremely complex, and only a very rough introduction to it is possible here.

Kant argues that, unlike judging a rose *as* a rose or a horse *as* a horse, which relies on concepts of those things, pure aesthetic judgements are not based on determinate concepts, but rather on feelings of pleasure and displeasure. The pleasure that arises in aesthetic judgement comes, Kant says, from the 'free play' of the imagination. Where concepts of the understanding say something about the world, pleasure and displeasure do not. Rather, Kant suggests, aesthetic judgements, which draw on the imagination, are 'subjectively based'. And though subjective, Kant argues, aesthetic judgements must be *disinterested* – contemplative and unconcerned with the object's actual existence. Taste, Kant says, is the ability to judge or present an object by means of liking or disliking, devoid of all personal interest in it. We call the object of such a liking 'beautiful', and because our judgements are made without personal interest, we frame them universally – we claim that everyone should make the same judgement, and discuss beauty as if it were a property of the object (though Kant believes it is no such thing). The beautiful, which is non-conceptual and arises from disinterested judgement, can thus be distinguished in Kant's view from the *good*, which in requiring a goal or purpose is conceptual, and the *agreeable*, which while non-conceptual, arises from *interested* judgement.

Where judging beauty requires taste, Kant argues, producing beautiful objects requires *genius*, an innate talent for art. However, because beauty is non-conceptual, genius cannot be taught, but rather 'rules' of art must be gleaned and abstracted from examples of beauty. That being said, Kant suggests, judging art *as* art tends to require concepts, as judging horses as horses does. And so we tend to judge an artwork not only purely – as a beautiful object – but also against its perfection as a *representation* of beauty.

Kant may very well be the most influential philosopher in the field of aesthetics since the ancients, and his influence was felt almost immediately. Within five years of Kant's publication, another German, Friedrich Schiller, published *Letters on the Aesthetic Education of Man*, arguing that the aesthetic experience plays a central role in both man and society. In the *Letters*, Schiller bemoans the current state of society, in which church and state, law and custom, have been fragmented. Man, too, Schiller argues, has suffered a split, setting in opposition man's sensuous and intellectual aspects. The key to reconciling these, Schiller suggests, is man's *play* impulse. In particular, beauty – the pleasure that Kant described as arising from the free play of the imagination – gives man a spiritual freedom, and allows him to realize his own humanity. The aesthetic experience, Schiller contends, at once allows man contemplative relaxation and dynamic engagement with his faculties. The experience of beauty, as such, provides a path from sensation to thought, allowing the sensuous man to become the rational man, and bringing his opposing aspects into harmony. In this harmony, Schiller supposes, man develops his social character, and where man finds his harmony, so too will society.

Schiller was followed in this line of thinking by another German, Friedrich Wilhelm von Schelling. In producing art, Schelling argues, the artist operates from a conscious goal, but at the same time operates on the basis of an unconscious creative power. In art, infinite, ungraspable 'Ideas' are formed into finite objects, and insofar as such Ideas are so united in art, that art is beautiful: the Absolute is revealed in the finite. And just as the artist finds satisfaction in this artistic process, so too does the art appreciator find satisfaction in the unifying experience of art. The observer of art, in contemplating such works, finds identity between his own viewpoint (the subject and finite) and the eternal Ideas (the objective and infinite).

This trend towards prioritizing art in the world of mankind reaches a head with the view of George Wilhelm Friedrich Hegel, who explicitly places the beauty of art above that of nature. Art, Hegel argues, is the product of mind and spirit, and so is able to represent divine ideals – what Schelling called infinite Ideas – while nature does not represent at all. Hegel postulates that art arises from a higher impulse in man, and satisfies his need to 'reduplicate' himself – to draw out and make explicit what he is. In so doing, man achieves consciousness and self-realization by forming an idea of himself to bring out. He moulds the outer world to reflect his inner self, and so comes to know himself. Thus, art is made, in Hegel's view, not only for sensuous appreciation, but also for apprehension by the mind. In expressing oneself through art, one becomes aware of one's inner state by externalizing it, and so is freed from one's emotions. The spiritual, Hegel says, is shaped by the artist to the sensual. And though its form is particular, Hegel suggests, the content of art is of a spiritual and universal sort. As such, Hegel argues, the goal of art is the universal 'Idea' of artistic beauty, the perfect coincidence of universal content and particular form.

1

Defining Art

Chapter Outline

I. *Fountain* (1917)

In 1917, the newly formed Society of Independent Artists held its first annual exhibition in New York City. Founded only the year before as an association for avant-garde artists, the Society opened its exhibition to any artist able to pay the six-dollar fee. Among the Society's founders and exhibition's directors was French artist Marcel Duchamp, only recently arrived from Paris, and perhaps best known at the time for his controversial painting, *Nude Descending a Staircase, No. 2* (1912).

As the story goes, with the exhibition only days away, Duchamp had yet to create a work for the show. But while at lunch with friends, he hit upon an idea. Travelling across town to J. L. Mott Iron Works (a specialist in plumbing fixtures), Duchamp purchased his urinal and returned to his studio. Duchamp's first New York studio was a curious place: chessboards

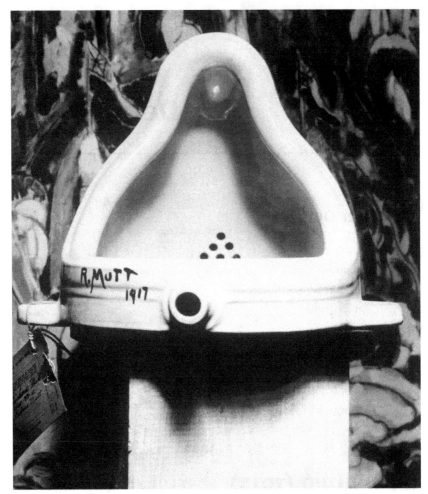

Figure 1.1 Marcel Duchamp, *Fountain* (1917). Photograph by Alfred Stieglitz.

leaned against one wall; near another, a bicycle wheel had been secured upright to a wooden stool. Overhead hung a snow shovel, and to the floor was nailed an ordinary coat rack. Duchamp's newest purchase was not out of place in the studio.

Duchamp turned the urinal on its back, painted 'R. Mutt 1917' on its rim and submitted it as *Fountain* to the exhibition under the name of Richard Mutt.[1] The Society's board was at a loss. Was *Fountain* art? If so, was it indecent? Although the exhibition had been advertised as having no selection committee, effectively accepting any submission, they hadn't anticipated *Fountain*. After some debate, the board narrowly voted to remove *Fountain* from view, either hiding it from view behind a screen or physically removing it from the show (reports vary).

Duchamp resigned from the Society, and the next month released the second issue of his self-published magazine, *The Blind Man*, with several pages devoted to *Fountain* and 'The Richard Mutt Case'. Although not Duchamp's first 'ready-made' artwork – the snow shovel hanging from his studio ceiling was the first work he called a 'ready-made' – *Fountain* is surely the best-known, despite having been thrown out shortly after the exhibition (he subsequently made several reproductions). And although the piece could easily have been forgotten as something of a joke, thanks to the controversy surrounding the exhibition, *Fountain* would go on to become one of the best-known works of the twentieth century. Indeed, a 2004 survey of British art experts named it *the* most influential artwork in the history of modern art (Picasso's first Cubist painting, *Les Demoiselles d'Avignon* (1907) took second place). But how could *Fountain* be art in the first place? Wasn't it just a men's room appliance?

II. On definitions

The issue of defining art is central to the project of contemporary aesthetics. Whether or not *Fountain* – or anything else – is art sounds like a simple question. After all, we know what art is, don't we?

Our contemporary concept of art is actually a rather modern notion. Although ancient Greece had no shortage of paintings, sculptures and great works of architecture, the Greeks did not have our concept of art. What they had was the term '*technê*', meaning skilful production. And while this did apply to sculptors, painters and architects, it also applied to carpenters, weavers and all manner of craftsmen. The Greeks simply had no word that distinguished what we call 'art' from what we would call 'craft'. Our word 'poetry' comes from the Greek word '*poiesis*', meaning any sort of production, and our word 'music' comes from the Greek '*mousike*', meaning any activity associated with the Muses – the mythical spirits of inspiration – and applied generally to anyone who was educated. The Latin '*ars*', the direct source of our current 'art', similarly referred to skill generally, and when the term 'artist' first came into use in the Middle Ages, it did not distinguish between skilled sculptors and skilled textile-makers. It was not until the eighteenth century that the concept of 'fine art' comes into play, collecting together the Arts with a capital 'A' and distinguishing them from other areas of skill.

Distinguishing the arts from other activities and products determines what it is we are looking to define, but it does not provide us with a definition. What is called a 'real' definition is meant to serve as an analytic tool for classifying and organizing our world. Ideally, a definition tells us how we *do* apply our concepts, and how we should do so in any case in the future. Leonardo da Vinci's *Mona Lisa* is an artwork, and Michelangelo's *David* is an artwork. The Society of Independent Artists had no problem here, but when it came to classifying *Fountain*, they were at a loss. Duchamp's work challenged their notions of art, and so the problem fell to the philosophers. Ideally, a definition should supply a set of necessary and jointly sufficient conditions for classification. We might, for instance, define a 'bachelor' as an unmarried male of marriageable status. That a person is unmarried, that he is male and that he is of marriageable status are each necessary for his being a bachelor. Your sister might be unmarried and of marriageable status, but she is not a bachelor. Your 6-year-old nephew may be male and unmarried, but in our culture he is not of marriageable status, so he isn't a bachelor either. Unless all of our conditions are met, our contender does not qualify, and so they are each necessary. But as soon as all of our conditions are met, the contender does qualify, and so they are jointly sufficient. The first challenge for any definition is for our set of conditions to match how we already use the concept at hand – how we divide up our world. Developing definitions can involve some bullet-biting, but the bullets shouldn't be overly large. If our definition of 'bachelor' includes or excludes Catholic priests, we may have to slightly reconfigure how we conceptualize our world, but if it includes my married father, we will have a serious problem. Likewise, if our definition of 'art' includes all the products and activities of ordinary plumbers, or excludes the *Mona Lisa*, we will still have some work to do. Ideally, a definition of art should be such that it encompasses not only all of those things we call art – painting, sculpture, literature, music, film, dance and so on – but also any new forms of art that might develop in the future.

III. Art as representation

As the ancient Greeks did not have our concept of 'art', and as their way of organizing their activities and products diverged so much from ours, they certainly had no definition of art. However, as they studied what we would call the arts, they observed that many of them seemed essentially imitative:

the painter imitated nature, the sculptor imitated the human form, and the poet imitated man's speech and actions. Plato condemned the arts for their imitation, and Aristotle praised them for the same, but lacking a general *concept* of art, neither set out imitation as a defining principle. It was not until the notion of 'fine art' developed in the eighteenth century that philosophers attempted to describe imitation or representation as an essential or necessary feature of art, and made the first moves towards a definition.

Although Immanuel Kant spends very little time on the notion of art, he makes perhaps the first attempt at defining it.[2] Unlike natural objects, Kant notes, works of art are artefacts – products of human intention and creation. And unlike scientific ones, artistic activities do not simply depend upon learned knowledge. As such, Kant distinguishes between art and technology. Kant puts fine art along with what he calls 'agreeable art' into the category of 'aesthetic art' – representational art designed towards evoking a feeling of pleasure. Where agreeable art gives rise only to immediate pleasure, the pleasure of fine art comes from the 'reflective power of judgement'. Today, we might make this sort of distinction between fine art and merely entertaining art. In the end, for Kant, fine art is 'is a way of presenting that is purposive on its own and that furthers … the culture of our mental powers to [facilitate] social communication'.[3] As such, while Kant does not formulate an explicit set of necessary and sufficient conditions, his view of art is that it is essentially representational, and that it has no function except to bring about reflective pleasure and to advance communication. So described, art is set apart from nature and from all manner of other human products and activities.

The view of art as essentially imitative or representational is perhaps not surprising given that up to the eighteenth century, with the possible exception of instrumental music, most art *was* centrally representational in nature (and arguments have been made that instrumental music imitates the form of the human voice, emotion or movement). However, as the eighteenth century gave way to the nineteenth, a new technology would have an enormous effect on the arts. In the 1820s and 1830s, a number of inventors worked to develop camera photography, in particular Louis Daguerre, creator of the daguerreotype photographic process. Where a painted portrait would take days, weeks or months to complete, an early daguerreotype could be completed in minutes. Advances in technology quickly reduced this time to seconds. Painting was also prohibitively expensive compared with photography, which could be afforded by the working class. With the swift advances in technology, its sweeping popularization and its ability to perfectly capture minute details, photography's effect on the business of portrait painting was immediate. Landscape painting felt similar pressures. As a result, painters began to explore the other possibilities of their art.[4]

Where art's representational elements once largely served to distinguish it from other human activities and products, the popularization of photography inspired artists to pursue new directions. French painter Claude Monet turned the tables on photography by insisting that a painting is, after all, ultimately a canvas covered in pigments, and that we should not be trying to look *through* it, but *at* it.[5] Monet helped to found *Impressionism*, a painting style characterized by its visible brush strokes, its emphasis on light and its attempts to portray movement. Following the Impressionists in the late nineteenth century were the *Post-Impressionists*, a loose collection of painters variously inspired by the Impressionists.[6] Henri de Toulouse-Lautrec alternatively produced textured paintings and lithograph posters consisting of outlined, flatly coloured figures. Georges Seurat introduced the technique of Pointillism, replacing brushstrokes with countless dots of colour. And perhaps the most celebrated of the Post-Impressionists, Paul Cézanne, worked (as one art historian has put it) to transform paint into 'a visible structure'.[7] In an effort both to capture the new directions in art as a result of photography, and in part to keep photography itself – seen largely as a technological and not artistic endeavour – from falling into the category of fine art, philosophers began to pursue the project of defining art with new vigour.[8]

IV. Art as form

Although it is perhaps difficult to imagine today, the work of the Post-Impressionists brought about a split among critics as well as the public at large. While one side praised the innovation of the new movements in art, the other flatly refused to recognize what they saw as art. Particularly enamoured of Cézanne and the Post-Impressionists was Clive Bell, who produced the most well-known *formalist* theory of art.[9] Bell argues in his 1913 book, simply titled *Art*, that Cézanne and the Post-Impressionists represented a return to the 'first-principles' of art. Although, like most of the painters that had come before them, the Post-Impressionists produced portraits, landscapes and still-life paintings, what set them apart was a focus on the painting as an image, rather than as a representation per se. As a result, Bell says, Cézanne and his contemporaries were able to create works that gave rise to a certain peculiar feeling in their viewers. Bell called this feeling the 'aesthetic emotion'. It is not the artwork-as-representation that provokes the aesthetic emotion, Bell argues, but rather the lines and colours that make up the artwork itself. Essentially, Bell contends, art is a matter of *form*, not of *content*. However, simply stipulating that art is form would not do as a definition. First, every visible thing has form: a blender has form, a goldfish has form, your hand has form. These are not art. Second, not every form gives rise to that peculiar feeling that Bell calls aesthetic emotion. Rather, Bell contends, what gives rise to the aesthetic emotion – and what sets art apart from other things – is '*significant* form'. So art is something with significant form, and significant form is that which brings about the aesthetic emotion.

Bell is clear that he is only discussing painting, the art form with which he is most familiar. It is not that he thinks there is nothing analogous to significant form, say, in music – it is just that he is not particularly sensitive to music's forms. We might further look to extend Bell's theory to something like significant form in dance, literature and other art forms. That a work has significant form is no guarantee, Bell says, that you will be sensitive to it, and if you are not sufficiently sensitive, it will not provoke in you the aesthetic emotion. However, a good critic might be able to guide you to see significant form you had previously overlooked. When you are made aware of the significant form, says Bell, you will receive the aesthetic emotion, and so recognize it as a work of art. It is the artist's job to combine forms so that they will move us, and insofar as he succeeds, he has made art. Representation, Bell suggests, is at best irrelevant to something's value as art, and at worst detracts or distracts from a work's significant form. When it comes to art, imitation is beside the point.

Why is it, then, that we find significant form in Cézanne, but not, say, in a sunset? Bell isn't entirely sure, but proposes what he calls the 'metaphysical hypothesis' as a possibility. Although the mechanism by which it does so is mysterious, Bell suggests, significant form moves us as it does because it expresses the aesthetic emotion of its creator. This would seem to explain why aesthetic emotion is provoked by art, but not by natural objects, which may have *beautiful* form but not *significant* form.

Although Bell's theory seems to have the advantage of tracking not only the trajectory of art, but also of aligning with one way that we evaluate it – not just *what* is represented, but *how* it is represented – it has several well-known problems which heavily outweigh its advantages. First, we might ask, what *is* significant form? Bell's only answer is that it is that which provokes aesthetic emotion in suitably sensitive viewers. So what is aesthetic emotion? Bell only says that it is that which is provoked by significant form. Although he does suggest *why* significant form brings about aesthetic emotion, in so characterizing art as something with significant form, and significant form as that which brings about aesthetic emotion, without telling us anything more, Bell's definition is rather empty. He has given us some new terminology, but little actual *meaning* to his terms. Significant form is simply that which brings about aesthetic emotion, and aesthetic emotion is simply that which is brought about by significant form. We are going in circles. However, this may be an intractable problem. Imagine that you wanted to describe what sadness felt like to someone who had never been sad, or what a headache felt like to someone who had never felt pain, or even what saltiness was like to someone who had never tasted salt. It may just be that (like emotion, pain or sense data) there is simply no real way to describe aesthetic emotion to someone who has not already experienced it.

The second serious problem with Bell's theory is that while it allows for varying degrees of quality in art (some works might produce stronger, or more pronounced, aesthetic emotion than others), it simply does not allow for the existence of *bad* art. As what is central to art's value is its ability to provoke aesthetic emotion (which is to say it has significant form), insofar as an item fails to produce this effect to any degree, it is not bad art – rather, it is not art at all. That there is simply no such thing as bad (or even mediocre) art seems out of step with our ordinary use of the term. Worse, perhaps, Bell's theory requires recategorizing some of our greatest works as non-art.

Figure 1.2 William Powell Frith, *The Railway Station* (1862). Engraving by Francis Holl (1866).

Bell singles out what he calls 'descriptive painting', which he says *suggests* emotion, conveys information or tells a story, but lacks significant form. Although such works may *interest* us, Bell says, insofar as they fail to provoke the aesthetic emotion, they are not works of art, properly speaking. A painting such as William Powell Frith's *The Railway Station* (1862), which depicts a raucous scene at London's Paddington Station, Bell says, gives us nothing more than a randomly taken photograph of the train station would, and probably less.[10] Although many people *like* the painting, he says, it seems fairly certain that no one has ever been so moved by it as to experience aesthetic emotion. So *The Railway Station* is not art. What else is thrown out? Without giving us any way to determine if something has significant form (aside from its production of aesthetic emotion, which, given our varying levels of sensitivity and Bell's lack of independent description of the feeling, is not a particularly useful determiner), we can't be certain. But in his outline of descriptive painting, we might reasonably exclude such masterpieces as Jan Vermeer's *The Artist's Studio* (1665–6) and Breughel the Elder's attributed *Landscape with the Fall of Icarus* (c. 1558), as well as all manner of straightforward landscape painting. Accepting Bell's definition would require us to exclude from the canon of art history some of what are taken to be its greatest works.

V. Art as expression

At about the same time that philosophers like Bell were developing formalist theories of art, another group of thinkers were working along another path in response to the apparent failures of the representational approach, and in the hopes of distinguishing art from other human activities and products. Following theories set out by Benedetto Croce and the novelist-turned-philosopher Leo Tolstoy, perhaps the clearest of this body of views comes from R. G. Collingwood in his book *The Principles of Art*.[11]

Collingwood seeks first to distinguish art from craft. With craft, Collingwood suggests, there is a necessary distinction between what the creator sets out to do (say, to arouse a certain state of mind in its consumer) and how he brings about that end (technique). The craftsman begins with the end (the product) he has in mind, develops a plan and uses skilled technique in his work to bring about that end. Poetry, Collingwood contends, provides a clear example of how art differs from craft. The poem, he says, is 'not an end to which there are means'.[12] While the poet may have a compulsion to produce something, the poem is not pre-planned, but rather arises within the poet as a reaction to this impulse. In art, there is not necessarily a clear means–ends distinction as there is in craft. Rather, the poet works out and clarifies her inner state *in* composing the poem. This is what Collingwood calls 'expression'. Prior to expression, the poet knows only that she feels 'something', but it is primal and undefined, and it is through this self-reflective process that she clarifies this inner something without knowing what the final product will be. As such, art seems to have a dual nature – we can talk about what results from this mental activity, and we can talk about the activity itself. Insofar as we want to distinguish art from craft, and insofar as we identify craft in terms of its products, Collingwood argues that we should identify art's essential nature as the mental activity and not the physical product. The product, for Collingwood, is really only a *byproduct* of art. Indeed, the artist – whether poet, painter, sculptor or composer – may work through this activity entirely on the mental plane, and so there may be no such externalization whatsoever of the product.

Where there *is* an external product, however, the medium enables communication of the artist's inner state to his audience. Collingwood writes: 'The characteristic mark of expression proper is lucidity or intelligibility; a person who expresses something thereby becomes conscious of what it is that he is expressing, and enables others to become conscious of it in himself and in them.'[13] That a work arouses emotions or thoughts in the audience does not make the work non-art, but if the artist sets out to *intentionally* arouse specific emotions in the audience, what he creates is only craft. With true art, insofar as there is an audience outside of the artist himself, the physical product is only a conduit to the true artwork – the clarified emotion of the artist. The painting, the poem or the song – if the artist is successful – allows the audience member access to the artist's internal state, ideally duplicating the true artwork in her own mind.

As with Bell's formalist theory, on Collingwood's view, representation is at best incidental to art. It may be that one's inner state is best clarified through representation, and it may not. An artist might seek expression through words, through music, through shape and colour, or through any other sort of media. As such, Collingwood's view of art has the distinct advantage of being able to apply equally well to all of the standard forms of art, where Bell's view struggles to find easy application to arts like literature and music which are not essentially visual. Of course, Collingwood's view has this advantage precisely because the product of art for him is to be distinguished from the art itself, properly speaking, which is essentially a mental and not a physical thing.

The renowned painter Henri Matisse perhaps predicts Collingwood's view, saying of his work: 'What I am after, above all, is expression … I am unable to distinguish between the feeling I have about life and my way of translating it.'[14] Matisse's approach to his art seems to fall in line with Collingwood's view. But is Matisse typical or atypical in this regard? It is difficult to say; we would need to interview a lot of artists to be certain. Still, Collingwood's seems a rather particular process to demand of artists.

In 1844, the French composer Hector Berlioz wrote his *Marche funèbre pour la dernière scène d'*Hamlet (*Funeral march for the final scene of* Hamlet). Like most funeral marches, his composition for *Hamlet* is written in a minor key, with the minor key noted for being 'soft', 'dark' and 'sad'. Unlike most funeral marches, however, this one was written for a fictional character. Now, it may be that Berlioz *was* in some particular emotional state when he composed the march, but insofar as he composed it *for* the audience of a production of *Hamlet* – either to entertain or to arouse a feeling of sadness – on Collingwood's view, Berlioz was not creating true art. Rather, if Berlioz was composing with the intent to arouse a feeling in his audience, as any funeral march might be expected to, he was creating what Collingwood calls 'magical art' (so named because it serves the same purpose as many religious artefacts). If he was composing simply to entertain the audience, he was creating 'amusement art' or 'entertainment art'. Neither of these, on Collingwood's view, is art, properly speaking; rather, both fall into the category of craft. Indeed, although he speaks of Shakespeare as a 'great artist', he elsewhere relegates the bard himself – or, at least, several of his works – to the realm of 'amusement art'. After all, they were written very much with the Elizabethan audience in mind. Along with Shakespeare, if we are to adhere to Collingwood's view, we will have to throw out a great deal of theatrical works, the great body of religious art (being magical art), presumably most portrait paintings and innumerable other works.

Finally, even if we were willing to bite these rather large and numerous bullets, Collingwood's view has one very conspicuous problem remaining: if art is essentially something mental, and not something physical, insofar as you are merely looking at a painting, watching a film or listening to a song, you are not experiencing art. On Collingwood's view, strictly speaking, neither the Louvre, nor London's National Gallery, nor New York's Metropolitan Museum of Art actually contains any art. Nor does any art hang on the walls of your home. Paintings and sculptures are, after all, not art at all on Collingwood's view, but simply the byproducts of it. So even more than demanding some very particular process of artists, and of throwing out as non-art a rather great number of acclaimed works, Collingwood's definition requires a radical rethinking of our basic concept of art, and most philosophers have found this simply too difficult and too radical to accept.

VI. Art and aesthetic function

To recall, Clive Bell grounds his formal approach in terms of significant form, and says that significant form is what gives rise to aesthetic emotion. However, Bell does not tell us what aesthetic emotion *is*, aside from saying that it is evoked by significant form. Although generally disavowing that there is some particular *emotion* to be associated with artworks, a number of philosophers following Bell have argued that art has something centrally to do with the *aesthetic*. In particular, several have argued that a work of art is, roughly speaking, an artefact which serves an aesthetic function. 'Artefact' seems an easy enough term – it is something made or modified by a person – but what is an 'aesthetic function'? Disagreements about this serve to largely distinguish between these 'functionalist' views of art.

Let's look at a handful of these definitions:

'An artwork is something produced with the intention of giving it the capacity to satisfy the aesthetic interest.' (Monroe Beardsley)[15]

'A work of art is an artifact of a kind whose main function is to provide aesthetic satisfaction to others.' (Oswald Hanfling)[16]

'[A] work of art is an artifact which under standard conditions provides its percipients with aesthetic experience.' (George Schlesinger)[17]

'An "artwork" is any creative arrangement of one or more media whose principal function is to communicate a significant aesthetic object.' (Richard Lind)[18]

What is clear, first, is that 'aesthetic' can be couched in a number of ways. Beardsley, perhaps the most vocal proponent of the functionalist approach, talks about aesthetic *interest*; Hanfling discusses aesthetic *satisfaction*; Schlesinger talks about aesthetic *experience*; and Lind about an aesthetic *object*. Philosophers also discuss aesthetic *contemplation*, aesthetic *attention* and so on. Which of these terms takes conceptual priority is a matter of some debate, but we can hazard at least a rough sketch of the issue here. To begin, philosophers of art tend to describe the aesthetic in terms of sensory experience – typically, although not always exclusively, in terms of sight and sound. This is roughly what Alexander Baumgarten meant when he coined the term in the eighteenth century. However, aren't all – or at least *most* – of our experiences sensory in nature? What marks off aesthetic experience is that it is focused *on* the sensory aspect of whatever has our attention. That is, when one listens to a sonata, one is concerned with it *as* a sequence of sounds, and when one looks at a painting, one is concerned with it *as* a field of colours – to the exclusion of other concerns one might have. If one is having an aesthetic experience, one is absorbed in the sensory experience itself afforded by the object of one's attention. Kant (and before him Anthony Ashley Cooper, 3rd Earl of Shaftesbury) called this absorption 'disinterestedness' – a special sort of interest in the thing *for its own sake*, or *for the sake of the sensory experience*, and not for any personal interest, say, in possessing, owning or otherwise exploiting the object.

Beardsley writes: "The painting and the music invite us to do what we would seldom do in ordinary life – pay attention *only* to what we are seeing or hearing, and ignore everything else."[19] And hasn't each of us, at one point or another, become 'lost' in an artwork? At a concert, lying back, closing your eyes and experiencing *only* the music? At the cinema, paying such close attention to the film that you become oblivious to your surroundings? Reading a book, and becoming so entrenched that you completely lose track of time? Each of these, and many others beside, are what aestheticians would call *aesthetic* experiences. Insofar as you listen to the music, read the book or watch the film so that you can have this sort of experience, you have an aesthetic interest in it. Insofar as you get what you want in this regard, you would seem to have aesthetic satisfaction. And the thing you are concentrating on – that purely sensory focus of your attention – is what we might call the aesthetic object.

Of course, the aesthetic is not solely an artistic matter; we find it in nature as well as, occasionally, in ordinary non-art items. What tends to distinguish art from non-art on these views is that art has the aesthetic as its *function* – the aesthetic is what art is *for*. But 'function' can be cashed out in a number of ways, too. For some, an artwork is like any other artefact: it has the function it has because it was *intended* to have this function; it was designed with this function in mind and to serve this purpose. The item on my bedside table is an alarm clock because it was designed to accurately show the time and to sound an alarm when it is time for me to wake up.

Similarly, something is an artwork because it was designed to provide an aesthetic experience or to yield aesthetic satisfaction. This approach is most explicit in Beardsley's definition above. On this view, an artist need not be successful in her intention for her work to be art; it is enough that this is what the work was designed to do. Even if she failed in her intentions, the work is art – it is probably just mediocre or bad art. Similarly, if the alarm on my alarm clock begins to fail, the object has not ceased to be an alarm clock – it is simply a bad or broken alarm clock.

Another way of looking at functions is not in terms of intent, but in terms of suitability. This is the approach taken, for example, by Schlesinger and Lind (although Schlesinger makes this explicit in his definition, and

Figure 1.3 'Studio 42' Olivetti typewriter, designed by Alexander Schawinsky, 1936. Photograph by ChristosV; image used under Creative Commons Attribution-ShareAlike 3.0 Unported license.

Lind does not). On this sort of view of functions, the worse an item is at performing some function, the more difficult it is to say that the item *has* that function. As the alarm begins to fail on my alarm clock, it seems to function only as a clock. And if the clock fails too, it seems to function only as a paperweight. It is now an alarm clock in name only. However, if I have another item around the house that can serve the function of reliably waking me up at the appropriate time, then *that* item can function as my alarm clock, regardless of whether or not it was designed to do so. Likewise, if we say that an artwork is any artefact that can serve to bring about pronounced aesthetic experience (or however we want to describe the aesthetic function), then any such artefact will be an artwork regardless of what it was originally designed to do. This may explain why certain items – like religious artefacts and cultural curios – make their way into art museums but which were perhaps not initially intended to serve such an aesthetic function. However, on this sort of view, the item created by the artist with the intent that it yield aesthetic satisfaction, but which fails to do so, fails to be art: it is not *bad* art; rather, it is *non*-art.

Of course, there is a difficulty in that some things serve multiple functions, whether because they were designed to do so or because we use them in multiple ways, or some combination of the two. Hanfling says that to be an artwork, the aesthetic function must be an artefact's 'main' one, and Lind says it must be the object's 'principal' function. Beardsley allows that the aesthetic function might be secondary to some other function the object is designed to serve, and Schlesinger only requires that under standard conditions, the object *does* serve that function. So, let's consider the case of the typewriter pictured in Figure 1.3. This particular typewriter – the 'Studio 42' model – was designed in 1936 by Alexander Schawinsky. Schawinsky was a student and later a teacher at the Bauhaus, an influential German art school that operated in the first third of the twentieth century. One of the primary objectives of the Bauhaus was to break down divisions between art, craft and technology – to meld the utilitarian and the aesthetic in one design. A Bauhaus-designed typewriter, chair or house was meant to fulfil an aesthetic function as much as the other function we normally associate with that object. This being the case, for Beardsley, Schawinsky's typewriter would almost certainly be art: it was intentionally produced with an aesthetic function in mind. For Hanfling, though, we face a question: can the 'Studio 42' have *two* primary functions? The very point of the Bauhaus movement was to design artefacts where the aesthetic and the utilitarian were inseparable. Someday, though – and probably someday soon – even a pristine-condition 'Studio 42' will cease to work as a typewriter, because nobody will be manufacturing typewriter ribbon any more. If we were to then put the typewriter on a shelf or mantle to serve as a 'significant aesthetic object', it would have become art, according to Lind. And if it can provide an aesthetic experience on that shelf today, then it probably always could – even when it sat on a writer's desk – and so, according to Schlesinger, it always *was* a work of art.

Whichever version of it you might prefer, a great advantage of the functionalist approach is that it seems like it may subsume both the formalist and expressionist views. These views, after all, capture *something* about why we appreciate art; they just seem to fail as definitions. If a functionalist definition allows that an artwork functions as an aesthetic object (whether by design or by use) because of its formal or expressive properties, all the better for the view. The problem with the functionalist approach tends to be a matter of which bullets one is willing to bite. On a view like Beardsley's, for instance, a toaster or coffee cup will be a work of art if its designer intended it to satisfy aesthetic interest, even if the designer wasn't a high-minded Bauhaus designer. Most of us, however, would be rather hesitant to allow simple toasters and coffee cups into the category of art without something further going on. On a view like Schlesinger's, as with Bell's, if something fails to have the right effect on its viewer, it isn't bad art – rather, it simply isn't art at all. Perhaps the biggest bullet of all, however, is the one that started off this chapter: *Fountain*. What are we supposed to do with *Fountain*? Whatever his motivation might have been, Duchamp's urinal was certainly not intended to satisfy aesthetic interest – frustrate it, perhaps, but not satisfy it. Beardsley famously throws up his hands and denounces (or at least openly doubts) the status of *Fountain* as art. The problem, as mentioned, is that art experts not only overwhelmingly think *Fountain* is art – they think it is great, important and indeed revolutionary art. *Fountain*, of course, is not the only example of what might be called 'anti-aesthetic' art, so there would be entire classes of art thrown out on this view. Others, like Lind, have suggested that even with *Fountain*, there is still an 'aesthetic object' to be beheld – it simply is not an *immediately* perceptible one, but requires both understanding *why* Duchamp created *Fountain* and actually seeing the piece. However, it isn't obvious that one would need to actually see *Fountain* in order to get Duchamp's joke (or artistic statement, or whatever it was he was trying to do by putting a signed urinal in an art show).

VII. On not defining art

As we have seen, philosophers of art have largely followed movements in art in an attempt to capture what is essential about art in a definition. As the Post-Impressionists had a generation before, Duchamp's *Fountain* caused an upheaval in the world of aesthetics. Although some held out on *Fountain*'s non-art status, as the work came to be not only accepted but *praised* in the artistic community, it simply could not be ignored. One group of philosophers argued that the artistic revolutions that allowed for artists like Cézanne and Duchamp not only showed problems with particular definitions of art; more than this, they argued, such works showed that a definition – at least the sort of definition that aestheticians had been so far attempting to formulate – was simply not *possible*.

The central problem with the definitional project, argues Paul Ziff, arises from the fact that 'artwork' itself is not a fixed concept.[20] As new movements in art arise – as with Cézanne and later Duchamp – critics must decide whether to extend the term 'work of art' to include these new items. Invariably, some will say yes and some will say no. Whether or not the extended use of the term is ultimately accepted depends upon the social consequences of doing so. Art plays a role in society, Ziff contends, and the question is whether the social consequences of accepting some new thing into the category of art are acceptable. Prior to the revolution brought about by photography in the nineteenth century, picking out a clear case of art was not difficult. We might select, say, the *Mona Lisa*, and with some thought, we might be able to describe the many ways in which such a work counts as a clear case or exemplar of art. When faced with some new item, say an early Post-Impressionist work by Cézanne, we are faced with a decision. If the new work does not fit our description of what makes the *Mona Lisa* an exemplar of art, we ask whether it is reasonable to expand our notion of 'artwork' to so include it. We might ask whether the new item reasonably extends the artistic tradition already in place, or whether the gap between accepted works and the new item is too wide to bridge. When Cézanne's work won out, our concept of art was successfully extended, and likewise it would seem for *Fountain*. But the project itself of defining art, says Ziff, is at best a matter of describing what counts as an accepted work at any one time; the hope of finding some 'real' definition of art – some set of necessary and sufficient conditions – is a fruitless one, as that definition is always subject to change with the next artistic revolution.

Following Ziff, Morris Weitz argues that the concept of art altogether defies definition – we cannot even find such a definition at any given time.[21] This, Weitz argues, is because none of the definitions of art we have so far considered is open to verification or falsification. Following the philosopher Ludwig Wittgenstein, Weitz asks, how do we *use* the term 'art' in our language? Weitz suggests the term 'art' works like the term 'game', one of Wittgenstein's central examples. We can, without much difficulty, provide a long list of things we accept as games: baseball, hide and seek, Monopoly, catch, solitaire, staring contests and so on. Each qualifies as an exemplar of 'game' as much as any other. However, Weitz says, we will not find any single trait that all of these games have in common. Some are competitive and some are not. Some involve multiple players and some do not. Some have a long list of rules and others do not. Rather, Weitz suggests, there is something of a 'family resemblance' between those things we call games: while there isn't any *one* trait that all of them have in common, any one game has much in common with several others, and so there is an overlap of such traits without any single common thread running through them all. Art, Weitz says, works the same way: looking at art, we will find no set of common properties, but only strands of similarities between works. As such, the hope for a set of necessary and jointly sufficient conditions is ultimately a fruitless one.

We might select an exemplar work of art, and say of it that it is an artefact, that it is a product of human skill, that it is representative of its subject, that it is expressive of its creator's mind, that it was created to serve an aesthetic function and so on. If some new item had *none* of these characteristics, we would be unlikely to describe it as a work of art. However, Weitz suggests, not a single one of these characteristics found in our exemplar is either necessary or sufficient for being an artwork. When it comes to determining whether or not some new candidate for the category of art should in fact be so classified, we cannot simply check against a list of conditions, as we might with 'bachelor'. Rather, Weitz argues, we must make a decision: does the new item suitably resemble in some way those that we already accept as art? Where 'bachelor' is a 'closed concept', 'art' is an 'open' one – it is always subject to extension and revision. In principle, we *could* close the concept of art – making the term 'art' operate like the term 'bachelor' – by deciding on some list of necessary and sufficient conditions, but to do so, Weitz says, is to stifle the very creativity that we so value in art. All of the definitions we have so far considered, contends Weitz, have value: they serve to point out criteria of excellence in art. That a work is formally excellent or serves well to express its creator's emotion, or that it is an amazing representation of its subject – all of these are things worth attending to in evaluating a work. But because art itself is a concept we must allow to expand to take in new works in the future, none of these criteria can qualify as *conditions* of being a work of art.

A number of challenges have been raised against Weitz's argument. First, Weitz rules out *all* conditions as necessary or sufficient to art. However, throughout all of the theories we have reviewed, one condition remains largely constant: for something to be art, it must be an artefact. Ziff, for one, explicitly accepts that this too is subject to change, but it is a much bigger bullet than most are willing to bite. That being said, even if artefactuality is a *necessary* condition, it clearly will not serve as a necessary and *sufficient* condition, so Weitz could accept this without great difficulty. Second, Weitz says that whether or not some new item qualifies as art depends upon whether it suitably resembles accepted works. But having let in *Fountain*, do we not have to let in all men's room urinals? After all, *Fountain* resembles other urinals much more than it resembles any other existing artworks. Having accepted *Fountain* but not the plethora of the world's urinals, something other than mere resemblance seems to be going on in our decision making, so at the very least Weitz has some further explaining to do. Finally, we might ask, if something becomes art by suitably resembling existing works of art, how did the *first* work of art come about, given that there was no art before it to resemble? So we are left with a rather gaping open question.

Weitz's paper, 'The Role of Theory in Aesthetics', may be the most-referenced essay on aesthetics in the twentieth century, but philosophers did not simply roll over on the project of defining art. Rather, with Weitz in mind, they took the project in a different direction. Maurice Mandelbaum, for one, points out that perhaps the reason Weitz cannot find an essential property of art is because he is looking in the wrong place – perhaps what makes something art is not some perceptible property it has, but rather some *relation* it holds to certain sorts of objects, practices or people.

VIII. Art and the artworld

Arthur Danto argues that what is required to see something like *Fountain* as art is 'an atmosphere of artistic theory, a knowledge of the history of art: an artworld'.[22] Without the history and theory of art, Danto argues, art itself would simply not be possible. Without an understanding of what art *is*, *Fountain* would just be a urinal, and the *Mona Lisa* would only be oil pigments on a piece of poplar. In order for you to see a work as representational, you must have some knowledge of the theory and practice of representation. In order for you to see a work as expressive, you must have some idea of what that means, and how expression has been used in art. This is not to say that in order to see art *as* art, you must have a complex understanding of the philosophy of art or an encyclopedic knowledge of art history. But you must have *some* understanding of what it means for something to *be* art, and some knowledge of what sorts of things we currently take and have historically taken to be art. Those who have such knowledge and understanding are together called the 'artworld'. Danto does not give us an explicit definition of art, but what he does tell us is that if you want to determine whether some item is art, you won't be able to do so simply by looking at it. Walking into a museum of modern art, you might encounter what looks like a dishevelled bed with stained sheets (Tracey Emin's *My Bed*, 1998), what seems to be commercial packaging for cans of juice (Andy Warhol's *Campbell's Tomato Juice Box*, 1964), or an otherwise unremarkable pile of lemon cough drops (Felix Gonzales-Torres' *'Untitled' (Throat)*, 1991). If you were to encounter these items outside of an art gallery, you might easily be forgiven for not knowing they were art. Indeed, the original *Fountain* might very well have been cleaned of its painted date and signature, and been installed in a men's room. Right this moment, someone might be urinating into what many consider the most important artwork of the twentieth century. How would anyone be expected to know? According to Danto, seeing urinals, messy beds, packages of juice, and cough drops as art already requires a knowledge of art. But how did these things become art in the first place? Is it the same way that the *Mona Lisa* or Georgia O'Keeffe's *Black Iris III* (1926) became art?

According to George Dickie, the answer is yes: what makes *Black Iris III* art is precisely what makes *Fountain* art, but in neither case will you be able to find this determining factor by looking at the piece. Rather, we must look outside the work to find our answer. Dickie produced two versions of his 'Institutional Theory of Art', and although he abandoned the first version, it is instructive for us to look at both.[23] In the first version of his theory, Dickie suggests that there are two conditions that must be satisfied for something to be an artwork, each necessary and together sufficient: (1) it must be an artefact, and (2) it must consist of a 'set of aspects' upon which has been conferred the status of candidate for appreciation by the artworld at large.

In other words, it must be something made or modified by a person, and it must be recognized as something to be appreciated by those people with a knowledge of art theory and art history. The artworld, Dickie suggests in this early view, is an institution like any other. For a marriage to be recognized, it must be performed within the bounds of a certain customary practice and by someone recognized as having the authority to perform such a practice. The same, Dickie says, rings true for art. For something to be recognized as art, it must be *christened* 'art' by some member of the artworld. So, who counts as a member? Dickie suggests that while artists, curators, critics and philosophers of art are obvious members, 'every person who sees himself as a member of the artworld is thereby a member'.[24] Essentially, the artworld consists of those people who are concerned with the arts.

Several problems with this first version of Dickie's theory have been pointed out. First, it seems to rule out private art or outsider art – works created without any notion of an artworld in mind, nor any actual christening taking place. However, such terms as 'private art' and 'outsider art' don't seem self-contradictory. Second, Dickie's theory seems to tell us little about how art is to be treated or appreciated – it might classify art, but that's about it, and we find ourselves wanting more. Finally, while the institution of marriage has certain set rules and laws, the institution of the artworld seems much looser than this. It is not like a state or a university or a corporation, so comparing a member of the artworld christening something 'art' to a minister or other official conferring a status of marriage seems misleading.

In Dickie's second version of his theory, he suggests something becomes art not in virtue of being *christened* 'art', but in virtue of being *used* as art. In the same way that a hammer might become a weapon by one's using it as a weapon, Duchamp's urinal became a work of art because he used it as a work of art – specifically, he created something of a kind to be presented to a particular group: the artworld public. This, Dickie says, is simply what it means to use something as art. The fact that *Fountain* did not actually *get* presented in the 1917 show makes no difference – this is what Duchamp *intended* for it, it is what he *attempted*, and this is enough for Dickie.

You should notice that Dickie is defining 'work of art' in terms of the artworld, and as you might expect, 'artworld' is going to have to be ultimately defined with reference to works of art. All told, Dickie provides five definitions:

'An artist is a person who participates with understanding in the making of a work of art.'

'A work of art is an artifact of a kind created to be presented to an artworld public.'

'A public is a set of persons the members of which are prepared in some degree to understand an object which is presented to them.'

'The artworld is the totality of all artworld systems.'

'An artworld system is a framework for a presentation of a work of art by an artist to an artworld public.'[25]

The fact that these five definitions form a fairly tight circle, says Dickie, should not overly concern us. The central concepts involved – artwork, artist, artworld public – all depend on one another because they are all parts of the same institution: that of art. One cannot have art without an artworld, and one cannot have an artworld without art. Of course, the matter is somewhat messier than this, as there are innumerable artworld systems – (at least) one for the visual arts, one for film, one for opera, one for comic books and on and on. That I have a knowledge of and interest in film does not mean I have a knowledge of and interest in, say, opera, so I will be a member of one such artworld public, but not the other, with each having its own history and theories of the sort Danto speaks of. Indeed, there might be artworld systems *within* artworld systems. The matter is bound to be messy, as the 'framework' of the artworld is not composed of laws, but of customs. But in this loose, yet institutional manner, something is a work of art in virtue of having been created to be presented to those who appreciate art – and this will be true whether that something is a sculpture, a painting, a song, an opera or one of Duchamp's 'ready-mades'.

There still remain a number of unanswered questions for Dickie's institutional view. Although the second version seems to allow for private art (Dickie says one can create something *of a kind* to be presented to an artworld public but then decide not to do so) it still seems to outlaw 'outsider art' – art created *outside* the institution. Further, Dickie's view leaves out any mention of how this institutional relationship between art and the public came about. If there cannot be art without an artworld, and there cannot be an artworld without works of art, did the two suddenly appear together? This seems unlikely. But if not, then there must have been art before the artworld developed (in which case, something other than the artworld must have made it art), or, less likely, there was an artworld before there were any works of art (in which case, one wonders what it was they were prepared to appreciate or understand).

IX. Art and art history

Jerrold Levinson agrees with Dickie that what makes some new item art is not some exhibited feature of the work, but rather a relationship it bears to something else.[26] However, he rejects the idea that this something else is any formal or informal art 'institution'. Levinson agrees with Weitz that what makes something art is a relationship it bears to pre-existing art, but rejects Weitz's idea that the relationship is one of resemblance. Nor, he says, is what makes something art to be found in our experience of it. Rather, Levinson argues, one makes art by intending one's creation to be treated or regarded as current or previous artworks have correctly or standardly been treated or regarded. Art, Levinson argues, is necessarily backward-looking.

Art is not created in a vacuum. Rather, new art depends upon art that has come before it, either by following, advancing or challenging existing traditions of art. Part of these artistic traditions is how audiences treat artworks at any given time. The composer of a new musical work does not expect her audience to treat the new work as some entirely new kind of thing. Rather, she expects it to be treated as musical works are normally treated. The director of a new film does not expect the audience to walk into the theatre and not know what to do with themselves. Rather, she likely expects the audience to take their seats, watch what is projected on the screen and follow the story. We variously expect artworks to be engaged with, contemplated, interpreted, evaluated and so on. Now, how we treat a piece of choral music is not how we treat a sculpture, and how we treat a fourteenth-century Dutch painting is not typically how we treat a twentieth-century abstract painting. In the former case, this is because choral music and sculpture have advanced along different lines of tradition. In the latter case, it is because, little by little, how we treat or regard artworks within a tradition changes, and new traditions arise from the old.

In the early part of the twentieth century, Isadora Duncan, who had been raised and trained in traditional dance, became disillusioned with the rigidity and structure of the form. Where classical ballet stressed upright posture and geometric formation, Duncan introduced a 'primitivist' style of improvisational dance focused on organic fluidity. Where classical ballet employs music either written for or easily suited to choreography, Duncan specifically chose music not written to be danced to. At about the same time, or shortly thereafter, dancer and choreographer Rudolf Laban was formulating detailed studies of human movement and dance, culminating in 'Labanotation', an extremely complex form of dance notation comparable to a musical score. By the middle of the twentieth century, dance had largely fractured into two camps, one following the tradition of Laban with his formal study of body mechanics, and the other following the tradition of Duncan and her focus on the 'body-liberating aesthetic'. Each of these paths responded to the tradition of classical ballet already in place, one seeking to advance it and the other to challenge it.

But what about works that represent an utter *break* with existing traditions? What about the work of the Post-Impressionists? What about *Fountain*? Surely we should not treat *Fountain* as we treat, say, a sculpture by Amadeo Modigliani of only a few years before. Modigliani's sculptures are of human heads and figures, and while they are wildly stylized – particularly drawing on African-art influences – they are certainly meant to be treated as representational and expressive things. *Fountain* seems neither representational nor expressive. It seems to be exactly what it is: an autographed urinal. If some new thing is art because it was intended to be treated or regarded as pre-existing work is treated or regarded, and if Modigliani's sculpture represents the furthest stretching of the sculpture tradition to that point, how could *Fountain* have been art in 1917? Surely, whatever he was thinking, Duchamp did not create *Fountain* as a representational or expressive sculpture. Here, Levinson offers a suggestion. Although Duchamp probably did not think of his work as representational or expressive, this is precisely what his audience expected to find in a 1917 art exhibition. If they had expected a plumbing fixture on a pedestal, *Fountain* wouldn't be at all shocking or interesting. Rather, it is *because* they were expecting ordinary sculpture that *Fountain* was so provocative (at least to those who actually got to see it). When we encounter some new work, we already have ways of treating art, and so we are bound to (at least initially) approach the new work in the same sort of regard. In order for revolutionary art to be revolutionary, Levinson suggests, it must be such that audiences come to it expecting to treat it as they treat other art, and are stymied in their attempts to do so. It seems not unreasonable to think that Duchamp wanted precisely this effect – in other words, he intended his creation to be regarded as artworks were at the time correctly or standardly regarded (thus satisfying Levinson's requirement for something to be art), but further intended for the audience to be rebuffed in this attempt. Indeed, it would seem, even artworks that represent smaller advances in traditions operate on the same basic principle. This is what makes new art interesting.

Now, given that new art depends on art that came before it, it seems that

Levinson's theory risks falling under the same objection that threatens both Weitz and Dickie: where does this chain begin? If some new item is a work of art because it was intended to be treated as earlier art was treated, how did the *first* art come about? Levinson suggests that at the end of the chain are 'ur-arts', the historical ancestors of art. What are these? Nobody knows, Levinson admits, but he suggests that we could find them by tracing our art traditions backwards, asking for art at some given time, what came before it such that the new art was intended to be treated as that earlier thing was. If we followed all of our chains backwards, we would eventually find a stopping point. It is at this point that we have the *ur*-arts. We could reasonably trace our current traditions of regarding art back to the eighteenth century when the notion of the 'fine arts' arose, beyond this through the Renaissance, the Middle Ages, to the ancient Greeks and beyond. Where does it bottom out? That seems more of a question for the anthropologist than the philosopher, but it doesn't seem unreasonable to think that what would become the arts began with either primitive religious articles or methods of communication (storytelling, representational cave painting) which came to be appreciated not for their original functions, but for something else, perhaps something aesthetic.

Robert Stecker suggests that Levinson's approach might be further simplified by looking to *functions* rather than to *intentions*. Stecker's view draws on Levinson's historical definition as well as those of the functionalists, discussed earlier this chapter. The aptly named 'historical functionalism' operates on the assumption that both the forms and functions of art evolve over time. Photography is a central art form today, though it wasn't a century ago. And landscape gardening, once central, has drifted more towards the periphery. Painting, sculpture, poetry and music, meanwhile, just keep chugging along in the nucleus of art. What counts as a work of art *today*, Stecker argues, depends in part on what constitute the central art forms today. So what counts as an artwork today might be very different from what would count as an artwork a century or a millennium ago. Something is an artwork at a given time, Stecker argues, just in case (a) it is in one of the central art forms at that time, and is made with the intention of fulfilling an artistic function at that time, or (b) it is an artefact that achieves excellence in fulfilling such a function.[27] So, first, being a painting or a photograph today is not enough to qualify something as art: although a child's finger painting qualifies as a painting, it may not thus be art, and not every snapshot you take on holiday will qualify either. However, if that finger painting or photograph was created to serve an artistic function, it will be art. So what counts as an *artistic* function?

As the functionalists would point out, not every use to which we might put an artwork is thus a proper function of art. Using a painting to cover up a stain on the wall does not make this a proper function of art, nor does buying a painting for its investment value. To cover up a stain is not to use something *as* art; to buy something for the purposes of turning a profit is not an *artistic* use of that thing. Stecker agrees with Beardsley and Schlesinger (among others) that art functions are normally tied to experience – to *aesthetic* experience. But artworks also *move* us, *enlighten* us and sometimes *terrify* us. As well, artworks *do* represent, they *do* express. Artworks may be created with any of these functions in mind, and all of these, Stecker suggests, are in the domain of artistic function (properly speaking) today.

Notice the second part of Stecker's definition. Something may not have been created with an artistic function in mind, and indeed may not even fall into a central art form, but may nevertheless be art *if* it excels at one of those artistic functions. Notice here that the bar is set quite a bit higher for things that don't fit neatly into the central art forms at some given time. On Stecker's definition, a painting or photograph today need only be created with the *intention* that it serve the right sort of function – it needn't actually *succeed* in that function. However, if something falls outside the central art forms, it needs not only to succeed, but to *excel* in achieving that function. Stecker's view does something interesting here: it makes sense of our sometimes honorific use of 'art'. Even if we do not treat video games or shoes as a central art form today (and even if we might hesitate to call video games or shoes a category of art at all), *some* video games and *some* shoes will rightly qualify as art if they excel at providing an aesthetic experience, or enlightening us, or expressing the mind of their creators. We can say the same for ancient artefacts or creations by art-outsiders that were never even intended to serve an artistic function: if they nevertheless excel at such a function, it is hard to deny that they are art.

Stecker admits, however, that *Fountain* continues to prove problematic. The work was an artwork in 1917, Stecker contends, but did not fall easily into any central art form at the time. In 1917, it would stretch credulity to call *Fountain* a sculpture. Rather, the work was (and is) a ready-made – a revolutionary and important art form, certainly, but hardly a central one. Stecker suggests that perhaps his view might be amended, broadening 'central art form' to include 'others recognizable as art forms through their derivation from the central ones'.[28] In other words, ready-mades are recognizable as something of an offshoot of the central art form of sculpture. The problem is that (given how *Fountain* was rejected by the Society of Independent Artists – surely among the most open-minded artists at the time) ready-mades were *not* generally recognized as an art form in 1917.

Chapter summary

We have seen throughout this chapter how developments in art have served to inspire philosophers to consider what distinguishes art from other human activities and products. Philosophers have moved from attempting to capture some essential quality in artworks (whether representation, form or expression) to seeking to define art in terms of its function, to questioning whether there *is* anything essential to art. In response to the scepticism of Ziff and Weitz, philosophers have begun to look for art's defining feature or features outside of the works themselves, in the relationships art bears to the artworld and to art history. Thinkers have moved from attempting to determine art's essential nature from existing works, to trying to provide definitions of art that will allow for unprecedented and unexpected future revolutions in art. Despite all of this, *Fountain* continues to be a thorn in the side of any compelling definition of art.

Historical timeline

	c. 360 BCE	Plato, *Republic*
	c. 350 BCE	Aristotle, *Poetics*
Leonardo da Vinci, *Mona Lisa*	1503	
Michelangelo, *David*	1501-1504	
Breughel the Elder (attributed), *Landscape with the Fall of Icarus*	c. 1558	
Jan Vermeer, *The Artist's Studio*	1665–6	
	1790	Immanuel Kant, *The Critique of Judgment*
First daguerreotype by Louis Daguerre	1837	
Hector Berlioz, *Marche funèbre pour la dernière scène d'*Hamlet	1844	
William Powell Frith, *The Railway Station*	1862	
Claude Monet, *Impression, Sunrise*	1872	

Georges Seurat, *Sunday Afternoon on the Island of La Grande Jatte*	1884–6	
Henri de Toulouse-Lautrec, *Moulin Rouge: La Goulue*	1891	
	1896	Leo Tolstoy, *What Is Art?*
	1902	Benedetto Croce, *Aesthetic*
Pablo Picasso, *Les Demoiselles d'Avignon*	1907	
Marcel Duchamp, *Nude Descending a Staircase, No. 2*	1912	
	1913	Clive Bell, *Art*
Marcel Duchamp, *Fountain*	1917	
Georgia O'Keeffe, *Black Iris III*	1926	
Henri Matisse, *Nude on a Yellow Sofa*		
	1931	Henri Matisse, 'Notes of a Painter'
Alexander Schawinsky, 'Studio 42' Olivetti typewriter	1936	
	1938	R. G. Collingwood, *The Principles of Art*
	1953	Paul Ziff, 'The Task of Defining a Work of Art'
	1956	Morris Weitz, 'The Role of Theory in Aesthetics'
	1958	Monroe Beardsley, *Aesthetics: Problems in the Philosophy of Criticism*
Andy Warhol, *Campbell's Tomato Juice Box*	1964	Arthur Danto, 'The Artworld'
	1965	Maurice Mandelbaum, 'Family Resemblances and the Generalization Concerning the Arts'
	1975	George Dickie, *Art and the Aesthetic*
	1979	Jerrold Levinson, 'Defining Art Historically'
		George Schlesinger, 'Aesthetic Experience and the Definition of Art'

	1981	Arthur Danto, *The Transfiguration of the Commonplace*
	1983	Monroe Beardsley, 'An Aesthetic Definition of Art'
	1984	George Dickie, *The Art Circle*
Felix Gonzales-Torres, *'Untitled' (Throat)*	1991	
	1992	Richard Lind, 'The Aesthetic Essence of Art'
	1995	Oswald Hanfling, 'Art, Artifact and Function'
Tracey Emin, *My Bed*	1998	
	2010	Robert Stecker, *Aesthetics and the Philosophy of Art: An Introduction*

Key terms and concepts

- The Aesthetic (p. 28)
- Aesthetic Art (p. 21)
- Aesthetic Emotion (p. 23)
- Aesthetic Experience (p. 28)
- Aesthetic Function (p. 28)
- Aesthetic Interest (p. 28)
- Aesthetic Object (p. 28)
- Aesthetic Satisfaction (p. 28)
- Agreeable Art (p. 21)
- Amusement Art (p. 27)
- Artefact (p. 21)
- Artworld (p. 35)
- Artworld Public (p. 37)
- Artworld System (p. 38)
- Closed Concept (p. 34)
- Entertainment Art (p. 27)
- Expression (p. 26)
- Family Resemblance (p. 34)
- Fine Arts (p. 19)
- Historical Functionalism (p. 41)
- Necessary Condition (p. 20)
- Open Concept (p. 34)

- 'Real' Definition (p. 20)
- Significant Form (p. 23)
- Sufficient Condition (p. 20)
- *Ur*-Arts (p. 41)

Further reading

In addition to the original sources for the theories discussed in this chapter, an excellent analysis of approaches to defining art after Weitz is Stephen Davies' *Definitions of Art* (Cornell University Press, 1991). Davies himself is a proponent of an institutional approach, following Dickie. A variety of new theories are offered in Noël Carroll's edited anthology, *Theories of Art Today* (University of Wisconsin Press, 2000). Of particular interest in Carroll's volume are Stecker's 'Is It Reasonable to Attempt to Define Art?' and Berys Gaut's '"Art" as a Cluster Concept'. Gaut, however, denies that he is offering a definition at all, but is returning to a sort of Wittgensteinian approach. The appeal of not defining art has gained new traction, and another Wittgensteinian, non-definitional approach is offered by Aaron Meskin in his 2008 article, 'From Defining Art to Defining the Individual Arts: The Role of Theory in the Philosophies of Arts' (in Kathleen Stock and Katherine Thomson-Jones's collection, *New Waves in Aesthetics*, Palgrave Macmillan, 2008).

Unresolved questions

1 Is 'art' something that *needs* to be defined? What happens if we are unable to settle on such a definition?
2 If our current concept of art did not arise until the eighteenth century, is it unacceptably anachronistic to apply our term to pre-eighteenth-century 'art'? Is it reasonable to use a work like the *Mona Lisa* (1503) to test our current definitions?
3 Philosophers like Levinson and Stecker have presented arguments that our concept of art is historically sensitive; should it be culturally sensitive as well? That is, should we say that while something is art, say, in contemporary America, it may not be art in contemporary Uganda?
4 Should a definition of art be expected to tell us anything about how art should be interpreted or evaluated? Why or why not?

2

Interpretation and Intention

I. 'Last Leaf' (2011)

Tom Waits, it is often said, has a cult following, and his albums are often described in terms of their accessibility, ranging from the more commercially friendly to the forbiddingly eclectic. One does not introduce the uninitiated to a Tom Waits album at random; one starts with entry-level Waits.

Waits's singing voice is practically synonymous with gravel, reportedly the deliberate result of decades of whiskey and cigarettes. Critic Daniel Durchholz describes it as sounding 'like it was soaked in a vat of bourbon, left hanging in the smokehouse for a few months and then taken outside and run over with a car a few times'.[1] And, despite (or perhaps because of) all of this, Waits is a haunting, unsettling vocalist, singing today with a voice from another time.

Rolling Stone places Waits at No. 55 on their list of the '100 Greatest Songwriters of All Time' and at No. 81 on their list of the '100 Greatest Singers',

Figure 2.1 Tom Waits. Photograph courtesy Anton Corbijn.

sandwiched between blues legend John Lee Hooker and 'punk poet laureate' Patti Smith. It's as comfortable a place as any for Waits, who is equal parts traditional and groundbreaking. Although he was inducted into the Rock and Roll Hall of Fame in 2011, a Waits song picked at random might as easily be a blues ballad or sea shanty. Waits himself says: 'I think what I do is try and write adventure songs and Halloween music.'[2] And those songs have been covered by the Ramones, Joan Baez, Johnny Cash and countless others. In 2008, actress Scarlett Johansson released her first studio album, *Anywhere I Lay My Head*, composed almost entirely of Waits cover songs. To describe Waits as having a 'cult following' rather severely underplays things: his cult followers are other musicians and music aficionados, his songs revered for their richness, their variety and their depth. As actor

Johnny Depp once put it, 'The devil doesn't have the best tunes. Tom Waits does.'[3]

And so, when Waits's producers asked Keith Richards of the Rolling Stones if he would contribute to Waits's 2011 album, *Bad As Me*, Richards did not hesitate. The album – Waits's seventeenth studio album, released after a seven-year wait – was met with enormous acclaim, and Richards's croaking voice joins Waits's on the waltzing ballad 'Last Leaf':

I'm the last leaf on the tree
The autumn took the rest
But they won't take me
I'm the last leaf on the tree

When the autumn wind blows
They're already gone
They flutter to the ground
'Cause they can't hang on
There's nothing in the world
That I ain't seen
I greet all the new ones that are coming in green

I'm the last leaf on the tree
The autumn took the rest
But they won't take me
I'm the last leaf on the tree

Some have suggested that having the seemingly immortal Keith Richards join Waits on this song is particularly apropos. Richards, like Waits, is a survivor in a world where superstars die too young. On her NPR show, *Fresh Air*, host Terry Gross interviewed Waits about the album:

GROSS: You have a couple of songs about death on the new album and …
WAITS: Oh, about death, oh yeah.
GROSS: Yeah. And you know – well, like one is explicitly about death, and one of them is kind of a metaphor for death, called 'Last Leaf'.
WAITS: Yeah.
GROSS: And …
WAITS: Well, I don't know. You could say it's a metaphor for death, or you could say it's really a song about the last leaf on a tree. You know, 'cause I did see a tree out in my yard; it had one leaf – one leaf left on it.
GROSS: Oh, really?
WAITS: And I looked at that leaf and I said, hang on, buddy.
(*laughter*)

WAITS: If you hang on, you can make it to the next season. And if you can make it to the next one, you might be here next year, greeting all the new ones. Hang on.[4]

So, 'Last Leaf' is about … a leaf? How should we take this? If Waits is right, is it because he wrote the song? Can Waits *be* wrong about his own song? If Waits *is* wrong, what justifies an interpretation other than his own?

II. On interpretation

When we ask what a given work *means* – what it is *about* – there are a number of theoretical positions. First, it might be suggested that there are *no* correct interpretations of the work – because no work really means any particular thing. We might as such call this view 'critical nihilism'. On this sort of view, Waits's interpretation of 'Last Leaf' as really being about a leaf is no better and no worse than the more widespread interpretation that the work is about death. Although this view may seem initially appealing, on reflection, the reason that Waits's interpretation is no better and no worse than the standard one is because, strictly speaking, they are both equally wrong. That is, on this view, the work doesn't mean a thing, so any attempt to find meaning in the work is doomed to failure. We cannot, if this view is correct, meaningfully disagree about the content of works of art because there is no such meaningful content. 'Last Leaf', on this view, is as much about the moon landing as it is about death – because it isn't *about* anything at all.

A second possibility is that, for any given work, there is *one* truly correct interpretation, a view called 'critical monism'. This would at least seem to align with how we often treat works of art: we discuss them, we disagree about them, we attempt to justify our interpretations. It seems we are – both individually and collectively – trying to find the 'right' answer. None of this, it should be noted, precludes the possibility of *partly* correct or correct-but-*incomplete* interpretations. It might be suggested, for instance, that 'Last Leaf' *is* about death, but that it is *also* about something more mundane – that the work has *layers* of meaning. So, it might be said, the song is about a number of things, and any interpretation that leaves out a layer of meaning will be impoverished to that degree. A *fully* correct account of the meaning of the song – one that leaves nothing out – will probably be several times longer than the song itself. All that such a fully correct interpretation cannot include are partial interpretations that flatly contradict one another. It cannot, for instance, say that a work is both ironic and not ironic, or that it is at one and the same time about death and *not* about death. A critical monist view as such allows us to say that the work is about a leaf *and* is about death, but yet allows us to deny that it is also about the moon landing. Where critical monists tend to disagree is on what it is that *determines* which interpretations are at least partially correct and which are flat-out incorrect.

A final possibility is that all of this talk about a *correct* interpretation of a work is misleading. Rather, some argue, a good work allows for *multiple* interpretations, each of which has as much claim to being right as any other, a view called 'critical pluralism'. On this sort of view, interpretations are neither simply 'correct' nor 'incorrect', but are, rather, 'valid' or 'invalid', 'acceptable' or 'unacceptable', 'plausible' or 'implausible'. If one interpretation is correct, then any interpretation that contradicts this one will be incorrect. But if a given interpretation is, say, 'plausible', this does not preclude the possibility of other plausible interpretations, even if they flatly contradict the first one. As such, at least in principle, we might have a plausible interpretation of a work that reads it as ironic, and another equally plausible one that reads it as not ironic, and we might accept that *both* are viable interpretations of the work. The same question that needs to be addressed by the critical monists also needs to be addressed by the critical pluralists, however: what is it that *makes* an interpretation plausible or implausible, acceptable or unacceptable?[5]

III. The Romantics

In his major work on aesthetics, *The Critique of Judgment*, Immanuel Kant suggests that producing great art requires *genius*, which Kant characterizes broadly as an innate talent for art.[6] Art, Kant argues, does not follow determinate rules – rules that can simply be explained to, and followed by, anyone else – and so genius cannot be taught. This is not to say, however, that genius is thus lawless and unconstrained. Where there is genius, Kant suggests, it can be *trained*, and so there may be better artists and lesser ones, but where genius is lacking, it seems, one is simply out of luck. An artist learns to create art by observing great beauty and practising one's art, but the aesthetic ideas with which the artist works are grounded in *intuition*, says Kant, not in determinate *concepts*, and so cannot simply be explained. In this way, Kant sums up a particular sentiment of Romanticism, a tradition that dominated art and intellectual thought in the eighteenth and nineteenth centuries. In the Romantic era, there developed a view of the artist as living in a sort of heroic isolation: the artist had something that the rest of us did not, and could not hope to gain. In Kant's terms, the artist had genius: a unique insight into man and the universe, and a unique ability to give his or her ideas form, whether through paint or marble or words.

Certainly, a great number of artists in the Romantic era were only too happy to accept and encourage this notion of the artist. In an 1824 journal entry, French Romantic painter and lithographer Eugène Delacroix writes about a gathering with friends discussing this very issue:

> At Leblond's. Interesting discussion about genius and unusual men. Dimier thought that great passions were the source of genius. I think that it is imagination alone, or better still, what amounts to the same thing, that delicacy of the organs that makes one see what others do not see, and which makes one see in a different way.[7]

So, on this view, the artist-as-genius is uniquely sensitive. But what, we might ask, does this have to do with interpretation, being the subject of this chapter? The upshot of the Romantic view is that artworks embody something that exists *within* the artist – something that, because we lack his sort of genius, we depend on the artist to communicate to us. The American Romantic painter Washington Allston writes:

> He, therefore, who possesses the power of presenting to another the *precise* images or emotions as they existed in himself, presents that which can be found nowhere else, and was first found by and within himself; and, however light or trifling, where these are true as to his own mind, their author is so far an originator.[8]

On this note, let us recall the view of R. G. Collingwood, discussed in the previous chapter. Although writing in the early twentieth century – after the Romantic era – Collingwood's theory of art is clearly influenced by Romanticism. On Collingwood's view, the artwork, properly speaking, does not exist as lyrics encoded on a CD or as paint on a canvas. Rather, the artwork is a *mental* thing that exists in the mind of the artist, and which (if the artist is successful) may be communicated through, say, a painting or a song to the audience. The painting or song is merely a conduit to the true artwork. This being the case, who but the artist could confirm or deny that you had properly understood the work? On this view, it would seem there is only *one* correct interpretation for any given work, and it is determined solely by what was in the artist's mind in the process of creation.

If, on this view, you take 'Last Leaf' to be about death and survival, and we can take Waits at his word, then you are quite simply wrong in your interpretation of the work. The work simply *is* about the last leaf on that tree. Now, if this Romanic view is sound, whose fault is your misinterpretation? Certainly, it might be yours – you might have uncultivated or insensitive taste, or perhaps you were distracted in your listening by your own mortality and were projecting onto the work. Perhaps you were simply giving Waits more credit than he deserves. But your misinterpretation might equally be Waits's fault: perhaps he possesses that special insight, that 'delicacy of the organs' that for the Romantics set the artist apart from the rest of us, but yet has not properly trained his genius, has not practised enough, and so has produced something that does not give appropriate access to that which exists in his mind. In whomever the fault lies, however, the final arbiter of meaning will be Waits himself, as on Collingwood's view, the work – the thing with *meaning* – is not the thing you read on a page or hear played over your speakers, but that to which the song is supposed to give you access.

Granted, Collingwood's overall view likely goes well beyond the positions held by the Romantics at large, but the implications for interpretation reflect the general sentiment of Romanticism: what a work means is determined solely by the artist who created it. Flaws or ambiguities in a work might *obscure* meaning, but they do not thus *determine* or *change* it. While this might seem an extreme view, in many ways it reflects how many of us continue to treat art. In 2007, Harry Potter author J. K. Rowling gave a reading of *Harry Potter and the Deathly Hallows* at New York City's Carnegie Hall. After the reading, Rowling participated in a question-and-answer session with the audience. One audience member asked whether Albus Dumbledore, the headmaster of the wizarding school that Harry Potter attends, had ever been in love. Rowling replied: 'My truthful answer to you ... I always thought of Dumbledore as gay.'[9] Rowling maintained script approval for all of the film adaptations of the Harry Potter series, and in reading one of the film scripts, she explained, she noticed that the scriptwriter had inserted a back-story of Dumbledore having had a childhood crush on a girl. Rowling made a note in the margin: 'Dumbledore is gay!' With these three words, Rowling made international headlines. Reactions were immediate and polarized, some applauding the inclusion of a character now revealed to be gay as central to such a popular series, while others arguing that the revelation served as more evidence that the books should be pulled from school libraries. What we did not hear, however, was anyone saying that Rowling was *wrong*. Rather, most seemed to at least tacitly accept Rowling's position: 'He is my character, and as my character, I have the right to know what I know about him and say what I say about him.'[10]

IV. Anti-intentionalism

In 1919, renowned poet T. S. Eliot published his essay 'Tradition and the Individual Talent', and inadvertently inspired a new critical movement.[11] In the essay, Eliot questions the Romantic idea that great works of poetry express the personal emotion of the poet. Rather, Eliot contends, artistic creation centrally involves surrendering oneself to artistic tradition. The mind of the poet, Eliot argues, serves as a catalyst for feelings and emotions arising in tradition, but these are not the poet's personal, *felt* emotions. Instead, the emotion in poetry – and the poem itself – is impersonal to its author. The poet, Eliot contends, must 'surrender' himself to the work. The emotion 'has its life in the poem and not in the history of the poet'.[12] As such, Eliot writes, 'Honest criticism and sensitive appreciation is directed not upon the poet but upon the poetry.'[13]

Literary critics in the 1920s and 1930s took Eliot's essay as a starting point for the theoretical position that would come to be known as 'New Criticism' (named for a later work by poet John Crowe Ransom). New Criticism in general rejected any literary criticism informed by sources outside the work itself, and so the author of a literary work was taken to have no more privileged a perspective on interpreting the work than any other reader. Without the authority of the author to turn to as an arbiter of meaning, the New Critics suggested instead that the only arbiter of meaning is the work itself. As such, New Criticism focuses on a very close reading of the text of a literary work, taking into account such formal elements as diction, metre and rhyme in addition to a work's characters, setting and plot. On the New Critical view, a literary work is an *autonomous* entity that exists apart from its author.

To illustrate, consider a particular case – Andrew Hudgins' 2001 poem 'In the Well':

1   My father cinched the rope,
2   a noose around my waist,
3   and lowered me into
4   the darkness. I could taste

5   my fear. It tasted first
6   of dark, then earth, then rot.
7   I swung and struck my head
8   and at that moment got

9   another then: then blood,
10   which spiked my mouth with iron.

11 Hand over hand, my father
12 dropped me from then to then:

13 then water. Then wet fur,
14 which I hugged to my chest.
15 I shouted. Daddy hauled
16 the wet rope. I gagged, and pressed

17 my neighbor's missing dog
18 against me. I held its death
19 and rose up to my father.
20 Then light. Then hands. Then breath.

So ... what does the poem mean? The approach of New Criticism demands that we look only at the poem itself: an autonomous thing. We cannot receive help from outside the words on the page. However, even with this limitation, there is certainly a lot to go on. On its face, the poem seems to be about a child being lowered into a well by his or her father to retrieve a neighbour's dog from the water at the bottom. On the way down, the narrator bangs his or her head. We might be naturally inclined to interpret the narrator as a boy because the poet is male, but this goes beyond what is in the poem itself. Since the poem does not tell us anything about the narrator's gender, New Criticism tells us the matter is indeterminate. However, we *can* reasonably infer that the narrator is a child because of what *is* in the poem: 'Daddy'.

Notice, though, the change in diction: at line 1, it is 'father', and 'father' again at line 11. Then, at line 15, it is 'Daddy', and back to 'father' again at line 19. What's happening here? One interpretation that fits the story is this: our narrator, the child, felt like an adult at the beginning of this ordeal. He or she was given an important job and felt brave (as children do when adults are around). But upon reaching the bottom, where it was just the child and the body of a dog, that bravery vanished, and 'father' became 'Daddy'. But, having been hauled back up to the top, our narrator is able to put on a brave face, and it's 'father' again.

At the end of the poem, there is breath, and we might ask, who is doing the breathing? There seem to be three options here: the child, the father or the dog. Although the dog would be the optimistic option, and the father is a possibility, the textual evidence seems to most strongly suggest that it is the child – the narrator – who is doing the breathing. At line 6, the narrator tastes rot, and at line 16, the narrator gags. Pulled up into the fresh air at line 20, the narrator can breathe cleanly again. Indeed, it's worth noting that throughout the poem, the focus is on the non-visual senses: what the narrator feels, tastes and smells. The child is in darkness.

Let's keep digging. The poem is written in iambic trimeter – three 'feet' of unstressed and stressed syllables: ba-DUM, ba-DUM, ba-DUM. The poem is made up of five quatrains (four-line stanzas) following an XAXA XBXB XCXC XDXD XEXE rhyme scheme (that is, the second line rhymes with the fourth, the sixth with the eighth and so on, while every other line – represented by Xs here – is unrhyming). This regular rhythm of loose-then-tight, loose-then-tight is form following content, mirroring the lowering and raising of the narrator on the rope: loose-then-tight, loose-then-tight. We see a repeated rhythm in the word choice as well: 'then ... then' (6); 'then: then' (9); 'hand over hand' (11); 'then to then' (12); 'then ... then' (13); 'Then ... Then ... Then' (20). Notice that in the final line, the repetition is sped up just as the child is nearing the top of the well.

The rhythm isn't perfect, however. Five of the 16 lines contain extra syllables. In line 10, the word 'iron' might be squished into a single syllable (a trick poets sometimes like to use), but notice that this occurs at a traumatic moment in the poem. This sort of divergence from form at an important point in the poem is not unusual in poetry. But our poem does more: notice that when the extra syllables occur at lines 16, 18 and 19, this is all after the narrator has gagged and would have trouble breathing normally. On the close reading that New Criticism demands, all of this – the plot of the poem, the diction, the rhythm, the metre – potentially contributes to meaning, and none of it should be dismissed out of hand. That being said, New Criticism does place limitations on interpretation.

I found a blogger who analysed the poem, writing: 'In the poem "In the Well" Andrew Hudgins tells the story of how he rescued a neighbor's [dog] from inside [a] well.'[14] Do we have any reason, though, to think that this poem is autobiographical? Not from a New Critical perspective: using this critical method, we aren't allowed to look outside the poem. So we also aren't allowed to take note of the fact that a number of Hudgins's poems are written from a child's perspective. Nor are we allowed to take note of the fact that the poem is reprinted in a later collection by Hudgins, *Ecstatic in the Poison*, where it is retitled 'Out' (serving as a sort of closing bookend to the collection's opening poem, 'In', which is also written from a child's point of view, and deals with a child's innocent ignorance about the world). Many have, as such, found New Criticism to be unnecessarily restrictive, especially given how much a broadened scope seems to provide to interpretation in examples such as this.

In 1954, literary theorist W. K. Wimsatt, Jr and philosopher Monroe Beardsley published 'The Intentional Fallacy', an essay growing out of the New Critical approach to interpretation.[15] In many ways, the view of Wimsatt and Beardsley reflects the approach of New Criticism, but in other ways allows for greater latitude in interpretation. Like the New Critics, Wimsatt and Beardsley suggest that literary biography – the study of authors, their motivations and their psychology – while a perfectly legitimate project, is nevertheless a project distinct from *poetic* studies and criticism. The central problem with the Romantic approach, Wimsatt and Beardsley argue, is that an author's intentions are simply not available to the reader for inspection. Not that this stops some readers. Hudgins reports that since his poem started being collected in anthologies for high school classes

> about twice a year I get anguished letters from high school students wanting me to assure them that the dog is alive. Or more rarely, from an outraged boy who knows the dog is dead but the class has sided against him in the discussion and implied he is morbid for thinking so.[16]

If Hudgins reassures students that the dog is alive (as our blogger apparently believes), does this mean the dog lived? Or if Hudgins tells the outraged boy that, yes, the dog is dead and his classmates are wrong, does that make it so? Should we *believe* the author *because* he's the author?

Let's look back at the case of 'Last Leaf'. Here, Waits seems to fairly clearly state that he wrote the song as being about a leaf, and so not about death and survival. Why not just take him at his word? After all, he was there when the song was written: *he wrote it*! Our first problem is that Tom Waits is a liar. Seriously, he's known for it. One writer notes:

> Tom Waits is, famously, not the easiest interview out there. Reporters often get frustrated with him because he speaks inaudibly or 'won't give straight answers.' (When, asked once why he had allowed six long years to pass between albums, Waits replied stonily, 'I was stuck in traffic.') He's notorious for telling make-believe stories about himself. Not out of malice, mind you. Mostly just to pass the time. He quite enjoys the lies that have been printed about him over the years.[17]

The fact that most of the lies have originated with Waits himself seems to make little difference. However, even when our author *isn't* a known liar – as, say, in the case of Hudgins or Rowling – it may be that the author doesn't always have the best access to her own intentions years after creating a work (or perhaps even at the time of creation). But even if we *could* trust the author, and *could* trust her memory and introspection, there is still an in-principle problem. Wimsatt and Beardsley do not want to deny the role that authorship plays in the *creation* of a literary work – what they deny, rather, is that the cause for a thing's existence should likewise serve as a standard of interpreting that thing.

What an author intended, Wimsatt and Beardsley argue, is a species of *external* evidence, to be distinguished from such *internal* evidence for meaning as syntax, form, plot and the like. Although knowledge of an author's biographical details (what works he is familiar with, the context in which the work was written, what he has said about the work and so on) may point us toward a particular interpretation, other interpretations of the work remain open. On this *anti-intentionalist* perspective, there is no reason why an author's intended meaning should trump any other competing interpretation. What an author *intended* a work to mean should be distinguished from what those words in that order *in fact* mean. Literary works, Wimsatt and Beardsley argue, are linguistic entities, and linguistic entities are *public* entities. The meanings of words are not determined by the speaker, but are constructed by the community that uses the language. On this view, competing interpretations are compared not against the author's intentions, but against the work itself. Which interpretation, we can ask, *best matches* what is written in the work? Which interpretation *most fully explains* the work? Which interpretation allows for the *richest reading* of the text? Perhaps it is the author's interpretation, but, it seems, it may just as likely not be. It is at this point that Wimsatt and Beardsley's anti-intentionalism diverges from New Criticism, strictly considered.

Wimsatt and Beardsley recognize that the best reading of a text may require looking outside the text itself. The song immediately preceding 'Last Leaf' on Waits's *Bad As Me* album is titled 'Satisfied'. It seems no coincidence that the song immediately precedes 'Last Leaf', as 'Satisfied' contains this passage:

> I will have satisfaction.
> I will be satisfied.
>
> Now, Mr. Jagger and Mr. Richards,
> I will scratch where I've been itching.
> Now Mr. Jagger and Mr. Richards,
> I will scratch where I've been itching.

Keith Richards, who duets with Waits on 'Last Leaf', is, like Mick Jagger, a founding member of the Rolling Stones, and the Stones' first international chart-topper was 1965's 'I Can't Get No (Satisfaction)'. This is a clear case of allusion: where a work refers to some person, thing or event outside the text. In this case, everything suggests that Waits's 'Satisfied' is in fact a *reply* to the Rolling Stones, and it would seem ridiculous to put all the evidence aside. In other cases, while references are not as explicit as they are in 'Satisfied', they seem nevertheless difficult to ignore. T. S. Eliot, discussed earlier in this section, is often referred to as an 'allusive' author: his works appear rich with allusive references, some clear and others obscure. A reader who is unfamiliar with the works apparently alluded to will find Eliot's work impenetrable; one who is familiar with the works will find Eliot's work extremely rich with meaning. Eliot himself famously refuses to explain the apparent allusions. On Wimsatt and Beardsley's anti-intentionalist view, if a poem is best read as alluding to another literary work – if, say, it best explains the poem – it simply does not matter if the author intended it to do so. As a thing autonomous from its author, it is centrally the *poem* that alludes, and not the author, so it is irrelevant whether the author intended the allusion that the reader interprets. Conversely, if an author *intends* her poem to allude to some other work, and this is not apparent in the text, the poem simply does not so allude – to intend your work to allude, they might say, does not thus result in your work alluding. This anti-intentionalist view will apply beyond allusion, taking in irony, metaphor and all manner of figurative language normally taken to be dependent on the author's intentions. As such, while interpretation of a work may stray beyond the words on the page, the meaning of that work will not be grounded in its author's intentions, but rather in the text itself.[18]

At least in principle, the anti-intentionalist view allows for multiple, competing and mutually exclusive interpretations of a work. It may be, for instance, that there is no clear answer as to whether or not a work is ironic or not ironic. It may be that each reading allows for an equally rich and meaningful interpretation of the work. And so an anti-intentionalist might hold the view that each is a 'plausible' or 'acceptable' interpretation of the work with neither having a claim to being the one single 'correct' interpretation.

V. Post-structuralism

Several years after Wimsatt and Beardsley published 'The Intentional Fallacy', French theorist Roland Barthes published his essay 'The Death of the Author' (1967).[19] In many ways, the content of Barthes's essay mirrors that of Wimsatt and Beardsley's. Like Wimsatt and Beardsley, Barthes decries the Romantic view of the author as arbiter-of-meaning. The notion of the author, he contends, is a modern invention, wherein great importance has come to be attached to the 'person' of the author:

> The image of literature to be found in ordinary culture is tyrannically centred on the author, his person, his life, his tastes, his passions, while criticism still consists for the most part in saying that Baudelaire's work is the failure of Baudelaire the man, Van Gogh's his madness, Tchaikovsky's his vice.[20]

In the shadow of the Romantics, Beardsley notes, we seek *explanation* for the work in the person of its author, with the author thought to *nourish* the work. Like Wimsatt and Beardsley, Barthes argues for a move away from the authority of the author. However, where Wimsatt and Beardsley contend that we should turn to the text itself as the source of meaning, Barthes suggests another direction.

Barthes argues that, by 'giving' the text an author, we impose a limit on the work – we 'close' the writing. Instead, Barthes argues, the creation of the work is an ongoing process – that every text is 'eternally written *here and now*'.[21] So far as meaning is concerned, Barthes suggests, the author 'dies' when the text is released to the public. From there on, the author becomes just another reader. And it is the reader, Barthes argues, who fills the work with meaning. Where the authority of an author 'closes' the writing, he suggests, the multiplicity of readers opens it again:

> Thus is revealed the total existence of writing: a text is made of multiple writings, drawn from many cultures and entering into mutual relations of dialogue, parody, contestation, but there is one place where this multiplicity is focused and that place is the reader, not, as was hitherto said, the author.[22]

With the author removed from the process, no longer is the text to be 'deciphered'; rather, it must be 'disentangled'. Where the deciphering of a code allows for only one correct answer, there are any number of ways that a text may be disentangled.

Barthes's essay helped to mark the beginning of a new critical movement, *post-structuralism*, a broad philosophical school of thought reacting to structuralism, an intellectual movement that dominated France in the 1950s and 1960s. Although post-structuralism is difficult to characterize as a whole, in literary analysis it is typified by the 'destabilization' of the author. Where the anti-intentionalism of Wimsatt and Beardsley replaced the author with the text, the post-structuralists replaced the author with the reader. In his 1969 essay, 'What is an Author?', another post-structuralist, Michel Foucault, suggests that the notion of the author is a functional principle that is imposed upon works to limit the composition, decomposition and recomposition of fiction, and to restrict the proliferation of meaning, something he suggests we actually fear.[23] Removing the author, on the post-structuralist view, does not leave the text as the arbiter of meaning. With the author removed (or, as Foucault might say, not imposed), the text itself is a mute thing; it has no meaning until it is engaged by the reader. Barthes suggests that the reader 'plays' the text, both as one 'plays' a game and as one 'plays' a musical instrument – that reading is an active, creative process.[24] In the search for meaning in literature, there is no longer *any* authority. There is no meaning in a text beyond what it means to *you*, the reader. And your authority is no greater than that of any other reader.

With its focus on the reader's role in creating meaning, post-structuralism thus gave rise to *reader-response criticism*, which operates according to the view that literature should be thought of as something of a performance art, with each reader as a unique performer. On this view, the meaning of the text is produced in the individual act of performance, and so there is no one 'correct' meaning for all readers – perhaps not even for the same reader at different times – although theorist Stanley Fish has suggested that readers may be grouped together in 'interpretive communities', groups who share a particular reading strategy or set of assumptions that inform their reading.[25] While reader-response critics in general agree that there is no single correct meaning for any given text, where they differ is on the degree to which the text should be thought to *constrain* meaning. Some, like Barthes, suggest that the text in no way constrains meaning, and that how readers 'play' with a text is an entirely open matter. Others, like Roman Ingarden, suggest the text serves to *guide* reading, but leaves open innumerable 'spots of indeterminacy', where details of a story or description are left unspecified and so left to each reader to fill in.[26] On this view, while there is no single 'correct' reading of a text, readings that contradict what is actually written in the text will nevertheless be 'incorrect' readings. And so, on a reader-response view, J. K. Rowling is perfectly free to read Dumbledore as gay, but this should not thus constrain *your* reading, and while Waits may interpret 'Last Leaf' as being about a tree, Terry Gross and others are perfectly free to interpret it as a song about death and survival.

Some contend that each way of reading or filling in a story itself creates a new work – a view called 'radical constructivism'. On this view, a work is identifiable with its meaning, broadly construed, and as meaning is determined by each reading, each act of reading creates a new work. When Rowling reads the Harry Potter series, she creates a work in which the character of Dumbledore is gay, and perhaps when you read the series, you create a work in which the character of Dumbledore is not gay. On a radical constructivist view, these are not conflicting interpretations, because they are about distinct works. On such a view, no one can ever be wrong in their reading of the Harry Potter series, 'Last Leaf', 'In the Well' or any other such work, because, strictly speaking, they are not reading *works*; rather, they are reading *texts* and *constructing* works (in the terminology of post-structuralism, 'text' is a very broad term: the words on the page of a poem are a text, but so are the images on the screen of a film, the words heard in a song and so on). The rather counterintuitive upshot of radical constructivism is that when Rowling was answering questions about *Harry Potter and the Deathly Hallows*, she was discussing a work that none of us will ever read, because only she herself has true access to it. When you sit down to read the novel, you will be creating a different work entirely, and nothing that Rowling says about the work *she* created applies to the work that *you* create – because they are different works. On this view, it seems it is simply not possible for two people to meaningfully discuss an artwork, because they will always be discussing different works.

A more moderate version of constructivism has been offered by Michael Krausz, who attempts to solve this problem by suggesting that rather than each reading (viewing, listening) creating some new distinct work, each such interpretation *contributes* to the work.[27] In reading the lyrics of 'Last Leaf' or listening to the song, Waits interprets it as a simple ode to a leaf, but when Gross hears it, she hears a song about death. In Krausz's terms, Gross and Waits have each picked out different features of the novel as 'salient' (significant, important), and so each 'imputes' (contributes) different properties to the work. However, Krausz says, 'When interpretations impute different properties, they must impute a sufficiently large number of properties in common to warrant the agreement that they are addressing a sufficiently common object-of-interest.'[28] That is, there must be enough overlap in the respective interpretations for readers to be said to reasonably be discussing the same work – the same object-of-interpretation – a relationship Krausz calls 'unicity'. Although Krausz does not precisely describe how much overlap there must be for unicity to be maintained, we might suppose that the relationship could be sustained, say, by requiring that all of the interpretations be grounded in and not conflict with the text itself. On Krausz's view, then, the work is nothing but this bundle or class of related interpretations, which is itself the thing being interpreted – the work.

There is a rather odd outcome for this view, however: if each reading or interpretation of a work (understood first as an object-of-interpretation) itself contributes to the work (also understood as the unicitous class of interpretations), then *each* such interpretation is actually an interpretation of itself, a strange sort of relationship to say the least. Robert Stecker points out a further problem: on Krausz's view, in interpreting the object, one is making a claim about it, but in doing so, one is also at the same time contributing to that object. Let us suppose that the interpretation in question is that 'Last Leaf' is about death. In what sense is this true or false? If the claim is true, it would seem, the song would already have to have had that property – which, on Krautz's view, it could not have until it was so interpreted. But if the song does not have that property prior to interpretation, it would seem that such a claim would have to be, properly speaking, false, but would be true thereafter on Krautz's theory. So, in first asserting that 'Last Leaf' is a song about death, one would be asserting something false, but any later reader who made the same interpretation would be saying something true about the same work.[29]

VI. Intentionalism revisited

Although popular, the moves to cut off works from their authors (first from the New Critics and then from the post-structuralists) did not serve to entirely eliminate *intentionalist* models of interpretation, holding that the author determines the meaning of the work. Perhaps the most outspoken of the twentieth-century intentionalists is theorist E. D. Hirsch, Jr, who outlines his central view in his 1967 book, *Validity in Interpretation*.[30] Hirsch argues that popularization of anti-intentionalist views is explained *historically* as a refreshing and invigorating change from the critical atmosphere instilled by the Romantics, but that it is not explained *logically*. In eliminating the author from the search for valid interpretations, Hirsch argues, critics had banished the only viable basis for validating interpretation – effectively destroying the project of interpretational validity altogether.

While granting that each reader might find different things in a work to be significant (or, in Krausz's terms, salient), Hirsch argues that *significance* should be distinguished from *meaning*:

> *Meaning* is that which is represented by a text; it is what the author meant by his use of a particular sign sequence; it is what the signs represent. *Significance*, on the other hand, names a relationship between that

meaning and a person, or a conception, or a situation, or indeed anything imaginable.[31]

The same work might have different significances for different persons at different times (or, indeed, the same person at different times), and this, Hirsch argues, is not problematic. But what a work *means* is logically prior to what any given reader *takes* it to mean (the distinction that seems to pose a problem for Krausz). For an interpretation to be valid, Hirsch contends, it must correspond to the *actual* meaning represented by the text. And this, he argues, is determined by the author. However, Hirsch does not suggest that this is always a simple matter.

Hirsch agrees with Wimsatt and Beardsley that an author's intentions probably cannot be known with certainty – perhaps not even by the author herself. However, he argues, that an author's intended meaning cannot *certainly* be known – that is, that such cannot be *confirmed* – should not thus sanction the hasty conclusion that the author's meaning is thus *inaccessible* and so a useless object in interpretation. In other words, that I cannot confirm that I have accurately understood the author's intentions does not mean that I have not done so. Understanding, he notes, does not require confirmation of understanding. Consider: if you are working through a mathematical calculation, you may afterwards want to work backwards to confirm that you have reached the right answer. If your answer is correct, however, confirmation is not what *makes* it so; rather, confirmation is only what *assures* you that you have understood it. Likewise, in interpreting a work of art, if your interpretation is the correct one, this does not depend upon confirming that it is the case.

The goal of interpretation, Hirsch argues, is to seek the most *probably* correct understanding of the work in question, and one does so by examining the text. It may be, he grants, that on very rare occasions an author's intended meaning will not be apparent in the text, but he argues that this does not lead to the slippery slope of discounting authorial meaning in general. When an author composes a poem, she usually intends it to be publicly understandable, and not to be obscurely private and autobiographical in meaning. That is, the author *wants* us to understand her meaning. In interpreting a text, Hirsch contends, we are only concerned with those meanings that are publicly shareable, and, he says, 'it is far more likely that an author and an interpreter can entertain identical meanings than that they cannot'.[32] Now, without confirmation being available to us as interpreters, we may be left with competing interpretations. If we are to choose between them, our goal is simply to show that a given reading is more *probable* than the others.

Noël Carroll offers another take on intentionalism.[33] He suggests that when we read a poem, listen to a song or contemplate a painting, we enter into a certain *relationship* with its creator – a relationship comparable to a conversation. Carroll argues that in art, the author wishes to *communicate* something, and, like any conversation, when it is rewarding, there is a sense of *community* or *communion*. Granted, unlike ordinary conversation, a poem or song or painting does not offer back-and-forth feedback with the creator, but, Carroll contends, we nevertheless have a stake in understanding the person 'speaking'. And so perhaps it is more like receiving a postcard from abroad than a face-to-face conversation. Nevertheless, Carroll argues, it is this sense of community that we are seeking when we engage with artworks: 'We want to understand the author, even if that will lead to rejecting his or her point of view.'[34] Conversely, he says, we also want to hold onto our own sense of self-respect in this conversation.

Carroll employs the example of Ed Wood's infamous 1959 film, *Plan 9 From Outer Space*. The plot of the film is pretty simple: aliens, concerned that humans are on the path to discovering and triggering a substance that will destroy the universe, implement 'Plan 9', a strategy to get the earthlings' attention by reviving their dead as zombies. Although featuring veteran actor Bella Lugosi (in scenes culled from an earlier, shelved project with the actor), the film is renowned for its problems. With continuity errors throughout, visible strings attached to wobbly flying saucers, and hackneyed narration, the movie has come to be known as one of the worst films of all time. Watching the movie as an attempt at a serious science-fiction/horror film almost inevitably results in groans and laughter in equal measure. Since it gained notoriety, however, some have started to look at the film as subversive – as a deliberate, self-conscious attempt to undermine standard filmmaking. Watching the movie in this light makes it seem like the work of a sort of cinematic genius: there is hardly a scene that does not turn serious filmmaking on its head. Strictly speaking, there is nothing in the film to indicate which sort of film it is – serious or subversive. As each interpretation matches the work, an anti-intentionalist view like that of Wimsatt and Beardsley would suggest that the correct way to interpret the work is the way that it comes off best. As a serious work, the movie is an abject failure, but as a work of subversive filmmaking, it is a complete success.

We know quite a lot about Ed Wood. After his death in 1978, Wood achieved a considerable cult status, with his life and films serving as the subject of numerous books, documentaries and biographical films. Throughout the 1950s, Wood wrote, directed and produced a string of cheaply produced films, including stories about teenagers on crime sprees, a mad scientist attempting to create a race of supermen, and a woman who falls in love with a gorilla in her basement. As Carroll notes, 'given the venue Wood trafficked in, it seems that the best hypothesis about his intentions is that he was attempting to imitate the Hollywood style of filmmaking in the cheapest way possible'.[35] That Wood had intentionally created *Plan 9* as a transgressive, avant-garde film, conversely, seems utterly implausible. Although watching *Plan 9* as if this was its design may make for a more interesting or enjoyable movie-going experience, Carroll argues, to do so is to trade in one's own dignity for the sake of an aesthetic high. We have, he argues, not only aesthetic interests in dealing with artworks, but also conversational ones – and we should not trade in the latter for the sake of the former. As in any mode of conversation, the speaker's central intention is to get her meaning across, and the listener's is to get to that meaning. Insofar as we have conversational interests in art, and insofar as conversational interests centre on the intentions of the artists, the artist's intentions cannot simply be disregarded in interpretation. In order to coordinate both our aesthetic interests and our conversational ones, Carroll suggests, the best policy would be to pursue aesthetic satisfaction *constrained* by 'our best hypotheses about authorial intent'.[36]

VII. Hypothetical intentionalism

Noël Carroll professes an intentionalist view on interpretation, but recognizes that our access to the actual intentions of an author is often limited. However, given our conversational interests in artworks – our desire to *commune* with their creators – he suggests we need to work with what we have available and make our best guess about authorial intent. On a similar line, Daniel Nathan suggests that we should, in our interpretative endeavours, consider the 'intentions' of 'an idealized, hypothetical author, an author who can be held responsible for everything in the text, being aware of all the relevant context, conventions, and background assumptions, an author for whom we may imagine everything is there by design, on purpose'.[37] Unlike Carroll, however, Nathan is an *anti*-intentionalist. Nathan certainly recognizes that artworks are artefacts – things intentionally created by people, but, like Wimsatt and Beardsley before him, he does not see the fact that a work *has* an author as reason to take that author's intentions as determining the meaning of the work. Rather, he suggests, we should imagine an author who *did* mean all of the things that the work *apparently* means. In this way, Nathan argues, we can avoid the problems of dealing with the unavailability of the actual author's intentions without thus slipping into the sort of 'anything-goes' approach suggested by Barthes.

Both Carroll and Nathan suggest that we should look to our best *hypotheses* regarding authorial intent – a view generally called 'hypothetical intentionalism'. But Carroll professes to be an intentionalist, while Nathan is an anti-intentionalist – so is hypothetical intentionalism an intentionalist view or an anti-intentionalist one? Is there any substantive difference between the views of Carroll and Nathan? In our case of 'Last Leaf', the reading of the song as being a simple ode to the leaf outside Waits's window, and the alternative interpretation of its being a broader metaphor about death and survival, are at least both in line with the words of the song. Imagine, though, that Waits had instead responded to Gross by asserting that the work is actually about the formation of the first star in the universe after the big bang – an interpretation, in other words, with absolutely no textual support. Carroll suggests that our only reasonable recourse in such a case would be to think that Waits was being *insincere* in his announcement – as we've noted, not an unwarranted thought when it comes to Waits – because, based on what is in the text, he could not reasonably have had such a belief.[38] In other words, such a claim on Waits's part would actually conflict with our best hypotheses about Waits's intentions. But what if we were further to discover (and authenticate) Waits's personal journals, composed during the period in which he was writing the song, and that these backed up his pronouncement? It seems that Carroll, an intentionalist, would have to take these into account; they would be data that 'our best hypotheses about authorial intent' would have to account for. Given the utter lack of textual support for what are evidently the author's intentions in this imagined case, it seems that in Carroll's view, we would have to conclude that this *is* what the work is about, and that (for reasons similar to Wood's *Plan 9 From Outer Space*) it is an abject failure. Nathan, an anti-intentionalist, would suggest that Waits's assertion and personal journals do not change what is actually in the text, and that we should instead hypothesize an author who intended what the work most clearly seems to mean. On Carroll's view, the meaning of the text is determined by the author, but in our limited position as readers we must hypothesize those intentions based on what trustworthy information is available. On Nathan's view, conversely, the meaning of the text is determined by the text itself, and from this we can hypothesize a *postulated* author whose imagined intentions may or may not align with the *actual* author's intentions.

Perhaps the most fully developed version of hypothetical intentionalism comes from Jerrold Levinson.[39] In trying to decide what determines the meaning of a work, Levinson considers a number of models of literary meaning. First, he considers, it might be that literary meaning is determined solely by word-sequence meaning – what those words in that order mean simply by virtue of the rules of language. The problem with this view, Levinson suggests, is that it entirely leaves out any notion of authorship. If your computer's printer developed a glitch, and starting churning out page after page of random sentences, we could talk about what those words in that order mean according to the rules of language, but it would be difficult to call such a project *interpretation*. Rather, Levinson argues, the very project of literary interpretation assumes that the literary text was intentionally created, and such a word-sequence-meaning approach to literary meaning has no use for this notion. So, it might instead be that literary meaning is determined simply by what the speaker or writer had in mind to convey by putting those words in that order ('utterer's meaning'). The problem here, Levinson argues, is that it eliminates the autonomy of the text. Interpreting a literary work is not like interpreting, say, a philosophical theory. If you are reading a philosophical essay, and you don't understand the view, you might, if she is available, simply ask the author what she meant. If the explanation is clearer, you don't need the essay any more, and can perhaps happily discard it. However, if, say, Andrew Hudgins had published in plain English an explanation of what he meant by 'In the Well', you would not as happily discard the poem in favour of the poet's explanation. We are not merely interested in what is *behind* the work; rather, we are interested *in the work itself*. With neither of these views seeming to offer a model of meaning commensurate with the project of literary interpretation, Levinson suggests that we should instead view the meaning of a literary work as determined by the 'utterance meaning': 'the meaning that such a [linguistic] vehicle ends up conveying in its context of utterance – a context that includes its being uttered by such-and-such an agent'.[40]

Here, Levinson refers to a view originally set out by William Tolhurst:

Utterance meaning is best understood as the intention which a member of the intended audience would be most justified in attributing to the author based on the knowledge and attitudes which he possesses in virtue of being a member of the intended audience. Thus utterance meaning is to be construed as that hypothesis of utterer's meaning which is most justified on the basis of those beliefs and attitudes which one possesses qua intended hearer or intended reader.[41]

Utterance meaning, as such, is tied to, but distinct from, utterer's meaning. It is our best appropriately informed projection of the author's intended meaning from our position as intended interpreters. An 'appropriately informed projection' is one made from our position as informed and sympathetic readers; it is principally an attribution most likely to be correct given the information available at the time of utterance, and secondarily one that is artistically most charitable to the author, so long as it is plausible.

Levinson considers that it might be better to speak of 'appropriate' readers, rather than 'intended' ones, as the latter threatens to drag us back into actual intentionalism. An appropriate reader will be one who is familiar with the tradition from which the work in question arises, is acquainted with the rest of the author's works to that point, and may be familiar with the author's public persona. Although his view suggests that we should be looking towards the actual author (and not an idealized, postulated author, as Nathan suggests), Levinson nevertheless describes his view as an anti-intentionalist one. Given the priority of the text, he argues, we should not be looking to the author's actual mental state at the time of writing in the sense that this would trump what is actually written in the text. Given the model of utterance meaning, Levinson suggests, literary meaning is generated out of knowledge shared between an author and her readers, but needn't rely on any 'inside' knowledge about the author's life. Authors, by and large, intend their works to be read, and readers ordinarily understand this much in their readings, so there is a sort of loose contract between the author and the reader. If information was publicly available to the reader when the work was released (either in the work itself, in the author's other works published before it, in the author's place in a literary tradition, and so on), the author could reasonably expect the reader to be familiar with it, and so to use it to inform an interpretation of the work. If, however, such information was not available (residing, say, only in an author's mind or in personal journals or as an inside joke between the author and a friend), the author could not expect this to contribute to a reading of the text – it would violate the contract, and so these intentions do not represent appropriate data for interpreting the work. The reader, in other words, would not be *justified* in such an interpretation. The sort of anything-goes approach suggested by Barthes and others, Levinson suggests, may be a perfectly interesting and harmless project, but it isn't literary interpretation.

VIII. The Patchwork Theory

In his essay 'Interpreting the Arts: The Patchwork Theory', Berys Gaut suggests that *no* global theory of interpretation – intentionalist, anti-intentionalist, hypothetical intentionalist or otherwise – is correct.[42] Rather, he argues, one needs a series of 'local' theories of interpretation.

Along with standard anti-intentionalist arguments, Gaut notes that simply interpreting a work as meaning what its author intended it to mean leads to unacceptable consequences. We want to say that an author may, for instance, fail in her intentions – that it may be that she intended for a sentence to mean something, but that this simply is not what those words in that order mean in the language in which she was writing. And it will not do, Gaut argues, to say that the meaning of a work is determined by its author's *fulfilled* intentions, as this will exclude all sorts of things that seem important to a work's meaning. Recall, for instance, Hudgins' poem, 'In the Well'. We might suppose it possible that the XAXA XBXB rhyme scheme was just an accident – that Hudgins couldn't think up enough rhymes for the AAAA BBBB rhyme scheme he really wanted. Still, we want to say that the loose-then-tight, loose-then-tight rhythm of the rhyme scheme contributes significantly to the meaning of the work, whether Hudgins intended it that way or not. In other words, we want, in such a case, to recognize a certain autonomy of the text itself.

However, Gaut argues that there are also problems for standard anti-intentionalist interpretative models. Despite the sorts of argument made by Wimsatt and Beardsley, for instance, Gaut contends that it simply does not make sense to divorce such literary properties as allusion, metaphor and irony from the intentions of an utterer. Consider again the case of a printer spilling out page after page of random sentences due to a computer error. It would be difficult to think of any sentence printed on these pages as being ironic, or as alluding to some work by the Rolling Stones, or as being metaphorical – and it would be equally difficult to think of any of them as being *non-figurative* in use. Rather, Gaut contends, it is simply much more reasonable to say that whether a use of language is or isn't figurative depends upon its utterer's intentions.

Finally, contrary to Levinson's hypothetical intentionalist view, Gaut suggests, correct interpretations may not be graspable by either a work's author or those who would have originally read the work (the 'appropriate reader' in the context of utterance). For instance, let us suppose we are looking to interpret Shakespeare's play *Hamlet*. On Levinson's view, we are restricted in our interpretation to those things that an audience member at the time of the play's creation could reasonably attribute to Shakespeare. Certainly discounted, then, would be a Freudian analysis of the play, as neither Shakespeare nor his audience would have been familiar with twentieth-century theories of psychoanalysis. However, Gaut suggests, when Shakespeare wrote the play, he presented the character of young Hamlet as a real person – a being with a psychology. As such, Gaut argues, it seems a not-unreasonable endeavour to attempt to analyse the character's psychology, and, on this basis, the play itself. If our advances in psychology allow us better insight into the character, why should the fact that Shakespeare and his contemporaries had no access to such psychological methods restrict us from using them?

In all, we might think of intentionalists like Hirsch as providing a *thesis* for interpretation, and anti-intentionalists like Wimsatt and Beardsley as providing an *antithesis*. Hypothetical intentionalists like Levinson, then, are attempting to provide a sort of *synthesis* of the views, taking the best from each extreme and hoping to weed out the worst. But whether thesis, antithesis or synthesis, each is attempting what Gaut calls a 'global' view – a theory that is meant to cover absolutely *every* aspect of interpretation, and this, Gaut argues, is where each is bound to fail. Although none of these views seems to work as a global view, Gaut argues, each seems to have something to offer 'locally' – that is, to *some* aspect of interpretation. Some properties of a work, Gaut suggests, have necessary and sufficient conditions fixed by the author's realized intentions – things like allusion and irony. With other properties, Gaut argues, intention plays little or no determinate role – things like metre, rhyme and diction are the way they are regardless of what was intended. Some properties seem determined by things outside the work *or* the author – things like the political atmosphere when a work was written – and still other properties, Gaut concedes, may be determined by the community of readers (here, we might consider an approach like that of reader-response criticism). This being the case, Gaut suggests, attempts at a global theory of interpretation should be abandoned in favour of a 'patchwork' of such theories, with some approaches applying to some aspects of a work and other approaches applying to others.

The difficulty, it would seem, is in knowing *when* to apply an intentionalist approach, when to apply an anti-intentionalist approach and when to apply a hypothetical intentionalist one. Gaut offers several examples for each, but does not provide any general means of determining when a given interpretative method should be employed. Perhaps, he might say, while there are some clear cases for using each of the various methods, there simply is no general schematic to be followed. Perhaps if there was, interpreting art would be a much less interesting project.

Chapter summary

As we have seen, the philosophical project of determining correct, plausible or meaningful interpretations of art has involved a lot of back-and-forth since the Romantic period. Intentionalists have argued that the meaning of a work is rooted in the author's intentions, while anti-intentionalists have argued that the author's intentions play no determinate role in meaning. Some anti-intentionalists, like Wimsatt and Beardsley, have argued that meaning is determined centrally by what is in the text, while others, like Barthes and Krausz, claim that the meaning or meanings of a work are determined primarily by its readers. Hypothetical intentionalists, like Nathan and Levinson, have suggested views that are best situated somewhere between intentionalism and strict anti-intentionalism, while Gaut has suggested that each view has its merits and drawbacks, and that each perspective has a role to play in interpreting art.

It should be noted that although discussion in this chapter has centred primarily on literary works, much of what is said here applies to other sorts of artworks as well, though it is more difficult to apply some of the views discussed to kinds of art that normally lack a narrative or representational element, such as instrumental music or abstract art.

Historical timeline

William Shakespeare, *Hamlet*	c. 1601	
	1790	Immanuel Kant, *The Critique of Judgment*
	1919	T. S. Eliot, 'Tradition and the Individual Talent'
	1954	Wimsatt and Beardsley, 'The Intentional Fallacy'
Ed Wood, Jr, *Plan 9 From Outer Space*	1959	
The Rolling Stones, 'I Can't Get No (Satisfaction)'	1965	

	1967	Roland Barthes, 'The Death of the Author'
		E. D. Hirsch, Jr, *Validity in Interpretation*
	1969	Michel Foucault, 'What is an Author?'
	1977	Roland Barthes, 'From Work to Text'
	1979	Roman Ingarden, *The Literary Work of Art*
		William Tolhurst, 'On What a Text Is and How It Means'
	1980	Stanley Fish, *Is There a Text in This Class?*
	1992	Noël Carroll, 'Art, Intention, and Conversation'
		Daniel Nathan, 'Irony, Metaphor, and the Problem of Intention'
		Jerrold Levinson, 'Intention and Interpretation: A Last Look'
	1993	Michael Krausz, *Rightness and Reasons*
		Berys Gaut, 'Interpreting the Arts: The Patchwork Theory'
	1996	Jerrold Levinson, 'Intention and Interpretation in Literature'
	1997	Robert Stecker, 'The Constructivist's Dilemma'
Andrew Hudgins, 'In the Well'	2001	
J. K. Rowling, *Harry Potter and the Deathly Hallows*	2007	
Tom Waits, 'Last Leaf'	2011	
Tom Waits, 'Satisfied'		

Key terms and concepts

- Allusion (p. 59)
- Anti-Intentionalism (p. 54)
- Autonomy of the Literary Work (p. 54)
- Constructivism (p. 61)
- Critical Monism (p. 50)
- Criticial Nihilism (p. 50)
- Critical Pluralism (p. 51)
- External vs Internal Evidence (p. 58)
- Genius (p. 51)
- Global vs Local Theories of Interpretation (p. 70)
- Hypothetical Intentionalism (p. 66)
- Intentionalism (p. 63)
- Interpretive Communities (p. 61)
- Meaning vs Significance (p. 63)
- New Criticism (p. 54)
- Patchwork Theory (p. 70)
- Post-Structuralism (p. 59)
- Postulated Author (p. 68)
- Reader-Response Criticism (p. 61)
- Romanticism (p. 51)
- Spots of Indeterminacy (p. 61)
- Unicity (p. 62)
- Utterance Meaning (p. 68)
- Utterer's Meaning (p. 68)
- Word-Sequence Meaning (p. 68)

Further reading

The topic discussed in this chapter is a lively one in aesthetics, with new approaches arising all the time. For the most part, however, the views of New Criticism and post-structuralism are studied under the banners of 'continental philosophy' and what is most often called 'critical theory', while the other perspectives in the chapter fall under the heading of 'analytic philosophy'. The two are only rarely discussed in the same place. Many of the analytic articles discussed in this chapter (and many others besides) are collected in Gary Iseminger's anthology, *Intention and Interpretation* (Temple University Press, 1992). For a quick, up-to-date lie of the land, I would recommend Sherri Irvin's 2006 article, 'Authors, Intentions and Literary Meaning' (*Philosophy Compass* 1 (2): 114–28). I would also strongly recommend Noël Carroll's spirited 2000 essay, 'Interpretation and Intention: The Debate Between Hypothetical and Actual Intentionalism' (*Metaphilosophy* 31: 75–95), an enthusiastic study of the line between Levinson's form of hypothetical intentionalism and the view that Carroll himself defends – what he calls 'modest actual intentionalism'. For views on post-structuralist and reader-response criticism, I would recommend Josuē V. Harari's anthology, *Textual Strategies: Perspectives in Post-Structuralist Criticism* (Cornell University Press, 1979) and Jane P. Tompkins's *Reader-Response Criticism: From Formalism to Post-Structuralism* (Johns Hopkins University Press, 1980).

Unresolved questions

1 What exactly *is* the act of interpretation? Performers of musical works are said to 'interpret' the works they are to perform. Is this activity the same as, or analogous to, what readers do when they interpret a work of literature? What about the interpretation that goes into an actor's performance?

2 How is art interpretation (its goals, its methods and so on) like or unlike other *non-art* activities, such as 'reading' body language, deciphering codes or finding imaginative shapes in clouds? How might this inform our understanding of interpretation in the arts? Should we think that interpreting art is utterly unlike any other human activity?

3 Is there any reason to think that the same interpretative theory applies to all works (of literature, or otherwise)? Could it be that some works should be interpreted according to an intentionalist model, others according to an anti-intentionalist model, and so on?

4 If there is a correct interpretation for any given work, and the author's intentions play some role in determining that interpretation, what are we to do when a given work has *multiple* authors, as is the case for most films, for instance?

3

Aesthetic Properties and Evaluation

Chapter Outline

I. *Black Square* (1915)

In 1915, Russian artist Kasimir Malevich contributed thirty-nine paintings to the '0,10' ('Zero-Ten') exhibition in the Dobychina Gallery, Russia's leading private commercial gallery. Subtitled 'The Last Futurist Exhibition', '0,10' is perhaps better known for its role as the first Suprematist exhibition. In the early twentieth century, the Russian art scene was undergoing a series of artistic movements tracing their origins to avant-garde art upheavals occurring in Western Europe. In 1907, Pablo Picasso had painted *Les Demoiselles d'Avignon*, generally recognized as the first Cubist painting. In the years that followed, Picasso and fellow French painter Georges Braque developed the principles of early Cubism, so named by art critic Louis Vauxcelles, who described a painting by Braque as being

Figure 3.1 Kasimir Malevich, *Black Square* (1915).

'full of little cubes'. Cubism, in turn, served to inspire the Italian movement known as Futurism, which, among other things, sought new ways to depict movement in the static form of painting. Malevich, inspired by both Cubism and Futurism, founded 'Cubo-Futurism', embodying principles from both European schools. However, within a couple of years, Malevich outgrew the movement he himself had founded, and created its successor, Suprematism.

Suprematism took the principles of Cubo-Futurism and extended them to what might be considered their logical conclusion. The Cubists had sought to find new ways to reduce three-dimensional objects to a two-dimensional picture plane, and the Futurists experimented with depicting dynamic action in a static form. Cubo-Futurism resulted in images of a kaleidoscope of interlocking geometric shapes, their subjects barely recognizable. With

Suprematism, Malevich threw aside representation altogether and concentrated instead on the geometric shapes themselves.

First shown in the '0,10' exhibition, and measuring over a metre on each side, *Black Square* is an oil painting essentially consisting of a flat black square on an off-white background.[1] (The network of white lines in the photograph is *craquelure* – a web of cracks in the paint brought about by age – and not what the work looked like in 1915.) Depending on how you look at it, one might say that the painting is *of* a black square, or alternatively, that the painting just *is* a black square. Perhaps resting on this ambiguity, Malevich called *Black Square* 'the beginning of true essence'.[2] Although there were many other Suprematist paintings in the same show (black circles, red squares, black crosses …), *Black Square* became something of an icon for the movement. This is due in no small part to its placement in the gallery. *Black Square* hung in a corner formed by right-angled walls, situated high up near the ceiling, higher than any of the other paintings in the room. This is the sort of unusual placement that, in a typical Russian home, would be reserved for a family's central religious icons – an area called the *krasnyi ugolok* – the 'red' or 'beautiful corner'. A home's beautiful corner was a place of reverence, a place where families devoted themselves to worship. Noting the painting's placement in the gallery, critic and painter Alexander Benois wrote:

> Black Square on a White Background – is not just a joke, not a simple challenge, not a small episode which happened to take place on the Field of Mars. It is an act of self-affirmation – the principle of vile desolation. Through its aloofness, arrogance and desecration of all that is beloved and cherished, it flaunts its desire that leads to deconstruction.[3]

Here, Benois unloads a rather unflattering description of the painting: it is 'aloof', it is 'arrogant', it 'flaunts'. It is unclear whether Benois means to describe the painting itself or Malevich's act in placing it where he did. Certainly, one might describe the painting as 'stark'. Others might say it is 'bold' or 'severe' (conversely, it would seem a mistake to describe the work as 'lively' or 'elegant' or 'delicate'). Our first question is, are these reasonable things to say of the painting if it simply consists of a plain black square on a plain off-white background? If we are to assert any of these of *Black Square*, would we also have to assert them of an indistinguishable scarf or tablecloth that consisted of a large black square with an off-white border?

A second question, which would seem to bear an important relationship with the first, is, is *Black Square* any good? Is this a question to which we should expect an answer? Should we expect any sort of general agreement on the matter? If it *is* good, what *makes* it good? Is *Black Square* any better or worse than, say, the *Mona Lisa*? If someone disagreed with you, what evidence could you point to? Is *Black Square* better or worse than 'Last Leaf'? Is this even a reasonable question?

II. On evaluation

There are certain words that we tend to use in evaluating artworks. We might call a drawing 'elegant', a piece of music 'insipid' or a novel 'dull'. Each of these terms usually indicates a value judgement on the part of the speaker. If a drawing is elegant, this typically counts towards the value of the work, and if a sonata is insipid or a novel dull, this usually counts against its value. We might also call a sculpture 'imposing' or a theatrical performance 'unsettling'. In these cases, without further information, it isn't entirely clear if the work in question is being praised or condemned – but it seems fairly clear that *something* evaluative is being said. However, if I say of Malevich's painting that it is 'black' or that it is 'square', this certainly describes the work, but seems to say nothing of its value. In Chapter 1, we considered a handful of functionalist definitions of art, which were couched in terms of art's 'aesthetic function'. There, we looked to Baumgarten's notion of 'aesthetic' as grounded in sensory experience – particularly visual and auditory experience. However, although they are the sorts of thing we come to know by sight, the blackness and squareness of the painting are not the sorts of properties that most philosophers would call *aesthetic*. Rather, most would describe these as merely *formal* properties of the work. Instead, the category of 'aesthetic properties' is typically reserved for those sensory attributes that essentially involve evaluation.

Although this chapter will centrally focus on the evaluation of artworks, there is nothing about most aesthetic terms that restricts their application to artworks. Certainly, a hand gesture can be elegant without being a part of an artwork. Likewise, a game of football might be dull, a wall imposing or a bit of news unsettling, and none of these are artworks. And many would argue that man has yet to produce anything as beautiful as a sunset – so it really is no great wonder that so many artists spend so much of their time attempting to capture the beauty of nature. The aesthetics of non-artworks will be the central focus of a later chapter, but the word 'beautiful' is worthy of particular note. 'Beautiful' is certainly an aesthetic property term – it is difficult to think of any use of the word that does not essentially involve evaluation, and at least central literal uses of the word pertain to objects of the senses. Moreover, it is difficult to think of any non-ironic use of the word that does not indicate positive evaluation. It is perhaps for this reason that beauty tends to serve as an exemplar for aesthetic properties generally, and has drawn the attention of philosophers for centuries.

Talk of beauty tends to revolve around two central questions: first, what *makes* something beautiful, and second, how do we *know* beauty when we see it? These days, the two questions tend to go hand in hand, and there is any number of positions that one might hold on the issue. One might argue, for instance, that beauty is an entirely subjective matter – that, as the saying goes, beauty is in the eye of the beholder. In general, we might call adherents to such a view *relativists* about beauty. On a view like this, if I say 'Black Square is a beautiful painting,' and you say '*Black Square* is not a beautiful painting,' all appearances to the contrary, we are not disagreeing. Rather, when I say, '*Black Square* is a beautiful painting,' I could only reasonably mean that *Black Square* is a beautiful painting *to me*, and when you say the painting is not beautiful, you could only reasonably mean that it is not beautiful *to you*. On such a view, provided you have a grasp of what the word means, you could never be wrong about whether the painting is beautiful, nor could I, even if we seem to disagree. Here, it might be suggested, to say '*Black Square* is a beautiful painting' is just to say, 'I *like Black Square*,' and to say '*Black Square* is not a beautiful painting' is simply to say, 'I *don't* like *Black Square*.' In so speaking, one is not reporting on properties of the work, but on one's own mental state, and who is anyone else to say what I do or do not like?

Conversely, one might hold the view that beauty is an entirely objective matter – that there is some fact of the matter about whether the painting is beautiful. In general, proponents of such a view are called *realists* about beauty – and if one is a realist about beauty, one is probably a realist about aesthetic properties in general. Of course, you and I might both be realists about beauty and still disagree about whether *Black Square* is in fact a beautiful painting. It might be, for instance, that we both think beauty is the sort of property that a given thing either has or lacks, but we might disagree about what it is exactly that *makes* something beautiful, or even if we agree about this, we might disagree as to whether *Black Square* has that special something.

Others might argue for a position somewhere between the extreme views of relativism and realism. One might argue, for example, that there *is* a fact about whether or not the painting is beautiful (and so be, strictly speaking, a realist), but argue that the matter is not so simple as the above account makes it seem. It might be suggested that whether *Black Square* is beautiful depends upon whether an individual with certain special qualities would *call* it beautiful – some ideal judge of beauty. What special qualities? Here, we might think of having properly functioning eyes and visual cortex, or of seeing the object in the right conditions, or even of having a certain body of knowledge – or some combination of these qualities. Here, you and I might disagree about whether *Black Square* is beautiful because we disagree about what makes for an ideal judge and whether either of us qualifies.

III. The search for objective beauty

As outlined in the Introduction, philosophical discussion on the nature of beauty stretches back at least as far as Pythagoras, the thinker most often credited with coining the term 'philosophy'. These days, Pythagoras is best remembered as a mathematician, and indeed mathematics was his central concern. Pythagoras and his followers did not merely explore mathematics for its own sake, however; rather, the Pythagoreans believed that mathematics was the supreme ordering principle of the universe – that, ultimately, everything was made of mathematical objects. As with everything else, then, beauty was believed to be quantifiable and objective in nature. In particular, the Pythagoreans argued that beauty arises out of mathematical harmony, order and regularity. As evidence, Pythagoras discovered that those musical intervals – harmonies – that people found beautiful were mathematically ordered, grounded in simple numeric ratios. And if this was true for musical beauty, why not for beauty in general?

One mathematical ratio that reportedly caught Pythagoras's attention was 1:1.6180339887 …, generally represented by the Greek letter phi (ϕ), though more commonly known today as the 'golden ratio', the 'golden section' or the 'golden mean' (as well as a litany of similar terms). The golden ratio would preoccupy not only the Pythagoreans, but also the Ancient mathematician Euclid, the German astronomer Johannes Kepler, the Renaissance painter Leonardo da Vinci and countless others. Why would a seemingly innocuous mathematical relation draw such attention? Here is what is fascinating about the golden ratio: first, draw a straight line (call this 'a'). If we divide the line so that the shorter segment ('b') bears a length ratio of 1:1.6180339887 … to the longer segment ('c'), we will note

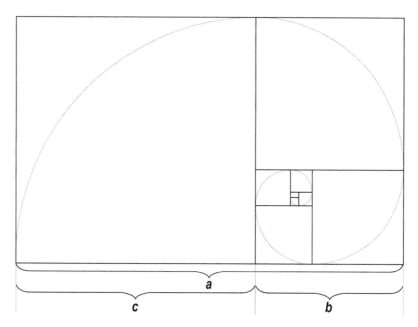

Figure 3.2 The golden spiral.

that the length of *c* bears the same ratio to that of *a* that *b* bears to *c*. We can keep dividing and subdividing and the strange ratio remains constant. You might say, this is all well and good for mathematicians, but what does it have to do with aesthetics? Many have argued that phi is, quite simply, *beautiful*, and objectively so – that wherever it shows up, there is beauty. From the phi ratio, we can form certain rectangles, spirals and other shapes – shapes that seem to keep showing up in both natural objects and artefacts that people revere as beautiful. It has been suggested that nautilus shells, sunflowers, the Parthenon and the Great Mosque of Kairouan all exhibit the phi proportion. The painter Salvador Dalí, the composer Frédéric Chopin and the sculptor Andrew Rogers have all created works specifically on the basis of the golden section. Even plastic surgeons have used the phi proportion to create models of beautiful faces that they could use to guide facial reconstruction.[4] If nothing else, the idea that beauty has an objective nature has continued to capture the attention of thinkers through the centuries.[5]

Following Pythagoras's example, a great number of philosophers have sought to determine the objective nature of beauty. In his dialogue the *Laws*, Plato suggests that beauty is found in certain proportions, harmonies and order.[6] On his metaphysical view, the beauty we find in natural and man-made objects is a reflection of the true 'Form' of beauty, something that exists beyond and before any given beautiful thing. On Plato's view, if two things are both beautiful, it is because they each reflect or embody this Form. So on Plato's view, there is some objective *thing*, beauty, and all beautiful things are a reflection of this. Following Plato, Aristotle suggested that beauty is bound up in size and order, although Aristotle did not believe in anything so obscure as Plato's Form. It is not, Aristotle suggests, because it reflects the true Form of beauty that we find some particular thing beautiful, but because it appears unified to the viewer – it is of just the right size and just the right arrangement.

The search for the objective nature of beauty would continue for centuries. The medieval philosopher St Bonaventure argued that beauty arises from proper proportion, that proper proportion arises from congruity, and that congruity emerges from quantifiable equality.[7] Ultimately, however, Bonaventure argued that the beauty we find in art and nature comes from the beauty of God, a notion he borrowed from an earlier philosopher, St Augustine.[8] At about the same time, St Thomas Aquinas suggested that beauty is solely a matter of three qualities: a thing's proportion or harmony, its integrity or perfection and its brightness or clarity.[9] In the Renaissance, Marsilio Ficino followed Aquinas by arguing that beauty was found in order, proportion and harmony, as well as in brilliance, and that we recognized beauty when it aligned with our shared innate idea of beauty – something we are born with.[10] And in the eighteenth century, Francis Hutcheson argued that beauty would be found in 'uniformity amidst variety', a bit of a difficult notion to get one's head around.[11] The central difficulty with claims such as these is that they are, at base, claims of fact. If beauty is objective, it would seem, each thesis should be easily testable – we should in principle be able to collect a bunch of beautiful and ugly things together and test the theories against them. And, certainly, each philosopher came ready to defend his thesis with a list of examples. The problem, of course, is that people can and do disagree about which things are beautiful and which are not, so we can imagine that the outcome of any such test is very much going to depend on who is doing the judging. But if beauty is objective, whatever the basis, why should this be the case?

IV. Taste

A recurring notion in the search for an objective basis to beauty is that beauty gives pleasure to its observers. In Plato's early dialogue the *Hippias*

Major, Socrates suggests that beauty is that which makes us feel joy through sight and sound – that beauty is a particular sort of pleasure-producing thing.[12] Aristotle, similarly, argues that beauty is ultimately a particular form of goodness and pleasure. That beauty is tied up with pleasure is something that philosophers in general have since largely agreed upon, whatever their views on what (if anything) provides the objective basis to beauty. After all, it would seem difficult to say that any given thing is beautiful if *nobody* enjoys it. But how are we to account for the fact that different people find different degrees of pleasure in attending to the very same things? If beauty is objective in its basis, then, it would seem, the fault must belong to the viewer.

The fifteenth-century artist and philosopher Leon Battista Alberti, while contending that beauty rests on objective grounds, argued that *judgements* of beauty depend upon an innate *sense* of beauty in man – a natural ability to recognize it and a natural tendency to be pleased by it. However, by suggesting that *every* man has this sense, and in arguing for an inviolate basis to beauty, Alberti concludes that there simply cannot be reasonable disagreement about beauty. This notion of a sense of beauty would be taken up again in the eighteenth century, first by Anthony Ashley Cooper – known more commonly as the 3rd Earl of Shaftesbury (or simply, Shaftesbury) – who suggests than man has an 'inward eye' which distinguishes the beautiful from the ugly, and then by Hutcheson, who compares this 'internal sense' to our external senses of sight and hearing. It is this internal sense that, when apprehending beautiful things, gives rise to aesthetic pleasure. Simply put, one apprehends a sunset, a painting or a song with one's external senses, and apprehends their beauty with one's internal senses. Hutcheson argues that, as with seeing and hearing, this sense of beauty is not equally acute in all people, but when it is particularly acute, Hutcheson says, we call it 'taste'. Both Hutcheson and Shaftesbury compared this inward sense to mankind's moral sense – an equally sticky matter, philosophically speaking. Shaftesbury contends that the moral sense and the aesthetic sense are one and the same faculty, while Hutcheson is less straightforward about their relationship.

Although Alberti, Shaftesbury and Hutcheson pioneered this notion of taste, it was the Scottish philosopher David Hume who would first tackle the problem of taste head-on.[13] Taste, Hume notes, varies among even those people who have roughly the same background and prejudices, and that as these become more varied, so too do tastes. You and your closest friend might share similar prejudices and have very similar upbringings, but disagree about whether Harper Lee's *To Kill a Mockingbird* is a better novel than, say, Suzanne Collins's novel *The Hunger Games*, or whether Adele is a better singer than Aretha Franklin. And it would be not at all unusual for you and your parents to differ in your artistic tastes. Worse, it seems that, with regard to any given thing, no side in such a debate seems to have any greater claim than the others to having the 'right' taste. Here, Hume asks us to notice the difference between *judgement* and *sentiment*. Sentiment, Hume argues, is like a sensation of pain or pleasure: one cannot be wrong about having because it is essentially about *you* – either you are in pain or you are not, and either you enjoy a particular novel, painting or musical composition or you do not. Judgement, however, is a determination of the understanding – and because it refers to something outside the judge, it *can* be wrong. Given this distinction, Hume suggests:

> Beauty is no quality in things themselves: It exists merely in the mind which contemplates them; and each mind perceives a different beauty. One person may even perceive deformity, where another is sensible of beauty; and every individual ought to acquiesce in his own sentiment, without pretending to regulate those of others.[14]

Although this seems a natural way to think about taste, Hume notes, there is another common sense suggestion that opposes it. It would seem absurd to say that a painting like *Black Square* is as elegant as a painting by the Chinese landscape painter Guo Xi. Guo Xi's paintings have been renowned for centuries, and while it seems on the one hand problematic to say everyone *must* agree about their aesthetic qualities, it is difficult to ignore such widespread and persistent agreement. Hume suggests that while lack of enduring assent will point to faults in a work, where a considerable uniformity of agreement exists, we might find something like 'perfect beauty'.

Observing beauty, Hume argues, has as much to do with the observer as it does with what is observed. While noting that there are qualities in objects which seem naturally suited to producing certain aesthetic sentiments, Hume notes, these qualities tend to be intermixed with other qualities, and require a certain 'delicacy of taste' to perceive and distinguish them. The better developed and more refined such a faculty, the better the judge. With experience, our feelings become more nuanced and exact, and we are better able to indicate qualities of praise or blame. After all, how much would you trust a film critic who had only ever seen one movie? The more works we are familiar with, the better we will be able to judge works we experience in the future. Indeed, judgement of any particular work of art may require more

Figure 3.3 Guo Xi, *Early Spring* (1072).

than one observation. At first, our judgements may be very rough, but with repeated viewings, we may observe the details, the relations between the parts, and on closer examination our judgements may contradict our earlier snap judgements. Although reason may not be essential to aesthetic taste, Hume argues, it is essential to checking the influence of prejudice. We tend, Hume notes, to be victims of sentimentality – preferring things that remind us of our homes, our own lives and so on. The critic's job is to become, as much as possible, a 'man in general'. Insofar as he is able to refine his taste, familiarize himself with a great many works and overcome his own prejudices, such a critic is on his way to becoming an ideal judge.

Taking up the problem where Hume leaves off is Immanuel Kant.[15] Kant argues that where, say, judging a dog show requires knowledge of show dogs, judging beauty is a non-conceptual matter – that is, such judgements do not draw on determinate concepts – rules that say when something is beautiful and when it is not. Rather, Kant suggests that aesthetic judgements – judgements of *taste* – are essentially *sensual* in nature, relying on feelings of pleasure and displeasure. With judgements of taste, rather than comparing some given thing – a painting or a sunset – against some ideal of beauty, one simply engages in what Kant calls 'free play' of the imagination.[16] We concentrate on the object of judgement but without any conceptual *goal* directing the process. Rather, we simply engage with the thing for its own sake. When this activity particularly excites the imagination, we recognize this by our feelings.

A pure aesthetic judgement, Kant contends, must be *disinterested* – that is, it must be unconcerned with the object's actual existence, and must be disconnected from any desire one might have, say, to possess the object being judged or to judge it again in the future.[17] Instead, a pure judgement of taste must be focused solely on the object's aesthetic qualities. To be personally interested in the object requires conceptualization of its place in the world – precisely what Kant believes we should avoid. As he puts it, '*Taste* is the ability to judge an object, or a way of presenting it, by means of a liking or disliking *devoid of all interest*. The object of such a liking is called *beautiful*.'[18]

Because such judgements are to be disinterested (that is, without any particular reference to oneself), they tend to be framed *universally*. That is, as one judges something to be beautiful, one presupposes that everyone else will as well, assuming they have the same basic faculties that you do – and so, for this reason, Kant argues that we discuss beauty as if it were a property of the object. So, Kant might say, although there are no *rules* that determine whether a painting or a sunset is objectively beautiful, we talk as if beauty is a property of the thing.

Kant wonders, then, as Hume did before him, how we are to deal with disagreements about taste. If beauty is non-conceptual, is there no fact of the matter about whether some given thing is more beautiful than another? Are disagreements just so much hot air? When judging a show dog, one has some *determinate* concept of what makes a good show dog – some list of qualities that would so qualify it. Judging beauty doesn't come with such straightforward rules. Rather, we know beauty by *intuition* – we know it when we see it. As such, we must be comparing objects of taste with *some* concept. Kant agrees, and argues that such concepts are *indeterminate* ones. Although we know beauty when we experience it – through the free play of the imagination – any attempt to explicate *rules* of beauty is bound to fail. We have what Kant calls *aesthetic ideas*, but these ideas are slippery things, and trying to grasp them is like trying to get a strong grip on jelly. This ability we have to judge beauty is something Kant suggests we are born with, but which needs to be developed, and so there may be better judges of beauty and worse ones.

V. Aesthetic properties

If Kant is right, then one simply cannot formulate a rule for what makes something beautiful. And, one might imagine, if judgements of elegance, boldness, insipidness and the like are also matters of taste, the same will be true of these. Now, let us suppose that you are discussing *Black Square* with a friend, and your friend declares it a beautiful painting. Let's further suppose that you disagree, instead declaring it altogether ugly. Is this simply a deadlock? Shall you both just throw up your hands and walk away from the discussion? Suppose your friend asks you, '*Why* do you think is it ugly?' or '*Why* don't you think it is beautiful?' Presumably, you will not be without an answer.

In his 1959 essay, 'Aesthetic Concepts', Frank Sibley outlines an approach to this issue.[19] He suggests that we can describe works of art in two sorts of way. First, we might describe a work in non-aesthetic terms. We might say of *Black Square*, for instance, that the painting measures 106.2 by 106.5 centimetres and that it consists of a black, nearly square quadrangle measuring about 84 by 84.7 centimetres, surrounded by an off-white border. This is the sort of thing that might be pointed out to anyone with normal sensory input and intelligence. Now, consider Hilda ('H.D.') Doolittle's famous 1915 poem, 'Oread':

Whirl up, sea –
whirl your pointed pines,
splash your great pines
on our rocks,
hurl your green over us,
cover us with your pools of fir.

We might describe Doolittle's poem as being written in an open form and consisting of twenty-six words, four of which are 'your'. However, Sibley notes, we might also say of Doolittle's poem that it is rhythmic, powerful and evocative. And we might similarly say of *Black Square* that it is bold and balanced, that it has a certain repose, but that it is generally lifeless. To describe a work in this way is to use aesthetic terms. And where seeing non-aesthetic or merely formal properties requires only normal sensory input and intelligence, seeing aesthetic properties requires the exercise of taste, perceptiveness and sensitivity – a certain faculty of discrimination and perception.

Sibley argues that a work's aesthetic qualities *depend* on its non-aesthetic ones. When your friend asks you to say why the work fails to be beautiful, you will point to its formal properties as evidence. And if she wants to defend its beauty, she too will point to formal properties. Thus we say of a painting that it is beautiful or bold or elegant *because* of its lines, its colours and its shapes, and we will say that a poem is delicate or sentimental *because* of its rhyme, metre, diction and the like. However, Sibley argues, no mere description of a work in non-aesthetic terms will ever justify the use of any given aesthetic term. And so, Sibley contends, aesthetic terms are not positively rule-governed. Granted, if I describe a sculpture as 'angular, large and brightly coloured' (all non-aesthetic terms), it might be difficult to think that the work could also be *graceful* or *delicate* (aesthetically speaking). However, 'angular, large and brightly coloured' perfectly well describes most sculptures by Alexander Calder, whose works are also certainly graceful and delicate. So while non-aesthetic qualities may count towards or against aesthetic ones, they do not guarantee them. Sibley does, however, allow for some instances of *negative* rule-governing: Suppose that I describe a work as consisting of an eight-foot by eight-foot by eight-foot cube, painted matte black. Here, Sibley supposes, we would be justified in concluding that the work is *not* elegant or graceful or delicate.

In general, Sibley suggests that the relationship between non-aesthetic qualities and aesthetic qualities is one of *supervenience*. Briefly, for property *A* to supervene on property *B* means that there can be no change to *A* without a corresponding change in *B*, though *B* can change without thus resulting in a change to *A*. In this case, Sibley suggests that aesthetic qualities supervene on non-aesthetic ones. So, if an artwork is, say, elegant (an aesthetic quality), we can say that this is *because* the work has certain lines, certain colours and so on (non-aesthetic qualities). And so, if we wanted to make the work *non*-elegant, we would have to change some of these non-aesthetic qualities. That being said, we *could* make some changes to the lines, colours and so on without *thus* making the work non-elegant – it could just be elegant in a different way.

In a later essay, Sibley goes into some greater detail on the relationship between a thing's aesthetic qualities and its non-aesthetic ones.[20] A thing will be *graceful*, to pick another aesthetic term, because it is curved. So we can say that the work's curviness is *responsible* for its gracefulness. Gracefulness is always a *meritorious* property – it always counts towards a thing's value – but curviness does not always produce gracefulness; indeed, curviness is not always a good thing for a work to have. Many a work is curved and yet not graceful. Because the relationship is supervenient, we *could* change the curves in a graceful work and still have a graceful work, but it will now be graceful in a different way (though still because it is curved). As such, a thing will be graceful not simply in virtue of being curved, but in virtue of being curved *in exactly the way that it is*. Given how particular this relationship is, then, and given the resources of language available to us, Sibley suggests that we are unlikely to ever find descriptions of a work's particular formal features such that we could conclude that it has any particular merit-quality, whether positive or negative, and this regardless of whether we are speaking on a very high level (using terms like 'beautiful' or 'ugly') or on a lower level (using terms like 'graceful' or 'garish'). Put another way, one must actually *see*, *hear* or otherwise experience a particular item to decide whether the application of the aesthetic term is warranted – whether one sees grace *in that particular line*.

It is worth noting, here, that Sibley is actually making two sorts of argument, one metaphysical and one epistemological. The metaphysical argument concerns the relationships between a thing's aesthetic properties and its non-aesthetic ones; the epistemological argument concerns what we can know about a work's aesthetic properties under certain conditions, and what we cannot. The case that started our chapter, *Black Square*, does nothing to hurt the metaphysical claim here. Sibley would contend that if *Black Square* is, say, bold, then this is because of its particular shapes and colours – and this seems reasonable enough. However, *Black Square* does throw something of a monkey wrench into the epistemological argument. Sibley's claim is that no mere *description* of a work's formal, non-aesthetic features will ever be sufficient to warrant knowledge of its aesthetic qualities. This, Sibley says, is because the relationship between a work's aesthetic and non-aesthetic features, while determinate, is *extremely* determinate, such that a slight change to a thing's curvature could turn it from graceful to clumsy, and our descriptive powers are such that they cannot so determinately and reliably make such distinctions. This seems a reasonable thing to say, for example, of a landscape painting by Guo Xi. However, consider again our non-aesthetic description of *Black Square* from the beginning of this section. Couldn't one, on such a formal description alone, make accurate conclusions about the painting's aesthetic features – its boldness, for instance? Now, it might be contended here that the only reason one is able to do so is because the work is so formally simple that one is able to form an accurate *picture* of the work in one's imagination, and that *this* is what one is judging. However, to concede this is to concede that one does not always have to *directly* experience a work to make warranted aesthetic judgements about it. Granted, this will be a very special sort of case, and will not apply to most works. Most paintings and sculptures will likely outstretch our descriptive capabilities, and to make an accurate judgement of even a simple poem's aesthetic qualities will likely require a description that ultimately reproduces a poem.

Roger Scruton argues that accurately reporting at least some of a work's aesthetic features depends upon actually experiencing that work for *another* reason.[21] Consider such terms as 'moving' or 'exciting' or 'enjoyable'. These sorts of qualities seem to depend not only upon the work, but upon the audience's mental and emotional lives. Scruton suggests:

> To see the sadness in the music and to know that the music is sad are one and the same thing. To agree in the judgment that the music is sad is not to agree in a belief, but in something more like a response or an experience; in a mental state that is – unlike belief – logically tied to the immediate circumstances of its arousal.[22]

Since knowledge is at very least a kind of belief, Scruton argues, one cannot strictly speaking *know* that a piece of music is sad, or that a novel is exciting, or that an opera is enjoyable – rather, one *experiences* sadness when listening to a certain piece of music, excitement when reading a particular novel, and enjoyment when experiencing a given opera. The relationship between art and emotion will be the central focus of an upcoming chapter, and so we shall not dwell on the matter here except to point out that if we can genuinely say that a work is sad, that sadness is an aesthetic quality of a work, and that making such an attribution depends upon actually experiencing the work, then there are at least some aesthetic qualities whose genuine application depends upon actually experiencing the work. That we can make accurate conclusions about *Black Square*'s aesthetic features might simply be because the painting fails to have such aesthetic qualities as sadness which depend upon actually experiencing the work.

Philip Pettit argues that even such properties as being sad or moving or exciting supervene on a work's non-aesthetic properties: for a work to change from being sad to being not-sad, something about its formal features must be changed as well – although, being a supervenient relationship, its formal features could be changed without the work thus becoming not-sad.[23] And to say that a piece of music is sad certainly takes the *form* of an assertion – the sort of thing that can be true or false. However, Pettit does not suppose that correct assertion of aesthetic properties has nothing to do with experiencing the work. Pettit argues that aesthetic characterizations are both *essentially perceptual* and *perceptually elusive*. They are essentially perceptual for the sort of reason that Sibley points out – one must actually experience the work in order to reach justified conclusions about its aesthetic properties (here, we can put aside our complicating case of *Black Square*). And aesthetic characterizations are perceptually elusive because seeing that a work is bold, elegant or exciting requires something more than working senses. Suppose you are listening to a funeral march like Berlioz's *Marche funèbre pour la dernière scène d*'Hamlet. It might be argued that the work is sad because of the particular arrangement of notes, the fact that it is written in the minor key and so on – and this fits perfectly well with Sibley's theory of supervenience. However, suppose you are listening to it full-blast on your stereo while you are being poked in the forehead with a sharp pencil. You would be unlikely to experience any of this sadness – that is, it would be difficult to hear the sadness under those listening conditions. This, Pettit says, is a matter of whether or not the work is being presented as it should be. Of course, it might be that you are listening to the funeral march exactly as you were intended to, and still fail to hear any sadness in it. Perhaps you did not know it was a funeral march, and, thinking it to be something else entirely, found it strangely upbeat. This would be an issue of what Pettit calls 'suitable positioning'. That you fail to hear the music as sad, Pettit would argue, does not mean it isn't. Rather, this might result from some failure in either its presentation or its positioning.

VI. Contextualism

Pettit, in speaking of suitable positioning, is drawing on a sort of contextualism, suggesting that seeing aesthetic qualities depends upon the context in which the item is experienced and perhaps on some knowledge of the viewer. In Chapter 1, we briefly discussed Arthur Danto and his view about the 'artworld'. Danto makes two sorts of arguments worth taking note of here. First, Danto notes, to *lack* a property is to *have* a property: the property of lacking the other property. And a negative aesthetic property (not-*K*) is just as aesthetically relevant as its positive inverse (*K*). So, for instance, where a Guo Xi landscape is elegant, *Black Square* is non-elegant. Where Hilda Doolittle's 'Oread' is moving, *Black Square* is not-moving. As such, Malevich's *Black Square* is just as aesthetically rich as a Guo Xi landscape or a Doolittle poem – it is just that, in these cases, all of *Black Square*'s aesthetic properties are in the negative. However, we could list some aesthetic properties that *Black Square* does have in the positive: it is *bold*, it is *stark*, it is *severe*. Perhaps, as Alexander Benois suggests, it is *aloof* and *arrogant* as well. If Sibley is right, these properties simply arise from the painting's formal properties. However, it would seem strange to say that a tablecloth is *severe*, that it is *aloof* and so on – even if that tablecloth was visually identical to Malevich's painting.

Danto argues that seeing the painting as having certain aesthetic qualities depends first upon knowing that it is indeed a painting – an art object. If one has no idea what art is, one is likely to describe the painting and the tablecloth in exactly the same way – because one will *see* them the same way. But if one knows that the painting is an artwork and the ordinary tablecloth is not, then one will look at them differently. If we look at a Rembrandt portrait, we can point at it and say: 'That figure is Rembrandt himself – it's a self-portrait.' Of course, what we are pointing at is simply pigmented oil on canvas, and someone who has never seen art before might be confused at our use of 'is' here. To recognize the painting as a portrait – to recognize those shapes and colours as a representation – requires some knowledge of what art is in the first place. Danto calls this the '*is* of artistic identification'. Now, what about *Black Square*? Perhaps, as suggested at the beginning of this chapter, *Black Square* is a painting *of* a square. Or, in another way of looking at it, perhaps it just *is* a square. Either way, in creating *Black Square* and the Suprematist movement in general, Malevich was responding to all of the artistic movements that had led up to it: Impressionism, Post-Impressionism, Cubism, Futurism, Cubo-Futurism ... To make art, Malevich is still relying on the *is* of artistic identification. In seeing the painting as art, there is more going on than in the visually indistinguishable tablecloth. Malevich is responding to – and perhaps rejecting – what has come before in order to produce *Black Square*. The tablecloth manufacturer, we can presume, is doing no such thing. As Danto famously writes, 'To see something as art requires something the eye cannot decry – an atmosphere of artistic theory, a knowledge of the history of art: an artworld.'[24]

Kendall Walton takes Danto's observation a step further, arguing that the aesthetic qualities that a work actually possesses are those that are found in it when it is perceived in the right art category.[25] By 'category', we might think of a number of ways that we categorize art: by media (painting, film, sculpture), by artistic movement (Impressionism, Cubism, Suprematism), by genre (romance, horror, magical realism) and so on. Features of works, Walton suggests, are either *standard, variable* or *contra-standard* with respect to a given category. Standard features are those that tend to determine category membership. Here, we might think of being composed of words arranged in sentences as standard to the category of literature, and being composed of paint as standard to the category of paintings. Contra-standard features are those that tend to negate category membership. Lacking words would, for instance, tend to keep some work out of the literature category, and being made entirely of carved wood would tend to keep us from identifying something as a painting. Variable features, meanwhile, are those that tend to be irrelevant to category membership, such as what colours are used in a painting or what words are used in a piece of literature. Whether a feature is standard, contra-standard or variable with regard to a given category might depend on any number of things – on the limitations of a given medium, on 'rules' for a given genre or just on artistic tradition.

When a work is taken to belong to a certain category (say, painting), but has features contra-standard to that category, this tends to be shocking, upsetting or controversial. For instance, paintings are *supposed* to be roughly flat picture planes, and we may have trouble dealing with paintings that have sculpted elements. Likewise, representational paintings are (in this sense) *supposed* to be in colour, and we are bothered by scenes painted entirely in shades of grey when their subjects would be in colour. When a work differs *too* much from standard works, we have difficulty perceiving it as belonging to the purported category. Sometimes such features become non-controversial, and we accept them as variable to the category. And sometimes we recognize a *new* category branching off from the first one. Futurist paintings, for example, are standardly representational, but not in a photographic sense. As such, viewed as a Futurist painting, *Black Square* is hollow, static and lifeless – it has no representational subject apart from the black square that it consists in. However, viewed in the category of Suprematist paintings, the work is not *expected* to have a representational subject, but only to consist of bare geometric shapes – and this it does exceedingly well. As a Suprematist painting, *Black Square* is bold, striking and, yes, perhaps a little arrogant. Whether the work *is* strange, stark and aloof, or whether it is bold, striking and arrogant, Walton says, depends upon whether the painting correctly belongs to the category of Futurist paintings or to that of Suprematist paintings.

Walton argues that the category to which a work *actually* belongs is determined by four conditions: (i) the category with regard to which the work has the most standard features, and the fewest contra-standard ones; (ii) the category in which the work comes off best; (iii) the category in which the artist intended the work to be perceived; and (iv) the category in which the artist's contemporaries perceived the work. These conditions are not equally weighted, however. Walton argues that, in almost all cases, one of the latter two conditions will trump the others. It would be strange, for instance, to suggest that a work belongs to a category with which its artist was unfamiliar. And, as discussed last chapter in the case of Ed Wood's infamous *Plan 9 From Outer Space*, that a work would come off best in some category does not seem sufficient reason to place it there – especially if we know that isn't where the artist or his contemporaries would have perceived it.

Let us return to Malevich's painting. Walton's first two conditions seem to properly place *Black Square* in the category of Suprematist paintings. However, as Walton notes, it is the third and fourth conditions – the 'historical' ones – that tend to disproportionately determine category membership. Regarding the third condition, Malevich almost certainly intended *Black Square* as a Suprematist painting – indeed, as one of the first Suprematist paintings. However, if we allow Malevich to simply create a new category for his painting, what is to stop every artist from creating a new ad hoc category for each work they create? Walton's fourth condition asks in what category the artist's contemporaries would have seen the work.

Given that the work was first displayed in a show dubbed 'The Last Futurist Exhibition', it would be understandable for the audience to perceive *Black Square* as a Futurist painting. Walton argues that the historical conditions tend to outweigh the others, but what if, as in this case, the artist and his contemporaries are likely to have seen the work in different categories? Suprematism eventually came to be viewed as its own category, but can a work change categories? It is difficult to see how, given that conditions (iii) and (iv) are firmly rooted in the time of the work's creation.

Most of the cases used to support contextualism are not real cases at all, but 'thought experiments' – imaginings of ways things *might* have been – and the thought experiment most frequently raised in this regard comes, itself, from a work of fiction. In 'Pierre Menard, Author of Don Quixote', Jorge Luis Borges presents the story of Menard, an early twentieth-century French writer, who took it upon himself to reproduce Miguel de Cervantes' seventeenth-century Spanish literary masterpiece, *Don Quixote*. However, Menard did not want to simply *copy* the work – he wanted to write it himself. Initially, Menard wanted to pull this off by *becoming* Cervantes, but ultimately rejected this as too easy a route. Instead, Menard decided he wanted to arrive at *Don Quixote* through his own experiences. And, after years of effort, Menard managed to reproduce a couple of chapters and a handful of fragments. The story's narrator writes of the contrast between the two works, Cervantes' and Menard's:

> ... the fragmentary *Don Quixote* of Menard is more subtle than that of Cervantes ...

> The text of Cervantes and that of Menard are verbally identical, but the second is almost infinitely richer. (More ambiguous, his detractors will say; but ambiguity is a richness.) ...

> Equally vivid is the contrast in styles. The archaic style of Menard – in the last analysis, a foreigner – suffers from a certain affectation. Not so that of his precursor, who handles easily the ordinary Spanish of his time.[26]

As a twentieth-century author, Menard is writing with the benefits and burdens of centuries of knowledge that Cervantes could not have had. Like any author, Menard is a product of his time, so when he writes about seventeenth-century Spain, he does so with hindsight, but also with the prejudices of his own time. Neither Menard nor Cervantes can be truly objective, though each may pretend to be. Menard's work can be evaluated in light of all of the artistic movements of the preceding three centuries, but Cervantes' cannot, as these came after his writing. Menard writes in archaic Spanish, where Cervantes' writing is not at all archaic – he was, after all, a seventeenth-century Spaniard. Comparatively, we might imagine a contemporary English poet who chooses to write in Shakespearean English, or a modern painter who consciously chooses to ignore the rules of perspective developed in the fifteenth century. A twenty-first-century student might complain that he finds Shakespeare's sonnets difficult to read, which is understandable, but it seems disingenuous to call this a fault of the poem. However, a contemporary poem written in Shakespearean English seems to be deliberately obtuse and evaluative as such. The contextualist argument is that whether a work is archaic, novel, ironic, rich or ambiguous is at least partly determined by who created it, when, and under what conditions. Insofar as these are aesthetic properties, or else directly contribute to a work's aesthetic properties, such properties do not simply supervene on the work's formal properties, but also upon its context of creation.

On this basis, we might say we have a way to distinguish between the aesthetic properties and value of a painting and of an exact forgery of that work. Contextualists argue that a forgery may not – and perhaps cannot – have the same aesthetic properties and thus value as the original, because each was created by distinct persons under distinct conditions of creation. Those who reject contextualism, however, argue that a work's aesthetic properties and value depend only on its formal qualities, and so claim that an exact forgery and the work it copies must have precisely the *same* aesthetic properties and value. However, when we discover that a work is a forgery, we hide it away or destroy it outright. It may have once sold for millions, but now can hardly be given away. Is there some *sort* of value that the original has that the copy lacks? Is there some particular *kind* of value of art?

VII. The value of art

Some might value art because it has a certain *exchange* value. In 2015, Willem de Kooning's 1955 abstract expressionist painting *Interchange* set an auction record, selling for $300 million. One might, as such, say that the artwork is valuable in the same way that anything else is valuable – real estate, gold, comic books; one could sell it and use the proceeds to buy something else. And, unlike most other things, the exchange value on fine art only ever seems to rise. The seller of de Kooning's painting could use the proceeds to purchase all manner of things – several mansions, a million flat-screen televisions or more art. Viewed in this way, the value of art is nothing special – it can serve as a commodity. But many argue that there is a value that art has that is peculiar to its nature *as* art.

In Chapter 1, we considered a variety of functionalist definitions of art, including Monroe Beardsley's: 'An artwork is something produced with the intention of giving it the capacity to satisfy the aesthetic interest.'[27] Reasonably, then, in Beardsley's view, something is *good* art if and to the degree that it *does* satisfy this interest. According to Beardsley's theory, a work's artistic value depends solely upon its aesthetic value, and a thing's aesthetic value is simply its capacity to produce (under suitable conditions) aesthetic enjoyment, a particular sort of pleasure. This pleasure, he argues, arises from three 'regional qualities' of what is seen, heard or otherwise apprehended: its *unity*, its *intensity* and its *complexity*.[28] If one work is more unified than another, then it is more coherent or complete; if it is more intense, then the pervasiveness of the feelings it gives rise to is stronger; and if it is more complex, then it has a greater range of distinct elements being unified or feeding into its intensity. It might be said, for instance, that *Black Square* has great unity, but lacks complexity, while Guo Xi's *Early Spring* comparatively has a lot more complexity, but less unity. Meanwhile, the two paintings seem arguably on a par so far as intensity is concerned – they are just intense in very different ways. It is worth noticing that in Beardsley's view, the value of a work of art arises entirely from the work's formal qualities. In this way, Beardsley's view fits quite well with the views presented by Sibley and Pettit. However, as one might expect, given his view of interpretation discussed in the last chapter, Beardsley's theory of value entirely leaves out the sorts of historical and contextual conditions discussed by Walton and the other contextualists.

On Beardsley's view, a work that is unified has the capacity to provide a unified experience, a work that is intense is one that that gives rise to an intense experience, and a work that is complex can give rise to a complex experience.[29] And so, Beardsley provides a straightforward analysis of artistic value: a work is valuable as an artwork if it gives rise to an experience that is unified, intense and complex, and such a work gives rise to such an experience if the work itself is unified, intense and complex. The value of art *as* art for Beardsley is simply aesthetic value – that is, a work of art is a good or valuable work of art insofar as (and to the degree that) it can give rise to this particular sort of pleasure. So, it might be suggested, de Kooning's *Interchange* has the exchange value that it has at least *in part* because of its aesthetic value. Some would argue that the aesthetic value of art, then, is, like its exchange value, just another sort of *instrumental* value. That is, we value art because it can give us something else (aesthetic enjoyment). Perhaps Beardsley at least has to allow for this possibility – although ordinary life rarely affords experiences that are as unified as our experiences of artworks, there is certainly nothing that in principle disallows such an experience outside of the realm of art.

Joel Feinberg argues that although we value art for something it gives us, we should nevertheless distinguish this sort of value from instrumental value, broadly speaking.[30] To value something instrumentally, Feinberg suggests, is to value something for what can be done with it. A clear case of instrumental value, then, would be valuing de Kooning's painting because it could be sold, and the proceeds used to buy something else. We could also instrumentally value the painting because it is precisely the right size to cover up that unfortunate stain on the wall. Of course, it might be said that we value de Kooning's painting because we can do *aesthetic* things with it, so this too would seem to be an instrumental value. However, Feinberg distinguishes instrumental value from *intrinsic* value – the value had in a thing in itself. The difference here, Feinberg suggests, is that intrinsic value is intimately connected with the object, while instrumental value tends to involve a lot of intervening causes. The aesthetic value of a work of art is immediate, and arises simply with the perception of the work. The work's exchange value, however, depends upon fluctuations in the market, being able to find the right buyer and so on. The aesthetic effects are immediate, while the economic ones are remote. So the difference, for Feinberg, is really one of degree.

Malcolm Budd argues that the difference between the intrinsic value of art and its instrumental values is not merely one of *degree*, but one of *kind*.[31] Valuing something for economic reasons or because it can cover up a stain on a wall – or, for that matter, to value it merely because of the pleasure it affords – is not, Budd suggests, to value it *as* art. The distinction, he argues, is whether what is being valued is itself a *part* of the very experience of the work in question, or merely a *product* of that experience. To value a work intrinsically on this view is to value it for the very experience it affords.

If you have a headache, and you know that either aspirin or ibuprofen will relieve your pain, you are unlikely to care which you are given. That is, it probably would not matter to you that aspirin works by blocking the body's production of prostaglandins and thromboxanes, and that ibuprofen works by inhibiting the enzyme cyclooxygenase. What you care about is the end result. So with headache medicine, if aspirin and ibuprofen work equally well, you will happily exchange one for the other. With art, however, we care about how the end result is brought about just as much as we care about the result itself. Budd writes:

> The effects of the experience of a work of art on an individual (its individual instrumental value) or on people in general (its overall instrumental value) are certainly of great importance; but it is the character of the experience the work offers, in conjunction with the nature of those who undergo it, that determines what the effects are likely to be; and it is not these effects themselves, but the character of the experience, that determines the artistic value of the work.[32]

So unlike headache medicine or other things that we value centrally for their effects, we value art as much for how the effect is brought about as for the effect itself. In this way, Budd's theory aligns nicely with a number of the views considered in this chapter. Kant suggested that when we engage with art or other objects of aesthetic interest, we should do so without an eye towards a goal, instead engaging in 'free play' of the imagination. Sibley argued that one is only justified in making aesthetic claims about those works one has actually personally experienced. And Scruton claimed that experiencing at least some of a work's aesthetic properties depend upon an emotional engagement with the work. For each of these philosophers, the value of art is intimately tied up with actually experiencing that art, and we would not happily exchange a work of art for a pill that would provide the same level of pleasure.

Robert Stecker, for one, has challenged Budd's claim that to value something *as* art is to value it non-instrumentally.[33] Stecker argues that although the *way* that the pleasure of art is brought about helps to shape that end, this is neither peculiar to art, nor does it negate the fact that what we ultimately care about is the end. First, although the value of art may be shaped by the art itself, this would also seem to be true for sporting events, the joy of cooking, the pleasure of a warm bath, and all manner of other experiences one might have. As such, it would seem that this will not serve to distinguish the value of art from the value of other sorts of experience. Second, Stecker notes, while it might be that the value of art can only be got from that very work – and so we might for this reason call such a value intrinsic – what we ultimately care about is the *experience*. And the experience of the work, Stecker argues, is a distinct thing from the work itself. It is ultimately the experience that we are after, and so it would be a mistake to think of the value of the artwork itself as anything but an instrumental value.

What all of these philosophers would seem to agree about is that artistic value is ultimately grounded – one way or another – in aesthetic value. Notice, however, that aesthetic value is something that can be found in a mountainscape, a sunset or a flower just as easily and as powerfully as it can be found in a poem, painting or play. And this is true whether that aesthetic value is intrinsic or instrumental, in the experience of the thing or in the thing itself. But it seems strange to say that a flower itself has artistic value, what with it not being art. Andrew Huddleston thus argues that '[w]hen aesthetic value is a value of art as art, it is only *because* this aesthetic value *has been achieved by an artist*.'[34] That is, any account of the value of art must at least include as a part of that account the fact that it is *art*, and understanding artistic achievement means understanding the thing as the outcome of an artistic project.

Chapter summary

Throughout this chapter, we have considered a number of interrelated issues and questions. Does beauty have an objective nature? Is taste simply subjective? Is there a *right* way to experience art? What sorts of properties are aesthetic properties, and what do they depend on? Does art have a unique *sort* of value – and if so, what kind of value is it? In general, since Pythagoras's time, what we have seen are attempts to ground beauty, aesthetic properties and the value of art in something determinable so that we have at least some basis for disagreements about particular cases of art and beauty.

Historical timeline

	c. 390 BCE	Plato, *Hippias Major*
	c. 360 BCE	Plato, *Laws*
	c. 350 BCE	Aristotle, *Poetics*
	398	St Augustine, *Confessions*
Guo Xi, *Early Spring*	1072	
	1259	St Bonaventure, *The Journey of the Mind to God*
	c. 1274	St Thomas Aquinas, *Summa Theologica*

	1435	Leon Battista Alberti, *De Pittura*
	1469	Marsilio Ficino, *Commentarium in Convivium Platonis, de Amore*
Leonardo da Vinci, *Mona Lisa*	1503	
	1711	Anthony Ashley Cooper, 3rd Earl of Shaftesbury, *Characteristics of Men, Manners, Opinions, Times*
	1725	Francis Hutcheson, *An Inquiry into the Original of Our Ideas of Beauty and Virtue*
	1757	David Hume, 'Of the Standard of Taste'
	1790	Immanuel Kant, *The Critique of Judgment*
Hector Berlioz, *Marche funèbre pour la dernière scène d'*Hamlet	1844	
Kasimir Malevich, *Black Square*	1915	
Hilda Doolittle, 'Oread'		
Jorge Luis Borges, 'Pierre Menard, Author of Don Quixote'	1939	
Willem de Kooning, *Interchange*	1955	
Alexander Calder, *Red Mobile*	1956	
Ed Wood, Jr, *Plan 9 From Outer Space*	1959	Frank Sibley, 'Aesthetic Concepts'
Harper Lee, *To Kill a Mockingbird*	1960	
	1964	Arthur Danto, 'The Artworld'
	1970	Kendall Walton, 'Categories of Art'
	1974	Frank Sibley, 'Particularity, Art and Evaluation'
		Roger Scruton, *Art and Imagination*
	1983	Philip Pettit, 'The Possibility of Aesthetic Realism'
	1994	Joel Feinberg, 'Not With My Tax Money: The Problem of Justifying Government Subsidies for the Arts'
	1995	Malcolm Budd, *Values of Art: Pictures, Poetry, and Music*

	1997	Robert Stecker, *Artworks: Definition, Meaning and Value*
Suzanne Collins, *The Hunger Games*	2008	
Tom Waits, 'Last Leaf'	2011	
	2012	Andrew Huddleston, 'In Defense of Artistic Value'

Key terms and concepts

- Aesthetic Ideas (p. 89)
- Aesthetic Properties (p. 80)
- Beauty (p. 81)
- Contextualism (p. 94)
- Disinterestedness (p. 88)
- Exchange Value (p. 98)
- Instrumental Value (p. 100)
- Intrinsic Value (p. 100)
- *Is* of Artistic Identification (p. 94)
- Judgement vs Sentiment (p. 86)
- Realism (p. 81)
- Relativism (p. 81)
- Sense of Beauty (p. 85)
- Standard, Contra-Standard and Variable Features (p. 95)
- Suitable Positioning (p. 94)
- Supervenience (p. 91)
- Taste (p. 84)

Further reading

The problem of taste is perhaps best initially set out by Hume in his 1757 essay, 'Of the Standards of Taste', and then further explored by Kant in strangulating detail in his 1790 book, *The Critique of Judgment*. For contemporary approaches to the central problems of beauty and taste, I would recommend Guy Sircello's *A New Theory of Beauty* (Princeton University Press, 1975) and Mary Mothersill's *Beauty Restored* (Oxford University Press, 1984). Both Budd's book, *Values of Art: Pictures, Poetry, and Music* (Penguin, 1995) and Stecker's *Artworks: Definition, Meaning, and Value* (Pennsylvania State

University Press, 1997) present robust views on the nature of artistic value and are worthy of serious reading. Also of interest are Alan Goldman's *Aesthetic Value* (Westview Press, 1995), in which he presents a view similar to that of Budd, and Noël Carroll's *Beyond Aesthetics* (Cambridge University Press, 2001), reprinting a series of the author's articles arguing against an aesthetic conception of the value of art. Finally, an interesting argument worthy of greater consideration is outlined by Anthony Savile in his book *The Test of Time* (Oxford University Press, 1982).

Unresolved questions

1 Is Hume's ideal judge even possible? Or is it just an ideal standard that a critic might get closer and closer to? Does it matter?

2 If some work of art is *about* something – say, ethical or political issues – does the artist even *want* us to be disinterested in our experience of it? Should this matter?

3 Is valuing something as an artistic achievement like valuing something as a culinary achievement or an athletic achievement? Can I value something as an artistic achievement without knowing anything about the artist's project or goals?

11   Unsolved questions

4

The Ontology of Art

I. *Alabama Tenant Farmer Wife* (1936) and *After Walker Evans: 4* (1981)

In 1935, St Louis-born photographer Walker Evans was hired by the US federal government's Resettlement Administration (RA) and Farm Security Administration (FSA) to document the effects of the Great Depression in America. Along with writer James Agee, Evans stayed with three families in rural Alabama, including a family of sharecroppers, the Burroughs, capturing images of them, their living conditions and their day-to-day lives. A number of the photographs Evans took were published in Evans's and Agee's 1941 book, *Let Us Now Praise Famous Men*, swiftly renowned for its journalistic innovation. Largely because of these photos, Evans went on to become one of the most praised American photographers of the twentieth century, later becoming professor of photography at Yale University. His

Figure 4.1 Walker Evans, *Alabama Tenant Farmer Wife* (1936).

RA/FSA photographs have become iconic images of rural America between the World Wars. John Szarkowski, curator of photography for the Museum of Modern Art, writes:

> It is difficult to know now with certainty whether Evans recorded the America of his youth, or invented it. Beyond doubt, the accepted myth of our recent pasts is in some measure the creation of this photographer, whose

Figure 4.2 Sherrie Levine, *After Walker Evans: 4* (1981).

work has persuaded us of the validity of a new set of clues and symbols bearing on the question of who we are. Whether that work and its judgment was fact or artifice, or half of each, it is now part of our history.[1]

In 1978, *First and Last,* a catalogue of 219 of Evans's 20,000 photographs, was published. It was not the first such collection of Evans's work, nor would it be the last. There seems little question that if you turn to page 73 of *First and Last*, you will see a copy of *Alabama Tenant Farmer Wife*, just as you can see Evans's work in the book currently in your hands. But things get a little more complicated from here.

In 1981, Sherrie Levine *re*-photographed a number of the images in *First and Last*, including Evans's *Alabama Tenant Farmer Wife* – a portrait of Allie Mae Burroughs – titling her 're-photograph' of Evans's iconic image *After Walker Evans: 4*. This, along with a series of other images photographed from *First and Last*, were displayed the same year in Levine's exhibition, 'Sherrie Levine After Walker Evans'. Levine is what is called an 'appropriation artist' – her works are primarily photographs of others' works. As Abigail Solomon-Godeau puts it, Levine 'does not make photographs; she *takes* photographs'.[2] *After Walker Evans: 4* is grain-for-grain indistinguishable from *Alabama Tenant Farmer Wife*. But is it, as such, the *same* photograph – the very same *work*? Suppose, in placing the images for this book, the layout designer had inadvertently swapped the photographs. If they are, in fact, just two copies of the very same thing, it should make no difference. But is the reverse also true? If swapping the photos would make no difference, would that make them the very same work?

In 2001, Michael Mandiberg scanned the same photographs from *First and Last* and posted them to his website, AfterSherrieLevine.com. If you visit the site, you can print out a high-resolution copy of the image originally taken by Evans – now titled *Untitled (AfterSherrieLevine.com/2.jpg)* – along with a certificate of authenticity. According to the certificate, if you follow the printing and framing directions, you will have in your hands an authentic copy of Mandiberg's work. But is it also Evans's work? Is it Levine's work? Have either Levine or Mandiberg created a new work?

II. On ontology

Put roughly, ontology is the study of what there is, and of the features and relations of those things taken to exist. Ontology considers such questions as 'Are material objects all that there is in the universe?' and 'If there were no red things in the world, would there still be the colour red?' Ontology in art begins with a seemingly innocuous question: what makes *this* thing the same as *that* thing, but different from that *other* thing? These are issues of identity and identity conditions.

When it comes to art, we might ask, are *Alabama Tenant Farmer Wife* and *After Walker Evans: 4* the same work of art or different works? And is there anything that makes Duchamp's *Fountain* different from the Bedfordshire-model urinal Duchamp made it from? Certainly, Evans's photograph and Levine's photograph *look* the same, but is this enough to say they *are* the same photograph, the same *artwork*? And certainly *Fountain* is made from the urinal, but is this enough to say it just *is* the urinal? Questions of ontology are often posed as questions of *essences*, but should not thus be confused with the central question being asked in Chapter 1. Although the definition of art and the ontology of art could both fall under the heading of 'What is art?', the project of the definition of art seeks simply to distinguish art from non-art. Questions of ontology seek to uncover something more about the *nature* of art. Rather than attempting to answer 'What makes art *art?*', we ask 'What is essential to *this work* of art or this *kind* of art?' Some philosophers argue that all art operates according to the same ontological model – that each work of art and each kind of art have the same *kind* of nature – and others argue that they can differ substantially. Most, however, do not assume that art operates according to some ontological model different than that of all non-art.

That being said, when it comes to ontology, there does seem to be an important difference between art in general and *some* kinds of non-art, and this is wrapped up in how we go about *determining* something's nature. We might ask, what is it that makes gold different from lead? They are both heavy and they are both fairly malleable metals, so this is of little help. It might be pointed out that lead is bluish or grey in colour, while gold is yellowish, so that's something. Of course, iron is also grey in colour, and the metal cesium is often yellowish, and if we want to distinguish gold from lead, we'll also want to distinguish these from the other metals. So we keep looking. As it turns out, what makes gold essentially different from lead is fairly straightforward. An atom of gold has seventy-nine protons in its nucleus, while lead has eighty-two. One simply cannot have an atom of gold or lead with fewer or greater protons than these, and the same model applies to all of the elements. Chemical elements are considered paradigm 'natural kinds' – what distinguishes one such kind from another is an issue of their *natural* make-up. We distinguish elements by *discovering* their essential natures – the same natures they would have regardless of whether people were around to discover them. The ontological model of natural kinds seems to work extremely well for chemical elements, and some have attempted to use the same model to differentiate biological species, sexes, races and so on, all to considerable debate. What seems fairly certain, however, is that artworks do *not* operate like natural kinds.

If we want to find the essential difference between gold and lead, we do so by *looking* at gold and lead. We look at them with our eyes. We look at them with microscopes. And if you are Ernest Rutherford, you finally look at them while firing alpha particles at them to see the effect. This methodology, however, doesn't seem to offer much hope of distinguishing one work of art from another. Suppose we are offered two word-for-word identical poems, one handwritten and the other typed, and we are asked if they are the *same* poem. Well, they *do* have the same words in the same order, so this seems to be *some* evidence of identity, but why should we ignore the manner in which they are written down? It seems that no matter how long or hard we look at them, we won't find a satisfactory answer to the question simply by looking. (Firing alpha particles at them is unlikely to help either.) Or suppose we seek to restore a centuries-old painting. If all that is required to restore it to its original condition is to apply a daub of paint to the lower-left corner, most would contend that we still have the same painting. But if what is required to restore it is to repaint everything *but* that spot in the lower-left corner, most would argue that the original painting has not survived, and so this is a different painting. But the result in each case is visually indistinguishable from the original. So it would seem again that simply looking won't help us to distinguish one work from the other. Or, at least, most of us won't be satisfied by an answer derived by simply looking.

What gold *is* seems to have little or nothing to do with how we use it, but the nature of art seems to depend very much on artistic practice. Many have argued that any ontology of art should be *guided* by artistic practice – how we treat artworks, how we judge them, how we differentiate them and how we evaluate them.[3] On one version of this approach, when a story about the nature of art comes into conflict with how we actually treat art, it is the story that must bend, not the practice. Some argue that there is some room for revision to practice. David Davies, for example, suggests that ontology must only conform to our practice to the extent that we deem those features of our practice acceptable on reflection.[4] For instance, if how we treat art conflicts with what it is we value about art, it might be reasonable to suggest that our practice should be revised to better match how we value art.

Amie Thomasson argues that not only must ontology be *guided* by artistic practice; any ontology of art must be *grounded* on practice.[5] That is, she suggests, in order for you to refer to Michelangelo's *David*, or Charles Dickens's *Hard Times*, or the film *Star Wars*, you must already have a background ontological conception of what kind of a thing the work is. And these background conceptions that we share are embodied in our practice. For instance, we might reasonably distinguish between the original 1977 theatrical release of *Star Wars* (in which Han shoots first) and the remastered 1997 Special Edition (in which Greedo shoots first), so a criticism of one does not necessarily apply to the other. But when it comes to watching the Special Edition on the big screen or on television, we are reasonably satisfied that both *are* the same film, so a criticism of one applies also to the other. These are matters of common *practice* – of how we treat, distinguish and evaluate artworks – and they serve to indicate just what it is we are referring to when we refer to a particular artwork. The goal of an ontology of art, Thomasson argues, is to sort out what kind of a thing a film or painting or poem is, *given* how we ordinarily treat it. When questions arise for which our practice provides no answers, the best we can do is try to come to a *decision* about how to deal with the issue. Unlike gold and lead, questions about the nature of art cannot be settled by simply looking at the work or kind of work in question.

On Thomasson's view, an ontological theory of art that flies in the face of ordinary artistic practice is a revolutionary one. Were we to accept it, it would require us to seriously rethink how we deal with art, saying that although we *do* treat art in *this* way, we *should* be treating art in *that* way. For such a revolutionary theory to have merit, it would have to have some extremely compelling argument to back it up. We might imagine that, once upon a time, people treated gold mined from mountains and gold sifted from riverbeds as two very different sorts of things, with the former being given a substantially higher monetary value than the latter. However, after discovering that there is nothing that differentiates them on a molecular level, people might be easily persuaded to stop thinking of them as essentially different. When it comes to art, however, what discovery could compel us to think of art very differently than we currently do is an open question.

III. Artworks as physical objects

Although Chapter 1 left us with unresolved questions about whether some things are or are not art, we can put aside questionable 'artworks' and 'art forms' for the moment. We will have more than enough to work with if we restrict ourselves to central art forms and fairly clear cases of artworks. Among the central art forms, we might include painting, both cast and carved sculpture, literature, music, architecture, dance, photography, film … When it comes to ontology, our first question might be: does the same *model* of ontology apply to all of these art forms? And, if so, what model might that be?

In his book, *Art and Its Objects*, Richard Wollheim considers what he calls the 'physical-object hypothesis': the view that artworks simply *are* physical objects.[6] As Wollheim puts it, 'Such a hypothesis is a natural starting point: if only for the reason that it is plausible to assume that things are physical objects unless they very obviously aren't.'[7] A theory that continues to gain ground both in philosophy and in the world at large is that the universe consists solely of physical or material objects – that ultimately this is all that exists. This theory would apply as much to artworks as to anything else, and some artworks seem to have a fairly clear claim to being physical objects. Consider a work like Michelangelo's *David*. The famous sculpture stands 517 centimetres tall, is estimated to weigh several tons and is composed entirely of blue-grey marble quarried from Carrara in Tuscany, Italy. *David* originally stood outside Florence's Palazzo Vecchio, but was moved to the nearby Accademia Gallery in 1873. These seem to be very much the sorts of things one could say of any material object – they seem to *describe* a physical object. In 1991, a man who had concealed a hammer under his jacket attacked the statue, breaking the second toe on the statue's left foot. The world was horrified not simply because a piece of marble had been damaged, but because (it seems) in damaging the marble, the man had damaged the work of art. There is a replica of the sculpture standing where the original was first displayed, and other full-sized replicas can be found in Buffalo, NY, in Las Vegas, NV, and on the campus of California State University, Fullerton. This last replica originally stood at the Forest Lawn Memorial Parks in Cypress, CA, but collapsed and shattered into several pieces in a 1987 earthquake. The pieces were collected and placed on the university campus exactly as they had fallen. But the destruction of this replica did not cause the horror that followed the breaking of a single toe of the original. Destroying a copy of *David* does no harm to *David*, it seems, but destroying the original would destroy the work itself. In this case, a copy of the work is not what we might call a genuine 'instance' of the work. In 2004, the Italian government considered moving *David* to a new location. Imagine now that the government had said they would move the work itself but not the piece of marble that Michelangelo carved – we simply wouldn't know what to make of this statement. This all seems fairly compelling evidence that Michelangelo's *David*, the artwork, just *is* that physical object.

We could tell parallel stories about any number of sculptures, paintings and drawings. Although the example of *David* is certainly compelling, the physical-object hypothesis runs into two sorts of problem. First, while there seems to be a physical object that we might identify with Michelangelo's *David*, the physical-object hypothesis does not seem to be a model that applies to art generally. What physical object might serve as a candidate for being, say, Dickens's *Hard Times*, or Beethoven's *Hammerklavier Sonata*, or the movie *Star Wars* in the same way that the piece of Carrara marble *is* Michelangelo's *David*? I have a copy of *Hard Times* on my bookshelf; perhaps you do too. There is almost certainly one in your local library. It might be said that these are *all* physical objects: they all take up space, and they can each be damaged or destroyed. But if I run my copy through a wood-chipper, I haven't in any way damaged the literary work that Dickens wrote. So it would seem my copy of *Hard Times* is not identical to Dickens's work – that is, *Hard Times* is not *just* my copy. And yet, if I have read my copy, we want to say that I have read Dickens's novel. We can say the same of the copy that sits on your shelf or on the shelf of your library. Perhaps, then, these are simply replicas of *Hard Times* in the same way that the shattered copy of Michelangelo's *David* is merely a replica and not the work itself (and so we would be confused in saying we had actually read the work). If that is the case, the clearest physical-object candidate for *being Hard Times* would be the manuscript actually handwritten by Dickens.

Dickens's original *Hard Times* manuscript, currently housed in the Forster Collection of London's Victoria and Albert Museum, was written in 1853 in iron gall ink, an ink rich in iron sulphate. Unfortunately, this sort of ink has the nasty tendency to slowly eat through the paper or vellum it is written on. What this means is that the original *Hard Times* manuscript is slowly eating itself, and it seems only a matter of time before it is destroyed completely. When and if this happens, does this mean Dickens's literary work will itself be destroyed? Certainly not. Let's consider another case: with the exception of *Nineteen Eighty-Four*, the original manuscripts for all of George Orwell's major works have been lost or destroyed, but this does not keep us from reading *Animal Farm*. When and if the manuscript for *Hard Times* turns to dust, we will still be able to study, enjoy and be frustrated by the work. Any copy is as good as any other, and it seems that as long as one accurate copy exists, the work itself exists. In this sense, a copy *is* a genuine instance. So, it might be suggested, *Hard Times* is not *this* physical copy or *that* physical copy, but rather the collection or *class* of all such physical copies. On this suggestion, *Hard Times* would be identical with all *copies* of *Hard Times*. But this raises some problems. Not all copies of *Hard Times* have the same apparent properties. My copy is hardcover and yours is a paperback. Mine is printed in a Garamond font, yours in Monotype Fournier. On the view presented, a work of literature is simply identical with all copies of itself, but not all such copies share the same properties – so which properties count? It seems we can only identify *Hard Times* if we already know what *Hard Times* is. This is viciously circular and terribly uninformative.

The second problem that arises for the physical-object hypothesis is that on further analysis the properties of a work like Michelangelo's *David* do not seem to line up exactly with any particular physical object. The 1991 attack resulting in *David*'s broken toe was neither the first nor the most substantial damage that the statue has taken since it was created. In 1527, the statue's left arm was broken off and shattered by a rioting mob who threw a piece of furniture off a nearby balcony. It was sixteen years before the damage was repaired, the original pieces reportedly being reassembled and fixed to the statue with copper pins. So prior to 1527 the statue consisted of a single piece of marble. After 1543, the statue consisted of several pieces of marble and a number of copper pins. The damage that *David* sustained was not irreparable. The statue has been damaged and repaired time and again over the years, persisting over time through periods of restoration. Though its material components have changed over the years, the statue remains, so the statue simply cannot be identical with any particular physical object or objects.

IV. Singular and multiple artworks

Although the physical-object hypothesis ultimately fails to describe the nature of artworks, our discussion of the hypothesis does help to indicate something peculiar about artworks in general: there seems to be an important distinction between works like *Hard Times* and works like *David*. Although Michelangelo's masterpiece cannot ultimately be identified with any material object per se (because the material components of the statue can change without *David* winking out of existence), it does seem that we can identify the artwork with a given particular thing. Even the most perfect copy of *David* is only a replica. Michelangelo's work is the thing standing in the Accademia Gallery, and which used to stand outside the Palazzo Vecchio – if this thing is utterly destroyed, the work will be lost. In other words, Michelangelo's *David* seems essentially singular. A work like *Hard Times* (or the 1997 Special Edition of *Star Wars* or Beethoven's *Hammerklavier Sonata*) exists in multiple genuine instances, each as authentic as the other. Destroying any one such instance will not destroy the work itself. Beethoven's handwritten score for the *Hammerklavier Sonata* is long since lost, and the original manuscript for *Hard Times* is slowly eating itself. But both of these works will survive or have survived the destruction of their original copies. In 2006, Lucasfilm announced that, in creating the 1997 Special Edition, it had to permanently alter the original negatives for the 1977 version of *Star Wars*. A decade later, however, a complete 35mm print of the 1977 film was discovered, and certainly, if you projected this 35mm film onto a screen, you will be watching the original *Star Wars*.

In his book *Language of Art*, Nelson Goodman introduces the terms 'autographic' and 'allographic' to determine what makes something a genuine instance of a given work.[8] If even the most exact duplication of some work will not count as genuine, that work is autographic; otherwise, it is allographic. On Goodman's view, then, Michelangelo's *David* is autographic – because a copy, no matter how perfect, will not be a genuine instance – while *Hard Times*, *Star Wars* and the *Hammerklavier Sonata* are each allographic. So, why the distinction? The distinction, Goodman suggests, is that allographic works allow for complete notation, while autographic works do not. Notation gives us a strict schematic to refer to for making new copies – it allows us to check a purported instance against what is essential to the work. Notation, for Goodman, consists of a system of characters with specifiable rules of use. The English language is such a system, as is the system of musical notation. To make a copy of a work of literature, Goodman says, one needs only put the right words in the right order. Likewise for performing a musical work – one needs only play the right notes in the right order, and one has performed that work. What Goodman suggests is that there is no equivalent notational system to refer to for things like sculptures and paintings, which would allow us to capture their essential structure.

Although Goodman offers the autographic/allographic distinction as an ontological one, he also suggests that conditions for authenticity arise as a result of cultural practice, and so how genuineness is determined is in principle subject to change. Some philosophers have suggested that it is only because we lack the necessary copying technology that we continue to think of paintings and carved sculptures as essentially singular, and that at some point in the future we may have to rethink the nature of these art forms. Others suggest that singularity is simply essential to the nature of something like Michelangelo's *David*, and that this is not subject to change. Conversely, on this view, one could not make a work of literature that is essentially singular – this simply isn't how we think of literature. This seems to depend upon the degree to which the ontology of art is grounded, guided or restricted by practice, and how much practice is open to change in a given culture.

However much Goodman's autographic/allographic distinction seems to line up with our current artistic practice in such cases as painting, carved sculpture, literature and music, it does have its problems. First, because art forms like printmaking, cast sculpture, film and photography do not have straightforward notational systems like those of literature and music, they would seem to fall on the autographic side of Goodman's distinction. However, we do treat these as art forms that allow for multiple genuine instances, and so for this reason they would seem to fall on the allographic side of the divide. Other art kinds, like theatre, seem to have *some* notational aspects, but are not *completely* amenable to notation, and so it is not entirely clear where they should fit in Goodman's system. For something to be a genuine instance of a cast sculpture, Goodman notes, it must be made from the original, authentic cast – otherwise it is a *mere* copy. Jerrold Levinson has suggested that we call a work autographic if it is *not at all* amenable to notation, and otherwise allographic. Levinson contends that this distinction will not distinguish between essentially singular and essentially multiple art kinds – as *all* allographic art forms, and *some* autographic art forms, will allow for multiple genuine copies – but will nevertheless broadly track how genuineness is determined in different kinds of art.[9]

With this in mind, let us briefly turn back to the case that opened this chapter: Walker Evans's *Alabama Tenant Farmer Wife* and Sherrie Levine's *After Walker Evans: 4*. Goodman does not discuss photography in particular, but he does discuss a similar art form: printmaking. For a print to be genuine, Goodman argues, it must be made from the original printing plates – merely looking like the genuine article will not suffice. This is a part of our cultural practice regarding the authenticity of prints. What, then, of photography? For a print of a photograph to be genuine, must it be printed from the original negative? Perhaps once upon a time, this would have been true, but even when negatives did serve as definitive templates, it was accepted practice that a new negative could be made by photographing an existing clean 'positive' print. In these days of digital photography, however, there *are no* negatives, so what are we to do? Will a photograph of the original photograph qualify as a genuine instance of the same photograph? Unfortunately, Goodman does not offer a suggestion, and because authenticity conditions can differ between seemingly similar art kinds, the example of printmaking may offer little or no help with photography. At the very least, we are left with some big open questions that can perhaps only be settled (if at all) by further investigating artistic practice. If Amie Thomasson is right, we may simply be left with a decision to make.

These issues aside, some philosophers have taken further issue with Goodman's suggestion that two novels with the same words in the same order are *necessarily* the same literary work, or that two pieces of music with the same notes in the same order are on this basis alone instances of the same musical work. But before we can get into this discussion, we need a little more background information.

V. Types and tokens

Turning from works taken to be essentially singular to works taken to be capable of existing in multiple instances, we might ask, how is it that one thing can be in many places at once with each being somehow the very same thing? It boggles the mind. The suggestion most often put forward is that what we are talking about are *abstract objects*, which have some peculiar sorts of properties.

To help understand the nature of such objects, Charles Sanders Peirce introduced what has become known as the type/token distinction.[10] Peirce offers the deceptively simple example of words to bring out the distinction. Count the number of *the*'s on this page. There are 35, and so in one sense, we can say they count as 35 words. In another sense, however, there is but one word 'the' in the English language. In the first sense, we are counting what we might call *tokens*; in the second sense, we are counting the *type*. Types are abstract objects, and tokens are their particular instances. At a first estimation, each token of the word 'the' counts as an instance of the type because it has the same letters in the same order, is being used in the same language and has the same basic meaning in each case. That is, what makes something a token of a given type depends upon whether the thing in question has the right properties. Artworks, many have suggested, work in the same way as words. But artworks tend to be much more complicated than individual words, so there is a great deal more to be said about them.

Although he does not use the type/token terminology, this sort of relationship between an artwork-type and its individual tokens was first introduced into aesthetics by the same philosopher who proposed and rejected the physical-object hypothesis, Richard Wollheim. Nelson

Goodman, too, in distinguishing between genuine and non-genuine copies, seems to be relying on the idea of abstract objects. An abstract object – in this case, a type – is not itself a physical thing. Rather, we experience or come to know the type by experiencing one or more of its tokens.

How we experience a token can vary with the kind of work we are talking about. A literary work may be experienced in many ways: it may be read from a printed copy, it may be heard at a spoken reading or it may be memorized. Centrally, musical works are performed. But they may also be recorded, and a recording may or may not be a straightforward recording of a particular performance. In the case of rock music, a recording will most often be cobbled together from the best bits of a number of performance-parts. Strictly speaking, however, a musical work cannot be written down. What is written down is the *score* for the musical work. Sometimes musicians simply work from *tablature* – a sort of musical shorthand. Scores and tablature are *instructions* for performing the work at hand. And whether or not a musical work (as opposed to instructions for performing such a work) can be memorized would seem to depend on whether we think of a musical work as being the sort of thing that actually needs to be *heard*, and whether ears are necessary for hearing. We might compare musical works with, say, dramatic works. A play like Shakespeare's *King Lear* or Amiri Baraka's *A Black Mass* is the sort of thing that is performed, using actors and sets and the like. But it also seems like the sort of thing we can read (most of us, I'm certain, read at least *some* of Shakespeare's plays in high school). So it might be asked, is reading *King Lear* like reading *Hard Times*, or is it more like reading the score for the *Hammerklavier Sonata* – or is it something else entirely? Is the script for a play an instance of the work or is it merely instructions for producing the work? That would seem to depend upon what we take to be essential to being an instance or a token of this kind of thing.

What is it that *makes* a given item a token of a particular type? It is at this point that philosophers tend to come to blows over the nature of artworks and over exactly what the type/token relationship – the relationship between a work and its instances – consists in, and what are the specific conditions required for something's being an instance of a given work. Goodman suggests that all that is required for something to count as an instance or token of a given literary work (what we might call the type) is strict word-for-word adherence. That is, *Hard Times* consists essentially of certain words in a certain order. On this view, anything that has those precise words in that precise order simply *is* a token of the type *Hard Times*.

Anything that fails to have those words in that order fails to be a token of that type. Likewise for notes and musical works. In other words, a literary work is essentially a word-sequence and a musical work is essentially a sound-sequence. Other sorts of works, Goodman suggests, may require something more – authentic cast sculptures must be made from authentic casts, and authentic prints must be made from authentic printing plates – but the requirements for literary and musical works are fairly simple. A number of philosophers have taken issue with the implications of this claim.

First, as many have noted, on Goodman's view, a copy of *Hard Times* with a single typo or misplaced comma is not, strictly speaking, an instance of the work. And a performance of the *Hammerklavier Sonata* with a single slightly misplaced note, or which is ever so slightly off in its timing, is not actually a performance of Beethoven's piece. The implications of this would seem to be staggering. There is hardly a book in existence (including this one) that doesn't have a typo, and so complex and demanding of the performers is the *Hammerklavier Sonata* that only very rarely (if ever) is a performance of it flawless in execution. On Goodman's view, it seems, most printed novels are not actually the novels they are purported to be, and most musical performances are not performances of the works they are said to be of.

Nicholas Wolterstorff suggests that this problem may be solved by thinking of works as 'norm-kinds'.[11] Wolterstorff suggests that an artist selects for a work certain properties as 'criteria for correctness' which specify what counts as a correct instance of the work. Where some item possesses all of the properties normatively associated with the work, that item is an instance of the work. And if some item comes *fairly close* to exemplifying those properties, we can call this an *incorrect* instance of that work. So a musical work with a misplaced note or a literary work with a typo will be actual instances, just flawed ones.[12]

However, Wolterstorff's suggestion does not help get around a second contentious issue with Goodman's theory: if a musical work is simply a sequence of notes (or, in Wolterstorff's terms, 'criteria for correctness'), and notes are simply specific sounds, then it would seem that strictly speaking no one ever *creates* a musical work. Rather, a sequence of sounds is the sort of thing that could have been sounded out at any time, and so all that a composer does is *discover* (or, at best, *select*) the work. And two composers who entirely coincidentally put the same notes in the same order (or select the same criteria for correctness) have merely *discovered* the same work. The sound structure itself has and will always exist. On this view, although we may owe Beethoven something for bringing the *Hammerklavier Sonata* to our attention, he is not *responsible* for the work's existence, because it always existed. The same would seem to be true of literary works – if such a work is simply a word-sequence, then so long as the words that compose that sequence have existed, the work itself has existed. It is like the sequence of nucleotides that make up human DNA: the scientists mapping human DNA are not *creating* human DNA; rather, they are in the process of discovering it. So, strictly speaking, Dickens did not create *Hard Times*; rather, he discovered it, and it could have as easily been discovered a decade before or a century afterwards.

This is a contentious matter in aesthetics. Some, like Julian Dodd[13] and Peter Kivy,[14] defend the view that things like musical works exist as *eternal types*. They argue that while a composer does not, strictly speaking, *create* a work, this does not detract from the importance of composition. After all, do we think less of the scientists mapping human DNA because what results is a discovery and not a creation? While such scientists perhaps do not *create*, it is argued, their activities are nevertheless *creative* – that is, discovery involves *creativity*. Others, like Joseph Margolis[15] and Jerrold Levinson,[16] argue that creation is essential to artworks and cannot be so easily disposed of. Back in Chapter 1, we noted that the one condition of art that seems most tenacious is that artworks are essentially artefacts – products of human intention or creation. To do away with this condition seems to fly in the face of one of the very few things we actually agree about when it comes to art.

Levinson suggests that rather than thinking of musical works as eternal types, we should think of them as *indicated types* – as sound structures indicated (or fixed, or determined, or selected) by their composers. In picking out such a structure, the composer creates the work. He may do other things as well, of course. He may, for instance, specify the instruments on which the composition is to be played – after all, the same notes played on a piano and on a saxophone will sound very different. But whether the composer does or does not specify the instruments involved, on Levinson's view, we distinguish between two musical works not on the basis of their sound structures alone (those notes in that order), but on the basis of when, by whom and under what conditions the sound structure was indicated.

In the previous chapter, we looked at Jorge Luis Borges' imagined case of 'Pierre Menard, Author of the Don Quixote', and the contextualist argument that a work's aesthetic properties depend in part upon the context in which that work was created. The same will hold true for all kinds of works, Levinson argues. Consider composer Johann Stamitz's *Symphony in E-Flat Major, Op. 11, No. 3*. Stamitz was a founder of what is known as the Mannheim school, an approach to classical composition characterized by a body of revolutionary orchestral techniques. The *Symphony in E-Flat Major* opens with one of the Mannheim school's innovations: the 'Mannheim Rocket', in which the notes that would otherwise make up a chord are played in ascending sequences, growing faster and louder as the notes rise higher and higher. In this late Stamitz symphony, the Mannheim Rocket is exciting. Had the same sound sequence been composed three-quarters of a century earlier by Antonio Vivaldi, however, the symphony would have been utterly shocking. Composed in today's context, the work might best be considered neither shocking nor exciting, but rather slightly comical. In general, however, if a work's context of creation contributes to its aesthetic properties (whether it is exciting, shocking or comical), and if two compositions differ in their properties, then they are distinct works, even if they are note-for-note identical. Two performances with the same sound structure would not necessarily be performances of the very same work, nor would two novels with the same words in the same order thus be tokens of the same type.

Finally, Levinson argues, while a performance of such a work may not be perfect – and so not, strictly speaking, an instance of the work – it will nevertheless count as a *performance* of the work if it is a reasonably or recognizably successful attempt to instantiate that work. Although Levinson is speaking specifically of musical works, we might generalize his view to account for other multiply instantiable art kinds as well, and so we might account for novels with typos, for instance.

In general, Margolis suggests that an artwork (the type) comes into existence with its first token (or, in the case of something like music, with the creation of its score – the *means* of instantiating a token performance). If someone in future comes along and strings the same words or notes together in the same order, they will have created an entirely *new* work, which only coincidentally is entirely similar to the earlier one in terms of its linguistic or sonic properties. Types, Margolis argues, cannot exist without their tokens, and a token is always a token-of-a-type. As such, if all of its tokens are destroyed (as well as all reliable means of making new tokens, as with musical scores), the work itself will cease to exist.

The nature of art, Margolis notes, is a strange one indeed. Artworks consist in abstract objects (types), which are always tied to instances (tokens), which are themselves embodied in physical objects (printed books, performances, prints and so on). However, Margolis further notes, tokens are not themselves identical with the physical objects that embody them, for the same sorts of reasons that Michelangelo's *David* is not identical with the physical object in the Accademia Gallery. After all, it would be strange to say that the physical grooves on a vinyl record constitute a token of the *Hammerklavier Sonata*, or that the millions of zeros and ones that are encoded on a DVD are a token of *Star Wars*. Sonatas are things that are heard, and movies are things that are seen. Rather, such physical things allow us accurate *access* to the work. Tokens are *concrete* (that is, not abstract), but they needn't be thought of as truly physical. All of this strangeness would seem to come back to the fact that artworks are things that arise from our cultural (and specifically, artistic) practices, and are treated in certain ways within our culture.

This view of artworks leaves us with some interesting questions. Although photographs are ordinarily treated as allowing for multiple genuine instances, is Sherrie Levine's *After Walker Evans: 4* merely an instance of Walker Evans's *Alabama Tenant Farmer Wife*, or is it something else? That is, is it simply a token of the same type – is *Alabama Tenant Farmer Wife* embodied in *After Walker Evans: 4*? Levinson's contextualist view suggests that where two art-objects are created in different contexts, the art-objects are distinct works. So if we think of Evans and Levine as independently creating distinct but visually indistinguishable art-objects, *Alabama Tenant Farmer Wife* and *After Walker Evans: 4* should be considered different works. But surely when the assistant at the print shop runs off copies of my photographs, he is not creating distinct works, but rather tokens of a type. Levine, after all, did not *coincidentally* produce an image visually indistinguishable from Evans's; rather, she *copied* Evans's photograph. If we are to distinguish what Levine does from what the print shop assistant does, how are we to do so?

Performance-based works like *King Lear* or the *Hammerklavier Sonata* raise further issues. Are two distinct performances of a play or musical work necessarily instances of the same work – simply tokens of the same type? The *Hammerklavier Sonata* consists of four movements of varying lengths, and the score specifies which notes should be played in what order. However, for instance, the third movement begins with the instruction 'appassionato e con molto sentimento' (play passionately and with great sentiment). What is a conductor to make of this? It tends to be played very slowly, but interpretations by composers have had it last anywhere from sixteen to twenty-five minutes. Is there a *right* way to play it? Mitsuko Uchida's take on the third movement has been called disastrously slow; Andras Schiff's has been called 'pure poetry'. Are these critiques of the sonata per se, or of

Uchida's and Schiff's respective interpretations of it? It seems the latter, but should we thus be treating these as works distinct from the *Hammerklavier Sonata* itself? One view is that in settling on particular ways of presenting the sonata, Uchida and Schiff have each produced new artefacts: Uchida's rendition of the *Hammerklavier Sonata*, and Schiff's rendition of the same. In that each of *these* can be performed, we might think of these as works distinct from each other, and also conceptually distinct from Beethoven's own work. Granted, our critiques of such works may be made on the basis of comparing a given interpretative performance with Beethoven's work itself, but we might also focus on those contributions intentionally contributed by Uchida or Schiff, treating it as its own work. The same issue arises in theatre, with a performance of a play (on stage at Sam Wanamaker Playhouse last Thursday night), the production that it is a performance of (the production directed by Ellen McDougall), and the play itself (Shakespeare's *Othello*).

VI. Constructivism

In Chapter 2, we discussed two versions of *constructivism*, which holds that in interpreting a work, you *create* a work, either by (i) creating a *new* work with each act of interpretation, or (ii) *altering* or *contributing to* a work already in existence. On the first, more radical, version of the theory, in writing the play, Shakespeare did not create a work; rather, the work is created when *you* interpret what Shakespeare wrote. That is, prior to interpretation, all we have are bare words (in the case of literature), sounds (in the case of music), shapes and materials (with sculpture) and so on. The problem many have pointed out with this view is that it implies you and I have never experienced the same work of art – indeed, you couldn't experience the same work of art twice – because each act of interpretation creates a new work. The famed critic John Ruskin praised *Hard Times* for its exploration of important social questions, while the playwright George Bernard Shaw criticized it for failing to accurately portray the actual social situation in nineteenth-century England. If the radical constructivists are right, Ruskin and Shaw are talking about entirely different works, each of which existed only in their respective imaginations – and you or I are in no position to agree or disagree with them, because we cannot experience those works. This, at least, is at odds with how we normally talk about, interpret and evaluate art.

The second, more moderate, version of constructivism offered by Michael Krausz suggests that each interpretative act *adds to* the work.[17] So the work is on this view a sort of abstract object – a class of interpretations – to be distinguished from any copy of the novel, or even the novel's word-sequence, and is continually being built by the novel's readers. However, it is this very point that bothers some philosophers. Robert Stecker points out that, on this view, *Hard Times* will seemingly never be complete.[18] Every time a new interpretation is made, the work – the class of interpretations and object of interpretation – grows. On this view, *Hard Times* is a *very* different work today than it was a century ago, and for reasons having little or nothing to do with Dickens. This outcome conflicts with our general shared belief that *Hard Times* was completed in 1853 when Dickens finished writing. However, this Krausz would chalk up to a fairly minor conceptual confusion on our part, and that what Dickens finished writing was the *text*, and that thereafter we could begin building the *work*.

VII. Mental works and action types

Back in Chapter 1, we discussed R. G. Collingwood's view about art as expression. Collingwood's theory not only attempts to distinguish between art and non-art, but also offers an ontological view of art. On his view, strictly speaking, what you see in a gallery, what you witness on stage and what you read in a book are not instances of 'art'. Rather, these things allow us *access* to the work itself. The nature of an artwork, Collingwood says, is that of a mental activity or object – the self-reflective clarification of the artist in producing the painting, sculpture, novel or other art-object. This physical product ideally serves as a conduit between the audience and the work itself, this internal state of the artist.

As a theory about what distinguishes art from non-art, Collingwood's theory runs into several problems. As an ontological view, however, it offers several apparent advantages. First, the view avoids the problems of identifying artworks with physical objects in that on Collingwood's theory artworks are *mental* objects; the material components of a sculpture like Michelangelo's *David* do not matter, so long as the sculpture continues to offer access to the mental object. Second, Collingwood's view seems to avoid the perplexities of abstract objects: there is not a type with multiple tokens, and some strange relation between them. Rather, each printing of a book, copy of a film or print of a photograph is simply something that offers the same access to the work itself. Third, Collingwood's view tracks our standard practice of treating artworks as things that are created and can be destroyed

– or, at least, lost. The work comes into existence as the artist creates the product, and if all copies of a printed novel are destroyed, our ability to access the work itself is lost. Finally, Collingwood's theory offers a view that applies equally to sculptures, paintings, novels, dances and so on; on his view, the artworks involved are all of the same ontological sort. Although Collingwood's view is criticized on the implication that sculptures, paintings and the like are not the physical things we see in galleries, the other views we have considered would seem to offer similar implications. Collingwood's view does, however, have some further implications that conflict with standard artistic practice. On Collingwood's view, as regards art, there is no difference between Michelangelo's *David* and an accurate replica of the same. Neither is the work itself, and so long as each offers the same access to the work, each is as good or as valuable as the other. So we could replace the object in the Accademia Gallery with a replica and we would be none the worse off. Collingwood's view also leaves some open questions: if the artwork is a mental object, something first experienced by the artist and hopefully later by the audience, what happens to it when nobody is experiencing it? Does it still exist? If so, how? Does it cease to exist? Does it exist as a *possibility* – something that someone *could* experience – and if so, how is this different from a time before the artist herself first experienced it? It is unclear how Collingwood could answer these questions without falling back on something like the type/token view. After all, if we want to say that you and I are accessing the same mental object – the work – it will have to be because our thoughts have the same mental content. And this would seem to be to say that we each have in our minds a *token* of the same mental *type*.

Although his own theory seems unsatisfying, in opening the door to alternative ways of thinking about the nature of art, Collingwood has directly or indirectly inspired several ontological theories, including those of Gregory Currie and David Davies, who argue that works of art are *actions*. Currie argues that artworks are action *types*, while Davies argues that we should think of them as action *tokens*. For the sake of space, we will concentrate here on Currie's 'action-type hypothesis' as outlined in his book, *An Ontology of Art*.[19] Like Collingwood, Currie suggests that one does not see or hear works of art, but rather imaginatively reconstructs them from the paintings one sees, the symphonies one hears and the novels one reads. The central difference in their views is what it is the audience is reconstructing.

To appreciate a work of art, Currie argues, is to appreciate the artist's achievement – not merely the end result, but how the artist came to create that product, including the goal the artist was attempting to reach and the problems he was attempting to solve. This is the artist's *heuristic path*, and Currie contends it is not simply what *leads to* the work; rather, it is an integral *part of* the work. In the case of the *Hammerklavier Sonata*, Currie suggests, the work consists in the discovery of the sound structure via the heuristic path that Beethoven followed. While accepting that a sound structure is itself an eternal type, and so is discovered and not created, Currie argues it is the *way* that the composer goes about discovering this structure that is central to our appreciation of it. Although the conditions under which the art-object was discovered is critical on this view, Currie argues (contrary to Levinson's contextualist approach) that the artist and time of discovery are not integral to the work. Rather, these merely serve to distinguish *tokens* of the action *type: discovery of structure S via heuristic path H.* Where any artist discovers the same structure (of notes, words, shapes, colours and so on) by the same heuristic path as another, they have instantiated the same work. Where either the structure discovered or the heuristic path by which it is discovered differs, a different work has been instantiated – or more properly, as such artworks are actions, works are *enacted*.

As with Levinson's contextualism, to fully appreciate a work on Currie's view requires exposure to more than the product. One must also know something about the history leading to the product, which will not be evident from an inspection of the product itself, however close. Currie's view, as such, may offer us the key to the problem of *Alabama Tenant Farmer Wife* and *After Walker Evans: 4* that opened this chapter. Although Walker Evans and Sherrie Levine produced visually indistinguishable works, Currie would argue, what we appreciate about them are the achievements of Evans and Levine, and it is on this basis that we can distinguish them. Evans set out to capture images of the American South during its worst economic disaster. Levine's project in capturing Evans's images was different. Levine states: 'What I think about in terms of my work is broadening the definition of the word "original." I think of originality as a trope. There is no such thing as an ahistorical activity.'[20] Simon Blond argues that if we compare Evans's work and Levine's, 'we can see that although the works are visually indiscernible they are conceptually different works: the Walker Evans is a work that pays homage to the fortitude and suffering of ordinary people during the depression in America's Deep South, while Levine's work has nothing to do with this – it's an interrogation of the nature of originality'.[21] To appreciate *After Walker Evans: 4* as a work of documentary photography or alternatively to appreciate *Alabama Tenant Farmer Wife* as a piece of appropriation art is to misunderstand the artistic projects of Levine and Evans. In focusing on their respective heuristics, Currie's theory gives us an understanding of the nature of the works as a means to interpreting and evaluating them.

Currie's view does, however, require us to bite some bullets. First, given this view of art, works are not created and cannot be destroyed, as it is always at least possible that someone else could in the future discover the same structure by the same heuristic path. As this would require more than mere structural similarity in two works, however, this is at least more palatable than some views that allow for the eternal existence of artworks. A second difficulty is more challenging: what we see when we see Michelangelo's *David* or hear when we hear the *Kammerklavier Sonata* is not an artwork, but only a structure. This much parallels Collingwood's view, but the implications of Currie's view are deeper: on Currie's theory, it seems, we can truly only encounter a work if we are present at the discovery of the relevant structure – otherwise, at best, we can hope to imaginatively reconstruct or understand what this discovery consisted in. As such, not only do we not experience works in galleries, theatres, books and the like – most of us are unlikely to *ever* fully experience *any* artworks unless we make them ourselves. Finally, we might ask, although as a matter of critical practice we *do* appreciate the actions of the artist in seeking, developing and solving artistic problems, is this *all* or even *centrally* what we appreciate about works? In focusing on one element of appreciation to the detriment of all others seems to be to throw out the baby with the bathwater.

Chapter summary

This chapter has focused on the nature of artworks, seeking to determine what kind of a thing an artwork is, whether or not all artworks are of the same kind, whether there is an essential difference between singular and multiple art-kinds, and how one distinguishes one particular artwork from another. In this pursuit, we have considered a number of views which track artistic practice to greater or lesser degrees. We have looked at the physical-object hypothesis, the view that any given artwork is identifiable with a particular material object, and at the other extreme, the views of R. G. Collingwood and Gregory Currie, suggesting that artworks should be identified with mental objects or human actions, respectively. We considered several takes on the idea that artworks are abstract objects, in particular the view that such works operate according to a type/token relationship, and views that suggest an artwork just is its interpretation or interpretations.

Historical timeline

Work	Year	Text
Michelangelo, *David*	1504	
William Shakespeare, *Othello*	1603	
William Shakespeare, *King Lear*	c. 1606	
Johann Stamitz, *Symphony in E-Flat Major, Op. 11, No. 3*	c. 1754	
Ludwig van Beethoven, *Hammerklavier Sonata*	1818	
Charles Dickens, *Hard Times*	1853	
	1906	C. S. Peirce, 'Prolegomena to an Apology for Pragmaticism'
Marcel Duchamp, *Fountain*	1917	
Walker Evans, *Alabama Tenant Farmer Wife*	1936	
	1938	R. G. Collingwood, *The Principles of Art*
George Orwell, *Animal Farm*	1945	
George Orwell, *Nineteen Eighty-Four*	1949	
Amiri Baraka, *A Black Mass*	1966	
	1968	Nelson Goodman, *Languages of Art* Richard Wollheim, *Art and Its Objects*
George Lucas, *Star Wars*	1977	Joseph Margolis, 'The Ontological Peculiarity of Works of Art'
	1980	Jerrold Levinson, 'Autographic and Allographic Art Revisited' Jerrold Levinson, 'What a Musical Work Is' Nicholas Wolterstorff, *Works and Worlds of Art*
Sherrie Levine, *After Walker Evans: 4*	1981	
	1983	Peter Kivy, 'Platonism in Music: A Kind of Defense'
	1987	Peter Kivy, 'Platonism in Music: Another Kind of Defense'
	1989	Gregory Currie, *An Ontology of Art*

	1993	Michael Krausz, *Rightness and Reasons*
George Lucas, *Star Wars Episode IV: A New Hope (Special Edition)*	1997	Robert Stecker, *Artworks: Definition, Meaning, Value*
	2000	Julian Dodd, 'Musical Works as Eternal Types'
Michael Mandiberg, *Untitled (AfterSherrieLevine.com/2.jpg)*	2001	
	2003	Robert Stecker, *Interpretation and Construction*
	2004	Amie Thomasson, 'The Ontology of Art' David Davies, *Art as Performance*
	2005	Amie Thomasson, 'The Ontology of Art and Knowledge in Aesthetics'
	2007	Julian Dodd, *Works of Music*
	2009	David Davies, 'The Primacy of Practice in the Ontology of Art'

Key terms and concepts

- Abstract Object (p. 119)
- Action-Type Hypothesis (p. 127)
- Allographic Art (p. 117)
- Artistic Practice (p. 112)
- Autographic Art (p. 117)
- Classes of Interpretations (p. 126)
- Constructivism (p. 125)
- Contextualism (p. 122)
- Criteria for Correctness (p. 121)
- Eternal Type (p. 122)
- Heuristic (p. 128)
- Indicated Type (p. 122)
- Natural Kind (p. 111)
- Norm-Kind (p. 121)
- Notational System (p. 117)

- Ontology (p. 110)
- Physical-Object Hypothesis (p. 114)
- Type/Token Distinction (p. 119)

Further reading

Beyond the books and papers discussed throughout this chapter, an in-depth and very approachable discussion of art ontology can be found in Roman Ingarden's *Ontology of the Work of Art* (Ohio University Press, 1989), focusing on music, visual art, film and architecture. And although Joseph Margolis gives treatments of the type/token theory in a number of places, his most thorough discussion is probably found in *What, After All, Is a Work of Art?* (Pennsylvania State University Press, 1999). Music probably draws more ontological discussion than any other art form. Of particular value on this topic are Jerrold Levinson's *Music, Art, and Metaphysics* (Cornell University Press, 1990), collecting a number of his seminal papers, and Stephen Davies' *Musical Works and Performances: A Philosophical Exploration* (Oxford University Press, 2001), in which he considers the topics discussed in this chapter, and a great number beyond. Some philosophers argue that we are still too coarse-grained in our ontology of art, looking for a one-size-fits-all view, and suggest a more particularized approach. See, for example, Sherri Irvin's essay, 'The Ontological Diversity of Visual Artworks' (in Kathleen Stock and Katherine Thomson-Jones's collection, *New Waves in Aesthetics*, Palgrave Macmillan, 2008).

Unresolved questions

1 How critical is it to our ordinary conception of artworks that we think of them as being *created*? How willing are we or should we be to let this go?
2 Could I, as a writer, just *decide* that my literary work is essentially singular?
3 If ontology is grounded on, guided or restricted by artistic practice, *whose* practice are we centrally concerned with: the artists who make the art, the general public that uses the art or the experts who study the art? What if their views or practices differ?

4 How should we characterize different versions, translations or adaptations of artworks? Are the original theatrical release of *Star Wars* and 1997 Special Edition the *same* work? Are these simply distinct works? Or are they distinct but importantly related works, and if so, what is the ontological relationship here? What about a novel or poem written in one language and translated into another, or a novel adapted into a play or film?

5

Emotions and the Arts

Chapter Outline

I. *The Exorcist* (1973)

The Exorcist is the story of Regan MacNeil, a 12-year-old girl who is possessed by a demon. To say that the movie has something of a reputation is to rather severely understate things: evangelist Billy Graham once suggested that evil was embodied in the very celluloid of the film.[1] In 1999, *Entertainment Weekly* released its ranking of the 'Scariest Movies of All Time,' and *The Exorcist* topped the list – ahead of *Alien*, ahead of *The Shining*, ahead of *Jaws*. Its review suggests, however, that 'scary' isn't a strong enough word to describe *The Exorcist*:

> A cat unexpectedly jumping from off camera is scary. But *The Exorcist* is so disturbing it will mess you up for months. Controversial and profane, *The Exorcist* remains the most viscerally harrowing movie ever made not only because it dares to question the existence of God but because it has the cojones to put Satan in the body of a 12-year-old girl. Moviegoers literally fainted as Linda Blair vomited pea soup on a priest.[2]

When *Entertainment Weekly* compiled its list, *The Exorcist* (directed by William Friedkin, and based on William Peter Blatty's bestselling 1971

Figure 5.1 Poster for *The Exorcist* (1973). Courtesy Warner Bros.

novel) was already more than a quarter-century old, first released in cinemas in 1973. The hysteria surrounding the original release of *The Exorcist* is difficult to describe – it puts the hype over the latest *Star Wars* movie to shame. During its initial run, cinemas reported widespread vomiting and fainting among patrons. One cinema usher said: 'We just make 'em lie down, keep 'em warm, and elevate their feet. One of the policemen showed us how to do it.'[3] A Chicago psychiatrist reported having to keep two patients in restraints for more than a week after seeing the film: 'My professional colleagues who have seen the film agree that there is no way you can sit thru it without receiving some lasting negative or disturbing effects.'[4]

In 1998, for its twenty-fifth anniversary, *The Exorcist* was re-released in cinemas as 'The Version You've Never Seen'. This was a year after Lucasfilm re-released *Star Wars* in cinemas, when patrons were willing to spend a little more money for the event of seeing a modern classic on the big screen. When the remastered version was released on video a few years later, it was with a tagline celebrating the honour bestowed on it by *Entertainment Weekly*: 'The Scariest Movie of All Time'. Even if you're not the sort to reel and pass out in the aisles of a cinema, noted one columnist during the film's initial run, 'It is perhaps a little indelicate, a mite insensitive, a trifle suspect – even a whit antisocial, as in having failed to swoon at the Beatles – not to have been scared by "The Exorcist".'[5]

In his 1973 review of the film, critic Roger Ebert gave *The Exorcist* four out of four stars, calling it 'one of the best movies of its type ever made'. But, he writes:

> I am not sure exactly what reasons people will have for seeing this movie; surely enjoyment won't be one, because what we get here aren't the delicious chills of a Vincent Price thriller, but raw and painful experience. Are people so numb they need movies of this intensity in order to feel anything at all? It's hard to say.
>
> Even in the extremes of Friedkin's vision there is still a feeling that this is, after all, cinematic escapism and not a confrontation with real life. There is a fine line to be drawn there, and 'The Exorcist' finds it and stays a millimeter on this side.

People certainly did see the movie; *The Exorcist* was a cultural phenomenon. It remains the highest-grossing R-rated film of all time (as well as Warner Bros's highest-grossing movie of any rating), and was nominated for ten Academy Awards, including Best Picture. Although it didn't win that highest award, it does have the honour of being the very first horror movie to be nominated for a Best Picture Oscar (and it *did* win the awards for Best Adapted Screenplay and Best Sound Mixing). In 2010, the US Library of Congress included the film in its National Film Registry, a collection of movies deemed culturally, historically or aesthetically important. Clearly, there is *something* that people like about *The Exorcist*. But do people *like* being scared? Is this even coherent?

Director William Friedkin suggests: 'It's about a real street in a real town with real people living in it – in the house – and upstairs, on the third floor of this house, is a real little girl who happens to be possessed by a demon.'[6] The original novel *is* based on a real exorcism, performed in Maryland in 1949. But that exorcism didn't take place in Georgetown, where the story in *The Exorcism* takes place. The house in *The Exorcist is* a real house – it's at 3600 Prospect St NW, in the Georgetown neighbourhood of Washington, DC. But the real house doesn't have a third floor – it was a façade added for the movie. The house isn't real. The story isn't real. Regan isn't real. Ebert is right: the film *isn't* about real life. So why, we might ask, is it scary at all? There's nothing, after all, to be scared *of* – it's fictional, and we know it!

Today, the movie is nearly half a century old, and still tops the list of scariest movies for most critics. And it still carries that tagline: 'The Scariest Movie of All Time'. But is this even a reasonable claim? What would we make of a claim to being 'The Saddest Movie of All Time'? Or 'The Happiest Movie of All Time'? When you come right down to it, on what grounds do we call it 'scary' at all?

II. On art and emotion

Emotion and art have been suggested to intertwine in a number of ways. It seems a hallmark of the arts that they are so able to capture, communicate and evoke emotions – indeed, many would argue that this is one of their chief values. As discussed in Chapter 1, R. G. Collingwood contends that the very essence of art lies in the artist's expression of some inner state – including emotions – and that the product ideally allows the audience to access this state. Two other thinkers, Benedetto Croce and Leo Tolstoy, have proposed related views.[7] Croce, like Collingwood, argues that a work of art is a mental object. However, unlike Collingwood, Croce does not anchor that object in the artist's mental state, but rather in that of the audience, such that each spectator is actually creating the work of art in her mind.[8] Tolstoy, who authored the great novels *Anna Karenina* and *War and Peace*, suggests that the function and value of art is to be found in its ability to act as a *conduit* for the artist's feelings, ideally reproducing that state in the audience (and so it has come to be known as the 'infection theory').[9]

Although as proposed *definitions* of art, none of these views have many adherents today, expression having been largely abandoned as the sole function or criterion of the value of art, we can nevertheless extract a view on the expressive qualities of art from these theories without suggesting that this is what makes art *art*. The view would run roughly like this: a piece of music, a poem, a painting or any other work is sad because it expresses the sadness of its creator. So, a musical work is sad because its composer was sad when he created it, and a painting is likewise angry because its creator was angry when she painted it. The first point worth noting is that musical works *aren't* sad, and paintings *aren't* angry. Works of art do not have mental states. And so, it would seem, in speaking of artworks in this way, we are at least speaking metaphorically or analogically. That is, we are justified in describing artworks in such ways not because such artworks *do* have emotional states, but because the works are somehow appropriately connected to *someone* having such states – on this view, the artist herself.

Guy Sircello is one such proponent of this view, which, for want of a better term, we might call a 'behavioural' theory. Sircello argues that in creating an artwork, one leaves traces of one's inner state in that work.[10] In this way, artworks are very much like our own behaviour. When I am happy, I smile; when I am angry, I scowl; when I am dumbfounded, I have a dumbfounded look on my face. When you see my expressions, Sircello suggests, you can see happiness, anger or dumbfoundedness *in* my behaviour. So one does not simply *infer* another's anger from the look on her face, but rather sees anger in the face itself. Likewise, Sircello argues, one sees the painter's anger in her painting, hears the composer's sadness in his sonata and so on. In essence, the work of art is part of its creator's behaviour, and so just as we are justified in calling a facial expression 'sad' on a behavioural basis, so too are we justified in calling a sonata sad or a painting angry for the same reason.

An obvious problem with this view is that we very often accept that a person's apparent behaviour can be divorced from her actual mental states, and if this is true for ordinary cases of behaviour, why not also for artworks? When actress Kristen Stewart – playing Bella Swan in *Twilight* – scowls, should we conclude that Stewart is angry? Of course not: *perhaps* she is angry, but more likely, she is simply producing an angry look on her face because that is what the scene calls for. One can *act* angry or happy or sad because one knows what behaviour is *normally* expressive of such emotions, and perhaps you would be *justified* in thinking your friend is angry when he scowls, but it may be that he is simply acting. Likewise, it seems a composer could create a 'sad' funeral march without being sad, an 'angry' painting without being angry, or a 'serene' sculpture while being anything but serene. It might be suggested that what makes the scowl on Kristen Stewart's face an 'angry' scowl is that it is the *sort* of look that is usually *indicative* of anger, even if, as the case may be, there is no actual anger there. We can perhaps expand upon this idea to take in artworks generally.

Peter Kivy suggests that we perceive similarities between the 'movement' in music and those movements, postures and other behaviours of the human body that naturally and typically express emotion.[11] Just as we describe, say, a slow-moving, dragging person as 'sad', so too would we describe a piece of music that dragged slowly as 'sad'. And as happy people tend to be 'upbeat' and 'bouncy', the same is true of music we would describe as 'happy'.[12] Ismay Barwell and Robert Stecker, among others, have suggested that the same moves can be made with regard to other art forms. An obvious form that we might discuss in this way is dance, but we can also expand into talking of painting, sculpture and other art forms that do not include literal movement. 'For example,' writes Barwell, 'I may describe some deep slashes in the wall of a house as "angry marks" and mean thereby that they are well suited to be the products of angry behavior, although I may know that they were caused by moving furniture.'[13] The marks may be said to seem 'angry' because of their shape. And we can similarly describe a soft and flowing line as 'calm', a jagged and rigid one as 'agitated' or 'pensive', and so on. As such, it might be said, while a line, colour, sound or movement may not be an *expression* of some emotion, it may nevertheless be *expressive* of that emotion, taking a *form* normally indicative of it.

This view, which has come to be called the 'local quality' theory, thus separates the expressive qualities of a line, colour, sound or movement from any actual emotion being expressed. The view thus rests on a resemblance between a visual or auditory input and a human behavioural expression. As is often the case with theories that rest on resemblance, however, there are questions that remain unanswered. First, there is the question of whether the resemblance features in the experience itself (that is, if it is a perceived resemblance), or whether it simply is that which causes the experience. That is, when you judge a bit of music as 'sad', is it because you *recognize* a resemblance, or do you judge it as 'sad' because there *is* a resemblance, whether or not you recognize it? Second, there is a question of why *these* resemblances and not others. That is, if the theory rests on an experienced resemblance, why should the mind connect the bouncy nature of a musical work with the gait of a happy person and not, say, with the rise and fall of the stock market, the turbulent heaving and surging of the seas or any number of other things? And if the theory rests on something causal in the resemblance, why should this resemblance cause the experience it does and not others? As well, while the theory focuses on particular qualities of particular works (this line, that melody), how are we to deal with complete works, which are composed of any number of these local qualities, which may (if the local quality theory is correct) conflict with each other? At the very least, the local quality theory leaves a number of open questions.

An alternative view is that we properly use expressive words to describe artworks because those artworks give rise to certain emotional responses in us, a view called the 'arousal theory'. Persuasive cases are not difficult to find. It seems reasonable, for instance, to describe a piece of music as 'exciting' just in case it excites listeners, a film as 'scary' just in case it frightens viewers, or a landscape painting as 'calming' only if it calms those who look at it. We can, as such, assess a work's 'expressive' properties in terms of actual emotions felt, but divorced from anything felt by the work's creator (and so putting aside the views of Collingwood, Croce and Tolstoy). Certainly, filmmakers have used the idea that certain music tends to give rise to certain emotions in selecting the soundtracks for films and television shows. In addition to setting appropriate moods, musical scores prompt us to anxiousness at the right points in thrillers, fear during the climax of horror movies and so on. Indeed, even when films were 'silent', they depended upon live musical accompaniment for screenings, so it is not surprising that music came to play an important role when the technology was developed for synchronizing recorded sound with film. We need only recall the screeching music played during the shower scene of Hitchcock's *Psycho* or the theme music from *The Exorcist* to realize the emotive role that music can play.

Predicates like 'exciting', 'scary' and 'calming' seem unproblematic for this view because they seem to describe the *effect* on the audience. But the theory can easily be extended to cover such emotional predicates as 'sad', 'angry' and 'pensive' insofar as the works in question make us feel these emotions. There is at least some scientific data to back up this idea. In the late 1970s, psychologist Alexander Schauss reported that a certain shade of pink produced a short-term calming effect on those who stared at it. On the basis of Schauss's research, the administrators of the US Naval Correctional Center in Seattle, Washington, painted the walls and ceiling of one of its admissions cells this particular colour (named 'Baker-Miller pink' after the administrators, and very close to the distinctive colour of Pepto-Bismol) and reported that after 156 days, there were no incidents of erratic or hostile behaviour among those confined to the room, with the calming effect lasting up to a half hour after detainees left the room.[14] On this basis, then, we might reasonably call Baker-Miller pink a 'calm' colour. And if this is true of a given particular colour, then, it might reasonably be suggested that the same could be true for other elements of artworks, visual or otherwise, and artworks taken as wholes. Certainly, I sometimes watch a movie, listen to a song or read a poem because it will put me in a certain mood, or I may do so to perpetuate a mood I am already in. There seems no question that art can have emotional effects.

Given this position, we can now make some sense of Roger Scruton's claim, discussed in Chapter 3, that some of a work's properties depend upon the audience's mental and emotional lives. To say that a given work is sad is to say that the work standardly arouses a feeling of sadness in those who view, read or listen to it. As such, Scruton argues, a full understanding of the work requires an imaginative engagement with it. Although reasonable on its face, this theory faces a couple of difficulties. First, there are all sorts of things that might move me to sadness or anger which we do not want to say are thus *expressive* of sadness or anger, so there is some more work to be done here. And second, what are we to say about those who look at a painting or hear a sonata and experience no emotional state as a result? Are they simply failing to actually experience the work? Granted, there are some forms of cognitive impairment, such as Asperger's syndrome, which can result in unusual emotional responses, and certain brain injuries can sometimes have peculiar results on one's emotions, but these are rare and certainly non-standard cases.[15] We might throw out some of these remaining claims as being cases of individuals who are generally emotionally stunted or who are insufficiently sensitive to music to feel its effects, but this latter move seems question-begging. And there will still be some people who don't cry at sad movies and don't scream at horror movies.

Derek Matravers suggests that these hurdles can be overcome with a sufficiently subtle understanding of what is happening in the mind of the person experiencing the work.[16] Although some report that they undergo no emotional change in experiencing a given work, Matravers argues that such reports are inconclusive. That one does not *recognize* that she is experiencing an emotional effect does not mean she isn't – and we can often point to changes in her behaviour (or, with suitable technology, to changes in her brain chemistry) as evidence of such a change in her emotional state. Granted, all manner of things can interfere with or influence emotional responses. When 20-year-old British musician Mike Oldfield released his prog-rock album *Tubular Bells* on 25 May 1973, it was immediately hailed as an important work. *Rolling Stone* critic Paul Gambaccini wrote:

> Trying to convey what *Tubular Bells* bears musical resemblance to is fruitless. I remembered music by Sam Cooke, J.S. Bach and Dick Rosmini when I first heard the album, but the associations are as personal as yours will be. People will hear different things in *Tubular Bells* because they will bring to it their individual musical experiences, some of which Oldfield will no doubt have incorporated.

That was probably true for about seven months. When *The Exorcist* was released in December of that same year, the opening piano solo from *Tubular Bells* was its theme music, and for most of us, Oldfield's work will forever be linked emotionally with the horror film. Today, that piano solo is almost universally described as suspenseful, chilling and creepy. Granted, *Tubular Bells* is something of an unusual work in this regard, and granted, some works will not have predictable emotional effects on even a majority of viewers or listeners, and so perhaps we would be unwarranted in such cases to describe these works using emotional predicates. But where a given work predictably brings about a certain emotional response in suitably positioned audiences (those, perhaps, who weren't first introduced to a song as the theme music for a horror movie), it may be reasonable to describe such works not only in such terms as 'exciting', 'scary' and 'calming', but also as 'sad' or 'angry'.

So far, we have primarily been discussing the emotional qualities of sounds, colours, lines and the like, and our examples have largely been drawn from music and the visual arts. When it comes to talking about art and emotion, the cases that seems *least* problematic are works with stories: narrative works. There are sad stories, exciting stories, scary stories, and we encounter these in novels, in plays, in films and in all manner of works where there is a narrative element. Even without settling the matter of what *justifies* calling a work 'sad', 'exciting' or 'scary', it seems obvious to say that *part* of what makes a story sad or exciting or scary is that it is about events and persons, and these are the sorts of things that are *unproblematically* sad, exciting or scary. However, the relationship between narrative works and emotions has troubled philosophers for millennia, especially when these narratives are fictional in nature.

III. The paradox of fiction

In his early dialogue the *Ion*, Plato presents a conversation between Socrates (his mentor) and Ion (a rhapsode). A rhapsode was a performer who gave dramatic readings of poetry – a job requiring comprehending, interpreting and embellishing poetic works. Ion specialized in the works of Homer, the attributed author of the epic poems the *Iliad* and the *Odyssey*. By Ion's time, Homer's poems were the most famous works of literature in the ancient world, the stories already well known to the general populace, having been passed along through the centuries by oral tradition.

As the dialogue opens, Ion has just won first prize at a festival of Asclepius, a celebration of arts and athletics. Ion meets Socrates, who congratulates him on his accomplishment. However, Socrates notes, it is strange that Ion, who has such ability with the work of Homer, has neither the interest nor the ability to present the works of other poets. Were his ability a *skill*, Socrates notes, then Ion should be able to apply that same skill to the other poets. As he cannot, Socrates suggests, there must be some other source to Ion's ability. Socrates suggests that, rather than being a skill, Ion's ability is something of a divine power or inspiration – something given to him by the gods. Socrates compares divine inspiration with a magnet: rub a magnet along a sewing needle, and, if it has the right iron content, that needle becomes magnetic. As such, the needle can be used to make more magnets the same way. A poet like Homer is inspired by the gods to compose his works: he does not work from skill – he cannot write at will, but only when 'possessed', when he is 'not in his right mind'. And as the poet is inspired by the gods, so the rhapsode is inspired by the poet, like one magnet creating another. As Homer is possessed by the gods, Ion is possessed by Homer.

Ion admits that, when reciting Homer, he is often overcome with emotion: '[W]henever I recite a tale of pity, my eyes are filled with tears, and when it is one of horror or dismay, my hair stands up on end with fear, and my heart goes leaping.'[17] Socrates points out to Ion that the same happens to audience members. They are awed by his performances, weeping at the sad parts of the stories, frightened by the scary parts. Like the magnetized needle creating another magnet, so the divine inspiration passes from the gods to Homer, to Ion, to the audience. As each is possessed, none is in his or her right mind.

Perhaps one could excuse Ion's audience for feeling sadness, excitement and other emotions during his recitals of the *Iliad*. The *Iliad* was, after all, a story of the Trojan War (believed by the ancient Greeks to have been a real historical event) centred on the hero Achilles (believed to have been a real person). But the Trojan War was supposed to have taken place centuries before Ion recited the stories, so what was the audience sad, excited or frightened about? Anyone who died was already centuries dead. The audience already knew the story, and knew what would happen next, probably almost as well as Ion himself. And all of these same issues seem to apply to Ion – why is *he* overcome with emotion when he tells the story? The only answer that Socrates can suggest is that Ion and his audience are all out of their minds – they are simply being irrational.

Perhaps the strangest thing about all of this is that it doesn't initially seem so strange at all. Someone who *never* responds emotionally to stories, fictional or otherwise, seems like a strange person. We don't all get scared by horror movies, we don't all get teary-eyed when we read sad stories and we don't all get excited by a play like *King Lear* – but almost everyone gets emotionally involved in *some* stories. So why should we think it is a problem that we do? The problem is particularly pronounced for fictional stories, and contemporary theorists have focused their efforts here. Let's suppose you are reading a story like Alice Elliott Dark's 'In the Gloaming', a story about Laird, a young man suffering from AIDS who has returned home to die. At the end of the story, as expected, Laird does indeed die, and no one is likely to blame you for getting choked up, for getting teary-eyed or for having any number of emotional reactions to the story. So what is the problem? The problem is that, in a very real sense, Laird hasn't died. Laird was never alive. Laird is not a real person. Laird, it seems reasonable to say, has only fictional existence. And it's not that you don't know this. You were well aware that 'In the Gloaming' was a fictional story when you started reading it. So who are you sad about? It seems thoroughly irrational to be sad about someone who you are fully aware never existed.

In more recent years, this problem has come to be known as the 'paradox of fiction', and was reintroduced by British philosopher Colin Radford.[18] The 'paradox' can be essentially broken down into three observations or premises:

(1) We believe the objects of our emotions exist.
(2) We know that fictional objects do not exist.
(3) We sometimes have extreme emotional reactions to fiction.

Regarding the first statement, as traditionally understood, for our emotional attitudes to be rational, they must be directed towards things we believe to exist (or, at least, to possibly exist). To be frightened of something that one *knows* does not exist is, it seems, to simply be irrational. The same, it seems, can be said for being sad about, nervous about or otherwise emotionally engaged with something one knows fails to exist. Now, as we have noted, almost everyone has *some* emotional reactions to *some* fictions. And yet, most of us have developed a clear enough understanding of fiction to know that the characters in fictions are not real people, the happenings in fictions are not real events and so on. And so, it seems, whenever we are having emotional reactions to fictions, while *knowing* they are fictions, we are simply acting irrationally.

Will it help to note that our responses to fictions and non-fictions are quite similar – that we react to the fictional Anna Karenina's fate in a way similar to that of the real person Anne Frank? Although this is certainly curious, our reactions to non-fictions are not problematic – if we believe that Anne Frank was a real person who truly suffered, there is no paradox: we are having emotional reactions towards real events. Likewise, if we take a work to be non-fictional when it has no basis in fact, there is no problem: the paradox arises from a conflict in our beliefs, not a conflict between our beliefs and facts.

A standard response to the paradox is to suggest that the reader or audience member is 'suspending disbelief', and that's all there is to it. The term 'suspension of disbelief' was introduced by the poet Samuel Taylor Coleridge in his 1817 work, *Biographia Literaria*. Coleridge's idea was that an author could give his work a 'semblance of truth' so that readers would put aside any implausibility of the story in an act of 'poetic faith'. Although 'suspension of disbelief' is certainly a commonplace term today, can it solve the paradox? That would seem to depend on what, exactly, suspending disbelief involves. In her essay 'Fiction and the Suspension of Disbelief', Eva Schaper attempts several interpretations of the notion.[19]

Could it be that to suspend disbelief is to willingly put oneself in a position of uncertainty regarding the truth of the story one is engaged with? If so, this would seem to solve our problem. In 1977, Jay Anson published his novel *The Amityville Horror: A True Story*. The book told the tale of the Lutz family – George, Kathleen and their three children – who moved into a home in Long Island, New York. A year before, the house was the site of the mass murder of the DeFeo family. As told in the book, the Lutz family quickly began experiencing an array of frightening paranormal and demonic phenomena. In less than a month, the family fled the home. Anson's novel was adapted into a film in 1979, with a remake released in

2005. Both the novel and the film adaptations have from the beginning been the subject of a great deal of controversy over the factual nature of the story. It is true that Ronald DeFeo, Jr killed six members of his family in their house in 1974. It is true that the Lutz family moved into the same house in December of 1975. And it is true that the Lutz family moved out again in early 1976. Beyond that, many of the allegations made in the story are questionable. Despite this, both film adaptations were marketed as being 'based on the true story'. Certainly *some* of the story is true, and one could perhaps be forgiven for suspending judgement about the rest. As noted, if one does not believe that the story is fictional, then the paradox does not apply to that case. And if one is uncertain one way or the other, then one does not believe the story is fictional *or* non-fictional. Rather, one is in a sceptical position. So could it be that, when dealing with any fiction, one puts oneself into the sceptical position of a reader of *The Amityville Horror*? The problem with this suggestion, Schaper notes, is that the suspension of disbelief is supposed to work while *knowing* that something or other is *not* the case, while in the *Amityville Horror* case, one is actually unsure about the matter.

Could it be, then, that in dealing with a fiction, say, *The Exorcist*, it is somehow the case that while you *know* that there is no 12-year-old girl possessed by a demon, you nevertheless *believe* precisely that? This, Schaper says, would seem to imply a state of utter mental confusion on your part – in other words, irrationality. However, it doesn't seem that you are typically experiencing any sort of confusion or derangement when dealing with fiction. You don't *forget* that you are sitting in your living room watching actors; rather, you *disbelieve* that you are witnessing real events or even re-enactments of real events. If an audience member failed to have the appropriate beliefs about what was real and what was unreal, we should want to say that he is simply hopelessly naïve, like a child who has not yet grasped the difference between fiction and reality.

Schaper suggests that the term 'suspension of disbelief' is actually something of a misnomer – that in dealing with fictions, we do not *suspend* or *put aside* any beliefs; rather, we *compound* beliefs. In watching a movie, you likely hold a number of true beliefs: that you are watching a film, that some actor is playing a role, that the script was written by somebody and so on. These are beliefs about the story's fictional nature, and we could list similar beliefs about plays, novels, video games, television shows and other sorts of fictions. Call these 'first-order' beliefs. If you are watching *The Exorcist*, you likely hold another set of beliefs: that Regan MacNeil has been possessed by a demon, that her mother is overwhelmed with grief and so on. These are beliefs *about* the story being told, and we probably want to say these are true beliefs as well (in the way that 'the priests all make it out of the MacNeil house alive' would be a false belief). Call these 'second-order' beliefs. Schaper argues that first-order beliefs are about *our* world, and that second-order beliefs are about the world of the story. Further, she argues, the second-order beliefs *depend* upon certain relevant first-order beliefs. That is, I believe in the existence of Regan MacNeil, but under certain conditions: I believe that she is a fictional character depicted in a certain movie – and so on. It is *because* I believe this that I can *also* hold the true belief that she is possessed by a demon.

As such, Schaper suggests that the paradox of fiction is dissolved by negating the second premise: that we know that fictional objects do not exist. Schaper's theory is that we *do* believe that fictional objects exist – specifically, we believe that they exist as fictional objects. And understanding that fictional characters are depicted in fictional worlds, we can then hold true beliefs about them, fictional though the objects of those beliefs might be. Now, if, by chance, someone thinks that *The Exorcist* is the recounting of a true story, and truly believes that a real person, Regan MacNeil, has been possessed by a demon, he will have a *false* belief, because he does not hold the relevant first-order belief that Regan is a fictional character. Rather, the belief will be a belief about a real person in the real world, and as there is no such real person, the belief will be a false one.

An alternative theory is offered by Kendall Walton.[20] Where Schaper concentrates on the second premise in the paradox, Walton focuses on the third: that we sometimes have extreme emotional reactions to fictions. Walton suggests that, immediate appearances to the contrary, we are *not* actually afraid when Regan is possessed by the demon, we are not truly sad when we read 'In the Gloaming', and in general, at least as regards those responses that concern us here, we are not having genuine emotional reactions to fictions. This may seem like a strange claim to make. Suppose you are at a horror movie. If it's a *good* horror movie, at certain points we might find you sitting on the edge of your seat, clutching at the armrests, ready to shriek if you are startled. Your heart rate will have increased, and perhaps you will be sweating. So you certainly *seem* afraid. And if we ask you if you're afraid, you are likely to answer in the affirmative. So you certainly *seem* afraid. But, Walton points out, while your experience may be *intense*, it seems different from ordinary cases of fear. If you were truly afraid, we might expect you to flee the cinema, to call the police or to perform some other preventative measures. What you are experiencing, Walton suggests, are *some* of the symptoms of fear – specifically the involuntary ones. What you lack are those symptoms of fear that depend upon *reasons*. Walton calls this state 'quasi-fear'.

Walton argues that 'quasi-fear' and other *quasi-* states arise from the activity of engaging with fiction. Fictional things are make-believe things, and we have been dealing with make-believe things since we were children. We played 'cops and robbers', make-believing that the sticks we carried were guns, that our bicycles were cars, that a garage was a bank and so on. Perhaps we made these 'rules' of the make-believe game explicit, but more than likely we picked up sticks, pointed them at each other and made gun sounds. It was the gun sounds we made that made it 'true' that the guns were firing. When we got on our bikes and chased each other around the neighbourhood, we did not need to point out that we were pretending to drive cars. It was because we were cops and robbers that our bikes 'were' cars. We imagined ourselves into a story with certain 'rules' of make-believe in force. And, of course, there was nothing to stop us from playing such make-believe games on our own, with entirely private 'rules' of make-believe in play. When we deal with fiction, Walton argues, we are doing essentially the same thing: we imagine ourselves into the world of the story. When the horrible green slime threatens the townsfolk, we imagine ourselves among the terrified citizens. Like the sticks in a game of cops and robbers, the film essentially serves as a *prop*, telling us to imagine what is true at any given point in the story.

When we imagine ourselves into the story, Walton suggests, we experience the symptoms of quasi-fear (or quasi-sadness, etc.). In kind, this is no different than the involuntary symptoms a child experiences in an imaginary game: increased heart rate, perspiration, anxiety. The only central difference is in an audience member's general inactivity: you sit in your seat and continue to eat your popcorn. Just as the child *pretends* he is afraid when he is being pursued, so you pretend you are afraid when you watch the horror movie by getting involved in the story: it is all part of the game. Because you are pretending to be afraid, it is *make-believedly true* that you are afraid. That is to say, you are 'afraid' as an imagined part of the story. But you are not *really* afraid. You do not *really* believe that you are in danger.

On this basis, Walton argues, the paradox is solved. You are not having real emotional reactions to fictions at all; rather, you are having *quasi-*emotions, and so it is only *make-believedly* true that you are having strong emotional reactions to the fiction. Walton argues that his theory has a lot of additional explanatory value. It explains, for instance, how we are able to enjoy repeated viewings of a movie or repeated readings of a novel. Although in fact you already know the plot, you *make-believedly* do not. The very *point* of engaging with fiction, he argues, is not merely to learn the outcome of the story, but to play a game of make-believe. Moreover, the theory explains how we are able to hold apparently conflicting desires. If you are watching a horror movie like *The Slumber Party Massacre*, you want a good bloodbath. If no character is threatened during the film, it would be difficult to call it a horror movie, and a horror movie is what you've paid to see. But, and seemingly at the same time, you might sympathize with the characters, hoping they will all escape the killer. On Walton's theory, it's true that you want the characters to die, but *make-believedly* true that you want everyone to survive.

David Novitz argues that the views of both Schaper and Walton are flawed.[21] On Schaper's account, it is because we know that we are dealing with a fiction (first-order beliefs) that we know statements within the fiction should not be taken as reports about real-world events (and so we can develop accurate second-order beliefs). The second-order belief that Superman is secretly Clark Kent, then, presupposes the first-order belief that this is not true of the real world (because there is, after all, no Superman in our world). The problem, Novitz argues, is that on Schaper's view, we must continually bear in mind that we are only dealing with a fiction, and that it has no bearing on the real world – indeed, is specifically *not* about the real world. However, Novitz contends, anyone who approaches fiction in this manner will be constantly distancing herself from the story. To so distance oneself is to prevent oneself from being 'drawn into' or 'caught up in' the world of the fiction. Walton suggests how it might be that we are so 'drawn into' the fiction, but Novitz finds his view equally lacking. Walton suggests that when you are watching a thrilling horror movie, your white-knuckled hands gripping the armrests, ready to scream at any moment, you are not *actually* afraid; rather, you are only *make-believedly* afraid. The problem here, Novitz notes, is that to *make-believe* something, *x*, requires that you *believe not-x*. Try to make-believe reading this book while, at the same time, actually reading this book (which would involve believing that you are doing so). *Pretending* something is the case requires believing it is not. We can only make-believe that we are scared, or sad, or excited, if we truly believe that we are not. So the problem is that many theatre-goers, movie-watchers and readers *do* believe they are frightened, upset and so on.

Novitz argues that proper understanding of a work of fiction requires that one be in a position to be appropriately moved by what is happening to the characters. However, this is not to say that one thus has to *believe* the story. Rather, Novitz suggests, one has to entertain the fiction in a special way: by taking it 'as-if' there is a girl named Regan MacNeil, or a man named Clark Kent, and that they do certain things. Contrary to Schaper's view, Novitz argues that one must render tacit the explicit knowledge that one is dealing with a fiction – that is to say, one should not attend to the fact that what one is reading or watching is a fiction.

Here is a way to think about tacit knowledge. Let's suppose someone is travelling by foot from Exeter International Airport to London's Heathrow Airport, some 160 miles. And let's suppose it takes her forty hours to make the trip. On average, how fast was she moving? The obvious answer is four miles per hour. But, it might be pointed out, at that latitude, the Earth is spinning at about 670 miles per hour, so she was really travelling at about 674 miles per hour. And, it might further be noted, the Earth is hurtling around the Sun at about 67,000 miles per hour, and that our solar system is spinning around the centre of the Milky Way as it wanders through endless space. Okay, you might say, that may all be true, but that's not what the point of the question seemed to be. Yes, the Earth is spinning on its axis, is orbiting the sun, and the whole solar system is moving around inside our galaxy, but we can safely ignore these facts when someone asks about how fast someone is moving between Exeter and London. The rest is *tacit* knowledge – something we know to be true, but shove to the background because it isn't relevant to what we are currently interested in. Likewise, Novitz argues that the knowledge that we are dealing with a fiction should be shoved to the background until it is relevant to our concerns.

Dealing properly with a fiction, Novitz argues, requires a certain sustained act of imagination, and to properly respond to the fiction imaginatively requires first that one think of the world described by the author, and second to do this without a mind to whether or not these descriptions are true or false in the real world. Rather, we simply take the story 'as-if' it is the recounting of certain persons or events, and we do not concern ourselves with the fact that it is a fiction. This is, as such, an imaginative act, but Novitz argues that this does not thus make our emotional responses imaginative or make-believe. Ultimately the act involved is little different from how we deal with much *non*-fiction, where we are similarly unconcerned about whether or not the story is a recounting of real facts. As such, we develop beliefs about the persons or events in a similar manner whether we are dealing with fiction or non-fiction. Our emotional responses, Novitz argues, are not irrational because they are about some creature of fiction – they can only be irrational if they are based on irrational beliefs about her. 'The mere fact,' Novitz says, 'that the object of one's emotion is fictional does not render the emotional irrational.'[22] And so, where Schaper attempted to dismantle the second premise in the paradox, and Walton the third, Novitz argues that it is the first premise that is faulty: that we believe the objects of our emotions exist. This, he argues, simply need not be true.

IV. The problem of tragedy

Like the paradox of fiction, the problem, of tragedy finds its roots in ancient Greece – perhaps unsurprising, as the Athenians invented its form.[23] Although most of the dramatic works of the ancient Greeks are long since lost, we know a great deal about the beginnings of tragedy from the surviving works of three playwrights: Aeschylus, Sophocles and Euripides. Between them, these three authors created hundreds of plays, but fewer than thirty have survived intact. Beyond these three authors, we owe much of what we know about Athenian tragedy to Plato's student, Aristotle. Aristotle wrote two works focused on issues in aesthetics: the *Rhetoric* and the *Poetics*, the former focusing on issues in persuasion, the latter on issues in dramatic poetry. Dealing with the classical forms of tragedy and comedy, only the first half of the *Poetics* has survived – the portion devoted to tragedy.

In what we have of the *Poetics*, Aristotle provides an exhaustive analysis of the tragic form as it existed in ancient Greece, characterizing tragedy as focused on the unfortunate things that happen to people of good character (as opposed to comedies, in which ridiculous things happen to people of poor character). Tragedies are stories about suffering. One of the most famous stories told in ancient tragedy is that of Oedipus, mythic king of Thebes, who unwittingly fulfilled the prophecy that he would kill his father and marry his mother, bringing disaster to all who knew him.[24] In Aristotle's view, it is through the plot – the ordering of events in the play – that the audience becomes wrapped up in the story: fortunes are reversed, characters move from ignorance to knowledge, and all (if the play is a good one, Aristotle contends) as a matter of a causal chain leading to the inevitable disaster. This, Aristotle argues, is the very *point* of tragedy; this is its central *function*.

The effect of tragedy (or, at least, good tragedy), Aristotle contends, is *catharsis*, which is usually translated as 'purging' or 'cleansing'. Although he devotes little space in the *Poetics* to the concept, the central idea is that the plot of a tragedy serves as a trigger for the audience to *vent* strong negative emotions. That is, rather than *soothing* the fears and anxieties of the audience, tragedy serves to force audience members to *engage* with their negative emotions through the play, and to walk away unscathed. It is the barrier between what is happening on stage and our own lives that allows us the necessary distance to safely engage with and purge pity and fear from our systems without getting dragged down by them. We might, as such, consider catharsis as Aristotle's answer to Plato's charge in the *Ion* that theatre-goers are out of their minds: the purging is a controlled and therapeutic engagement with one's darker emotions.

Aristotle's concern in the *Poetics* is with the ancient Greek form of tragedy, but much of what he and others have to say about tragedy can be applied outside this very particularized form. We can, of course, look to other classic tragedies – to such Shakespearean plays as *Hamlet, Julius Caesar* and *King Lear*, and to works by Shakespeare's contemporary, Christopher Marlowe. Theatrical tragedy has been pursued and developed through the centuries, and so we could look to Pierre Corneille's *Le Cid*, which sought to break down the classical tragedy–comedy distinction, or to a more modern work like Arthur Miller's *Death of a Salesman*, which challenged the traditional restriction of tragedies to those in the upper classes. However, we do not have to restrict discussion of the topic solely to tragic plays. We might look to all manner of horror in film and literature, like *The Exorcist*, which gives rise to similar problems. And, of course, we can look to such novels as Tolstoy's *Anna Karenina*, and any number of soap operas that viewers tune into every day. Of all these works and many more besides, we can ask, how is it that we can (seemingly at one and the same time) have both positive and negative responses to the same events being portrayed? Why is it that we, or at least many of us, seek out such experiences when there are so many comedies to be had? Why is it that, so often, the more tragic the work, the greater its artistic value?

In 1757, David Hume published 'Of Tragedy', an essay looking to further explain how it is that audiences of dramatic tragedies feel pleasure as the direct result of feeling sorrow, terror and anxiety in response to the events depicted onstage.[25] Indeed, it seems, the more tragic the events onstage, the greater our resulting pleasure – the stronger our negative emotions in witnessing the theatric tragedy, the stronger the ensuing positive emotions. As such, it should be noted, this is not a simple case of what the Germans call *Schadenfreude*, a pleasure derived from the misfortune of others, typically describing the sort of pleasure one experiences when watching someone slip on a banana skin, or perhaps when an enemy gets his comeuppance. The difference is that with tragedy, we do not merely feel pleasure; rather, it is a positive emotion that results from feeling negative emotions. Perhaps most curiously, Hume notes, precisely what pleases us in tragedy would seem to have the opposite effect in real life. Rarely are we in any way pleased by tragedies that befall us in our own lives or in the lives of those we know. But what gives us pleasure by watching it onstage is precisely what would give us only pain when witnessed in the real world. As such, he contends, it cannot simply be that theatre-goers seek merely to avoid boredom: there is more than enough tragedy in the real world, but we go out of our way to avoid this while seeking out the same in fiction.

The solution, Hume suggests, is that what our pleasure arises from is not the displeasure itself, but rather the artistry involved in presenting the tragedy: the abilities of the playwright, actors and others to create the story and pull us into it. In this way, tragedy is not unlike other imitative art forms: witnessing it is, by its nature, pleasurable. When dealing with tragedy in the real world, our predominant emotion is negative, and so we should not expect to feel anything but this. However, with theatrical tragedy, our predominant emotion is positive – the pleasure in imitation – and the negative emotion is subordinate to this. The predominant pleasurable emotion, Hume argues, *converts* the subordinate negative emotion into a positive one. This might seem a strange claim, but perhaps it is helpful to think of it this way: imagine a river blocked by a bunch of logs. The logs, if there are enough of them, will slow or halt the flow of the river. This is how we might think of positive emotions being blocked by negative ones. But if the river manages to dislodge the logs, then they flow *with* the river, adding their bulk to the rush of the water, making it all the much more powerful. Likewise, since the emotion with which one engages fiction is positive, the negative emotions of pity, fear and the like only add more power to the positive emotions, rather than blocking them.[26] But, through all this, the negative emotions do not lose their character – we do not now *merely* feel pleasure – rather, they are simply in service of the predominant positive emotions.

In his first published book, *The Birth of Tragedy*, Friedrich Nietzsche suggests that the pleasure of tragedy arises from something else.[27] The ancient Greeks, Nietzsche theorizes, lived a dichotomous existence, constantly pulled at by two opposite poles: the 'Apollonian' (named for the Greek god Apollo) and its opposite, the 'Dionysian' (named for the Greek god Dionysus). Where Apollo served as a symbol of light, order and civilization, Dionysus was a symbol of darkness, chaos and the savagery of nature. Apollo was, among other things, god of the plastic arts – sculpture, painting and architecture – while Dionysus was associated with the revelry of music and dance. These two poles, Nietzsche contends, are brought to a head in Greek tragedy, with the Dionysian aspect being embodied in the music of the chorus and the Apollonian in the play's dialogue.[28] Further, the audience bears witness to the tragic protagonist trying to make sense – to find order – in the chaos befalling him. As such, the theatre-goer was able to experience in one setting both poles battling over humanity. The audience (here, Nietzsche speaks of the ancient Greeks, but this could as well apply to us) does not stand apart from the events onstage, but enters a 'dream-state' and becomes fully engulfed in the story. And although Apollo ruled over dreams, once in this state, the audience could now access the more primordial Dionysian nature flowing within mankind and society. Through tragedy, the audience could directly experience Dionysian revelry within ordered Apollonian form – allowing for a balanced appreciation of both aspects of humanity. In doing so, theatre-goers were thus offered a glimpse of what Nietzsche refers to as the 'Dionysian abyss' of humanity, and so return to their civilized Apollonian lives with renewed insight and self-affirmation.[29]

Although taking her cue from Hume, Susan Feagin's approach to the problem of tragedy borrows the central notion of self-reflection and affirmation from Nietzsche.[30] Following Hume, Feagin notes that tragedies both produce and are *designed* to produce a certain sort of pleasure in the audience, but without supposing any special callousness or insensitivity on its part. Indeed, Feagin suggests the answer to the problem is to be found in the very opposite supposition. Hume's suggestion was that because the artistic form of tragedy – imitation – is naturally pleasurable to us, it 'converts' our unpleasurable responses to the events onstage to pleasurable ones. However, Feagin finds this notion perplexing. What mechanism or process is responsible for this conversion? How can emotions which seem by their very nature negative, such as pity, fear and terror, become positive emotions while at the same time retaining their original character (that is, still *being* pity, fear and terror)? Feagin argues that they cannot. Moreover, she notes, the 'pleasures' of tragedy are not of an excited sort, but amount to serenity, calmness and feelings of satisfaction. So we are dealing with two very different sorts of emotions, and we need to account for both.

Feagin argues that, in responding to tragedy, we *do* experience unpleasant or negative emotions such as fear, pity and horror. This 'direct response' is not at all surprising, and is in kind no different than the sorts of emotions we feel when witnessing or experiencing unpleasant events in the world outside the theatre. There is, in other words, no deep mystery to be explained with regard to these responses. However, in addition to these direct responses, we also experience 'meta-responses' – that is, responses to our responses. Where the direct response is a response to the events portrayed onstage, the meta-response is a response to our own mental states. The direct responses are unpleasant, while the meta-responses are pleasant, and arise from our awareness of those direct responses. In particular, Feagin argues, we *appreciate* that we have negative responses to things like villainy, treachery and injustice (the hallmarks of tragedy), and this appreciation yields satisfaction. This is not the feeling of a cathartic release, but rather arises simply from the judgement that our initial reactions were appropriate. We have, in other words, affirmed our own good nature – we know what is admirable and what is deplorable, and we have confirmed this fact. This relationship between direct responses and meta-responses is not solely to be found in the domain of fiction, Feagin suggests, but with fiction one's direct responses have *closure* – plays invariable end – and so we are allowed the opportunity to step back and evaluate our initial responses. In real life, meta-responses tend to remove us from our current situations, where these situations call for continued direct responses.

If Feagin is right, then we shouldn't actually enjoy ourselves *at* a performance of *King Lear* or a screening of *The Exorcist*: the enjoyment, if it's going to come at all, will come later – with our meta-responses. Aristotle's notion of catharsis suggests something similar: that the experience of a staged tragedy should not *in itself* be enjoyable – that enjoyment will come with the relief of purging one's negative emotions. But this seems at odds with the ordinary theatre-goer's (or horror junkie's) experience of actual enjoyment *during* the performance. Some philosophers have suggested that enjoying a tragedy or a horror movie is, in this way, similar to enjoying a roller-coaster ride or skydiving. Roller coasters are fun so long as you believe the car will stay on the tracks and stop where and when it's supposed to stop. We can enjoy the ride so long as we believe that any real risk is remote. Skydiving is fun so long as you believe that the parachute will deploy when you pull the ripcord. John Morreall suggests that we can enjoy the heightened alertness, the increased bloodflow and the rush of adrenaline that come with these sorts of activities.[31] But, Morreall suggests, this enjoyment depends on the belief that things are under control, and when this belief is erased – when the ripcord fails – excitement turns to real terror. Control, Morreall argues, is the key to enjoyment in extreme sports and roller coasters. Similarly, Marcia M. Eaton suggests, 'A horror story is fun to read only when we are in control of the situation in which we read it.'[32] That is, if you're looking for a good scare, a horror movie might be exactly what you want, and if the movie is scary, you're more likely to enjoy it. On the other hand, if you *weren't* looking for a horror movie, and just stumbled across *The Exorcist* on television late at night, you might not enjoy yourself so much. Centrally, Eaton and Morreall argue, the key to enjoying tragedy and horror lies in keeping just on the other side of believing we are in *real* danger. When you start seeing things in the shadows, it's time to turn off the movie and go to bed.

Chapter summary

This chapter has focused on a few of the philosophical issues pertaining to art and emotion. We began by discussing how emotional terms like 'sad' and 'exciting' and 'angry' might be reasonably predicated of artworks, including such approaches as the local quality theory and the arousal theory. The local quality theory suggests that whether or not a work (or any part thereof) is, say, 'sad' depends centrally on its formal qualities and their resemblance to the qualities of sad persons. The arousal theory, conversely, suggests that it is appropriate to call a work 'sad' if that work standardly produces sadness in its audience members. The remainder of the chapter was devoted to discussing two philosophical issues arising from narrative works: the so-called paradox of fiction and the problem of tragedy. With the paradox of fiction, we looked at Plato's classical introduction of the problem in the *Ion*, Colin Radford's more modern formulation, and solutions proposed by Eva Schaper, Kendall Walton and David Novitz. On turning to tragedy, we discussed Aristotle's *Poetics* and his notion of catharsis, David Hume's outline of what has come to be known as *the* problem of tragedy, Friedrich Nietzsche's take on the matter, and contemporary theories proposed by Susan Feagin, Marcia M. Eaton and John Morreall.

Historical timeline

Homer, *Iliad*	c. 725 BCE	
Homer, *Odyssey*	c. 800 BCE	
	c. 380 BCE	Plato, *Ion*
	c. 350 BCE	Aristotle, *Poetics*
William Shakespeare, *Julius Caesar*	c. 1599	
William Shakespeare, *Hamlet*	c. 1601	
William Shakespeare, *King Lear*	c. 1606	
Pierre Corneille, *Le Cid*	1636	
	1757	David Hume, 'Of Tragedy'
	1817	Samuel Taylor Coleridge, *Biographia Literaria*
Leo Tolstoy, *War and Peace*	1869	
	1872	Friedrich Nietzsche, *The Birth of Tragedy*
Leo Tolstoy, *Anna Karenina*	1878	
	1896	Leo Tolstoy, *What Is Art?*
	1902	Benedetto Croce, *Aesthetic*
	1938	R. G. Collingwood, *The Principles of Art*
Anne Frank, *The Diary of a Young Girl*	1947	
Arthur Miller, *Death of a Salesman*	1949	
Alfred Hitchcock, *Psycho*	1960	
	1972	Guy Sircello, *Mind & Art*
Mike Oldfield, *Tubular Bells*	1973	
William Friedkin, *The Exorcist*		
Stephen Spielberg, *Jaws*	1975	Colin Radford, 'How Can We Be Moved by the Fate of Anna Karenina?'
Jay Anson, *The Amityville Horror*	1977	
	1978	Eva Schaper, 'Fiction and the Suspension of Disbelief'
		Kendall Walton, 'Fearing Fictions'
Ridley Scott, *Alien*	1979	
Stanley Kubrick, *The Shining*	1980	

Amy Holden Jones, *The Slumber Party Massacre*	1982	Marcia M. Eaton, 'A Strange Kind of Sadness'
	1983	Susan Feagin, 'The Pleasures of Tragedy'
	1984	Robert Stecker, 'Expression of Emotion In (Some of) The Arts'
	1985	John Morreall, 'Enjoying Negative Emotions in Fiction'
	1986	Ismay Barwell, 'How Does Art Express Emotion'
	1987	David Novitz, *Knowledge, Fiction and Imagination*
	1989	Peter Kivy, *Sound Sentiment*
	1990	Kendall Walton, *Mimesis as Make-Believe*
Alice Eliot Dark, 'In the Gloaming'	1994	
	1998	Derek Matravers, *Art and Emotion*
Catherine Hardwicke, *Twilight*	2008	

Key terms and concepts

- Apollonian and Dionysian (p. 154)
- Arousal Theory (p. 141)
- Behavioural Theory (p. 139)
- Catharsis (p. 152)
- Direct and Meta-Responses (p. 155)
- First- and Second-Order Beliefs (p. 147)
- Infection Theory (p. 139)
- Local Quality Theory (p. 140)
- Make-Believe Truths (p. 149)
- Paradox of Fiction (p. 144)
- Predominant and Subordinate Emotions (p. 154)
- Problem of Tragedy (p. 152)
- Quasi-Fear (p. 149)
- *Schadenfreude* (p. 153)
- Suspension of Disbelief (p. 153)
- Tacit Knowledge (p. 151)
- Taking 'As-If' (p. 151)

Further reading

Many of the philosophical problems of fiction (and stretching beyond those outlined in this chapter) are explored in *Truth, Fiction, and Literature: A Philosophical Perspective* (Clarendon Press, 1994) by Peter Lamarque and Stein Haugom Olsen, and in Lamarque's *Fictional Points of View* (Cornell University Press, 1996). Stephen Davies gives an extensive overview of theories of art and expression in *Musical Meaning and Expression* (Cornell University Press, 2004), and Mette Hjort and Sue Laver provide a great collection of articles in *Emotion and the Arts* (Oxford University Press, 1997), including approaches to the paradox of fiction not included in this chapter, and discussion of the 'hypothetical persona' theory of expressiveness, originally proposed by Jerrold Levinson in his 'Musical Expressiveness' (included in his collection *The Pleasures of Aesthetics*, Cornell University Press, 1996) and modified by Jenefer Robinson in her *Deeper than Reason: Emotion and its Role in Literature, Music, and Art* (Oxford University Press, 2005). Also worth reading are Robert Stecker's 2011 article, 'Should We Still Care about the Paradox of Fiction?' (*British Journal of Aesthetics* 51: 295–308) and Noël Carroll's book, *The Philosophy of Horror, or the Paradoxes of the Heart* (Routledge, 1990).

Unresolved questions

1 Should we be 'realists' about emotional qualities of artworks? Is it any more or less problematic to say a work *is* sad, angry, scary or exciting than it is to say the work is beautiful, ugly, bold or elegant?

2 What, if anything, is the relationship between a work's emotional qualities (or our emotional responses to a work) and the *value* of that work? Is a work always better insofar as it results in positive emotional responses? What if a work predictably results in only negative emotional responses – is it thus a *bad* work?

3 Video games are very likely a form of art, and many such games might reasonably be called 'fictions'. In these cases, are the excitement, fear, sadness and the like in any way problematic? Is the issue the same with fictional movies, novels and plays, or is something else going on that needs to be considered?

6

Art and Morality

I. *Helena* (2000)

Marco Evaristti's *Helena* is certainly not the first piece of installation art to invite audience participation. Briefly mentioned in Chapter 1 was Felix Gonzales-Torres' 1991 work *'Untitled' (Throat)*, consisting of an ordinary pile of packaged cough drops on an ordinary handkerchief. This work was just one in a series of works in which audience members were encouraged to take part of the work with them – in this case, a lozenge. Carl Andre's 1969 installation, *144 Lead Square*, still housed in New York's Museum of Modern Art, consists of 144 square lead tiles arranged in a 12-by-12-foot grid. It was Andre's hope that visitors might not even notice the piece, and either purposely or accidentally walk across it. So, as a work inviting audience participation, *Helena* is not unique. Rather, the difference lies in what the audience was invited to do.

Originally installed in Denmark's Trapholt Art Museum, *Helena* consists of ten water-filled Moulinex-Optiblend 2000 blenders, each containing a live goldfish. The blenders were plugged in and fully operational, and museum

Figure 6.1 Marco Evaristti, *Helena* (2000). Installation view from the exhibition at Trapholt Museum of Modern Art. Courtesy ME contemporary.

visitors were told that they could press any blender's on-button were they so inclined. Evaristti's idea was to divide visitors into three categories: 'The idiot, who pushed the button, the voyeur who loves to watch and the moralist.'[1] Reportedly, at least one visitor to the Trapholt did, indeed, push the button. And Peter Meyer, director of the museum, suddenly found himself being fined for cruelty to animals. Rather than paying the fine, Meyer took the matter to court, where the fine was ultimately dropped. According to Judge Preben Bagger, the fish were killed instantly and humanely. In his defence, Meyer suggested that there is a bigger issue at play: 'It's a question of principle. An artist has the right to create works which defy our concept of what is right and what is wrong.'[2] In other words, Meyer contended, the artwork – and perhaps the artist himself – is outside the reach of moral judgement.

Is the matter so clear? If art exists in a moral vacuum, what are we to make of Evaristti's pronouncement that the work is fundamentally *about* morality? Can Evaristti and Meyer have it both ways? What about the gallery visitor who turned the blender on? Was she just helping to make the art? If so, should she be held morally responsible for her actions? How, in general, should we consider the relationship between art and morality? If *Helena* is immoral, would this be because Evaristti is himself immoral? Or because his act of creating the work is immoral? Or because someone used the work to kill a goldfish? Or would it be immoral even if no one had ever pushed the button? And if *Helena* is immoral, should it be removed from exhibition?

After the initial public outcry, the work remained on display at the Trapholt, but with the blenders unplugged. In 2006, the work was moved to Austria's Kunstraum Dornbirn gallery, with the blenders once more operational. And again, a visitor pressed the button, pulverizing another goldfish – this time with full knowledge that she was being videotaped.

II. On ethics and aesthetics

Aesthetics and ethics each deal with sorts of value. We evaluate works of art, non-artefacts and certainly each other aesthetically; and we evaluate actions, events and persons ethically. In many ways, these two areas of study raise many similar problems. What does it mean to say something is good, whether in the aesthetic or ethical sense? When is it appropriate to so judge a thing? Are ethical or aesthetic judgements merely subjective? If not, how do we *know* when something is good – and is it the same *sort* of knowing in both ethical and aesthetic cases? If a work of art is aesthetically bad, is it thus ethically bad? If it is ethically bad, is it thus aesthetically bad? Today aesthetics is sometimes lumped together with ethics under the banner of 'value theory', although certainly aesthetics has concerns beyond questions of value. But the intertwining of aesthetics and ethics goes back to Western philosophy's beginnings in ancient Greece, long before either had truly become its own discrete area of concern.

In the *Republic*, his most famous work, Plato discusses how the ideal city-state might be designed.[3] The sort of utopian city that Plato has in mind is one in which each individual has one (and only one) function, and performs that function in harmony with those of others. This is at the core of Plato's concept of justice. Famously (or infamously), in attempting to determine how such a utopia might be created, Plato outlaws art from the city. Specifically, Plato outlaws poetry, but his arguments might be easily extended to art in general. Plato has two reasons for barring poetry, one arising from the other, and ultimately tied to his notions of harmony and justice. First, Plato argues, poetry is by its nature imitative. The imitation inherent to poetry, he says, gives us only the dimmest reflection of reality. It cannot, for instance, tell us anything about virtue, but rather can only give us the *appearance* of virtue by imitating virtuous men. Imitation, as such, is far removed from the truth, and so inferior to it.

Second, Plato contends, imitation appeals to the non-rational part of us. In the previous chapter, we looked at Plato's *Ion*, in which he suggests that the poet's ability arises not from some sort of skill or knowledge, but only when he is 'not in his right mind'. As the poet is overcome, so too is the rhapsode who performs his works, and ultimately so too is the audience member who witnesses the performance. Audiences follow a talented poet with sympathy, Plato says, praising those so able to affect us. But, he notes, when we are on our own, we praise ourselves for our ability to keep calm and strong. It is our rationality that normally keeps our emotional aspect in check, and these, along with our will, usually act in harmony. But imitative poetry, which appeals to our emotions, allows our emotions to overrun our reason. Worse still, when the emotions overtake reason, the effect typically lasts longer than the duration of the reading itself, doing further damage to the normally harmonious relationship of emotions, reason and will. How can we admit to the ideal society something that serves to violate the very principle of harmony and justice upon which the city is to be built? Although he allows in hymns in praise of the gods and heroes, Plato generally ejects the imitative arts, arguing, 'if you allow the sweetened Muse of lyric or epic, pleasure and pain will rule in the city instead of custom and the rational principle which in any given instance seems best in the opinion of the community'.[4]

Outlawing poetry for its deleterious effects, the *Republic* is often cited as one of the first arguments for censorship of the arts. It is an argument made on ethical grounds: art harms us by driving us out of our right minds, and so should be censored. Plato's argument might seem a little far-fetched, but he certainly wasn't the last to make it. In the 1950s, psychologist Fredric Wertham argued that comic books were a major cause of juvenile delinquency, testifying to that claim before the US Senate, and calling for their censorship. At the same time, rock and roll was being blamed for its effects on teenagers: kids were dancing in the aisles at concerts, girls were breaking into fits of crying and screaming as Elvis Presley gyrated his hips – clearly they were all out of their minds. In more recent years, violent video games have been claimed by some to cause aggressive and violent behaviour in teens and preteens, and in 1997 a subcommittee of the US Senate met on the topic 'Music Violence: How Does it Affect Our Youth?', prompted by claims that listening to music by Marilyn Manson had driven a 15-year-old boy to suicide.

Certainly, we might judge a work to be aesthetically bad – this was one of our central concerns in Chapter 3 – and it seems not entirely unreasonable that we might judge a work to be morally bad; at the very least, we have been doing so since Plato's time. But does the one have anything *to do* with the other? That is, could a work be aesthetically bad *because* it is morally bad, or morally bad because it is aesthetically bad?

Even before Plato, philosophers were wrestling with the relationship between 'beauty' and the 'good'. At one point, Socrates treats beauty as synonymous with the good, suggesting that something is 'beautiful' when it is well suited to its purpose. So, just as we might have beautiful works of art, we have beautiful hammers and engines and equations. Later, he contends that beauty is that which makes us feel joy through sight and sound, tying the notion to both our senses and our emotions, and separating it from the good in general. Plato's student Aristotle suggests that beauty is simply one *form* of the good. And, centuries later, St Thomas Aquinas suggests that where the good is what we aim towards, beauty is something we contemplate. Among the many views that were considered, however, beauty and the good – aesthetics and ethics – were almost always tied together, treated as related in *some* way, if only on the grounds that each involves *judgement*. In the eighteenth century, philosophers concerned with how we come to know beauty and the good took a new tack on the relationship between ethics and aesthetics.

As discussed in Chapter 3, Shaftesbury suggests that our ability to discern what is moral and our ability to judge what is beautiful are one and the same. This sense, Shaftesbury contends, distinguishes the beautiful from the ugly, the good from the bad, immediately. He writes:

> Is there then ... a natural beauty of figures and is there not as natural a one of actions? No sooner the eye opens upon figures, the ear to sounds, than straight the beautiful results and grace and harmony are known and acknowledged. No sooner are actions viewed, no sooner the human affections and passions discerned ... than straight an inward eye distinguishes and sees the fair and shapely, the amiable and admirable, apart from the deformed, the foul, the odious or the despicable.[5]

This 'inward eye', Shaftesbury contends, applies to both the ethical and the aesthetic, distinguishing harmony and proportion from their opposites in both arenas. In short, although their objects might be different, there is for Shaftesbury no difference between the ethical *sense* and the aesthetic one – a sense he describes as 'taste'. Following Shaftesbury in the eighteenth century, Francis Hutcheson calls the power to perceive regularity, order and harmony the 'Internal Sense', and the determination to be pleased with the contemplation of virtues a 'Moral Sense'. But, at the same time, he discusses the aesthetic and the moral as two *forms* of beauty, implying a more complex interrelation between our moral and aesthetic tastes.

At about this same time, the notion of the 'fine arts' – 'Art' with a capital 'A' – was developing in Europe and elsewhere. French philosopher Charles Batteux had published his 1746 treatise *Les Beaux-Arts réduits à un même principe* – an attempt to systematize what we today call the fine arts – and the practice of art criticism was becoming a going concern. French writers Étienne La Font de Saint-Yenne and Denis Diderot published now-famous accounts of the annual art 'Salons' of Paris, offering descriptions and judgements of the contemporary works on display, with their publications becoming more renowned than the Salons themselves. Before long, the fledgling artworld was littered with critics.

Immanuel Kant observed that, strangely and almost as a rule, those critics most celebrated for their taste in art were equally known for their poor moral fibre. And so, looking to the work of Shaftesbury, Hutcheson and others, Kant suggested it would be a mistake to take the relationship between the moral and the beautiful too far. Stating that an interest in the beautiful *in art* is no evidence of that person's having moral goodness, Kant nevertheless contends that an interest in *natural* beauty is always a mark of a good soul, indicating 'at least a mental attunement favorable to moral feeling'.[6] The difference between judging the aesthetic in nature and that in art, Kant says, is that the former is typically *disinterested*, while the latter tends to be tainted with personal interests on the part of the critic, and an eye towards the *goal* of art. As with pure aesthetic judgement, Kant contends, moral action must arise from disinterestedness: one's moral decisions should not depend on special consideration for oneself, one's position or one's advantage. So where there is overlap in pure judgements of beauty and moral judgements, for Kant, judgements of art will typically be found on the outside. This is not to say, however, that we cannot properly assess fine art. What distinguishes a great artist, Kant suggests, is that he or she has *genius* – an innate talent for art – as well as *taste*, an intuition for judging beauty. In the artist, taste serves to discipline, polish and civilize genius. For the rest of us, taste allows us to judge something aesthetically without a concern for its purpose or our own interests in it. As much as possible, then, we should judge a work of art on its own merit and defects.

This sort of thinking helped give rise to a perspective on art coined '*l'art pour l'art*' or 'art for art's sake', a phrase most often credited to nineteenth-century French art critic Théophile Gautier. The idea behind 'art for art's sake' was that art is its own reward, and constitutes a realm outside of moral or social utility. Writing during the heat of the French Revolution of 1848, Gautier says:

> A dynasty has been overturned and the Republic proclaimed: but art pays no heed to such events. Art is eternal because it is human; systems of government may change but it endures … Smoke from the fray fills the public squares and hides the plunging perspectives; but soon enough a wind comes up and blows away the whiff of powder, sweeps away the opaque clouds, and the temple of art appears again in its white serenity, cast against the unalterable azure of the sky.[7]

A quarter-century after Gautier's writing, Oxford critic Walter Pater published his *Studies in the History of the Renaissance*, mirroring many of the same ideas. His work concludes: '[A]rt comes to you professing frankly to give nothing but the highest quality to your moments as they pass, and simply for those moments' sake.'[8] Pater and his followers came to be known as 'aesthetes', and their movement as 'aestheticism'. And so, while Kant's idea of artist-as-genius was a hallmark of Romantic thinking, his notion of disinterestedness would fuel the nineteenth-century aestheticism movement. The artist, it was accepted, possessed special insight and abilities, and so was outside the common man's judgement. His works were to be judged on their own merits, in something of a protected bubble. The appreciation of art, it was felt, should be divorced from political, social and moral considerations.

The art-for-art's-sake movement in many ways fell in line with both the intentionalist perspective of the Romantics and the anti-intentionalism of the New Critics and formalists, discussed in detail in Chapters 2 and 3. In interpreting and evaluating works, the Romantics looked to the artist-as-genius. The New Critics and formalists, insofar as it was possible, looked only at the work itself. For the Romantics, the artist stood apart from the rest of us. For the New Critics and formalists, the work stood apart from the artist. But, notably, for both schools of thought, art existed in a realm outside of politics, of society and, importantly, of morality.

The most significant upheaval of this sort of thinking came from perhaps a surprising place: the feminist movement. In the 1960s and 1970s, the United States saw the birth of social activism focused on the rights, roles and general social perceptions of women, with the movement quickly growing beyond American borders. Although the movement targeted a number of both social and legal issues, it resulted in a broad, general reconsideration of the many roles that women had been placed in, and those that they had been excluded from. The artworld did not escape scrutiny. Austrian artist Valie Export writes:

> THE PLACE OF ART IN THE WOMEN'S MOVEMENT IS THE PLACE OF WOMEN IN THE ART MOVEMENT
> THE HISTORY OF WOMAN IS THE HISTORY OF MAN,
> precisely because man has defined the image of woman. men create and control the social and communicative media like art and science, word and image, dress and architecture, social intercourse and the division of labour … to change the art imposed on us by man is to destroy the facets of woman constructed by man. through the processes of civilization the new values we bring to art will assign new values to us as women. art can be significant for the women's movement to the extent that we strike new meanings – our meanings – from art.[9]

The feminist movement served to undermine the schools of both Romanticism and New Criticism. Although the Romantic notion of the artist focused on the creator of fine art, the problem was that rarely were women among this group. In *Gender and Genius*, Christine Battersby notes that the Romantic notion of the artist-as-genius is almost entirely exclusionary to women.[10] Although often characterized in traditionally feminine or female terms, described as 'intuitive' and as a painful birthing process, genius was generally treated as a transcendence of one's nature (where such characteristics were simply natural to women). In 1971, art historian Linda Nochlin published her article 'Why Have There Been No Great Women Artists?' in which she argues that the entire art profession, built on the notion of artist-as-genius, has systematically made it difficult for women to emerge as great artists.[11] Although there certainly *have* been women artists, Nochlin argues that the artworld *system* has developed to keep them from elevating to the status of *great* artists.

In principle, on the New Critical perspective, the critic is meant to ignore biographical facts about the artist and conditions under which the work was created, thus eliminating anything outside the work itself. As well, the critic is meant to put aside his or her own personal position as a reader, viewer or listener. The problem, feminist artists and philosophers have noted, is that we cannot read, view or listen to a work from a position entirely devoid of perspective. And the 'default' perspective that society has historically impressed upon us is one rife with assumptions about our various roles. However, those who produce art and those who consume it each exist in their own particular social situations. Some are wealthy, some are impoverished, some are conservative, some are liberal and – importantly – some are men and some are women. Each of these domains brings with it certain assigned social roles and norms. Each of us, then, has a certain 'situatedness', defined by the roles we are assigned and the norms we are judged by. As such, Anne Eaton argues that the sort of disinterestedness suggested by Kant and promoted by aestheticism is a myth. She writes: 'it is impossible that taste can be disinterested; that is, free from the influence of the particularities of one's constitution and situation, and without regard for one's personal preferences, inclinations, peculiarities, tolerances, or orientations'.[12] This will be equally true for both artist and audience. If we cannot escape situatedness, then to attempt to remove the peculiar position of either the artist or critic from the equation is at best naïve and at worst serves only to perpetuate the historically dominant 'default' position – one which assigns both women and men their respective roles, and treats them as absolute.

Works of art, in other words, are things created and consumed under certain circumstances. As cultural artefacts, they play political, social and moral roles. The effect of this movement on the philosophy of art is difficult to overstate. The wide-sweeping effects of the feminist movement helped give rise to a number of the schools of thought we have considered in earlier chapters. The idea that the conditions under which a work is created are critical to both its interpretation and evaluation was the seed from which the contextualist movement grew, and the spirit of the feminist movement is evident in the theories of Kendall Walton and Jerrold Levinson, to name just two. At the same time, looking to the role of the audience, the movement of post-structuralism (and, in particular, reader-response theories) expanded on the idea that none of us are ever truly disinterested or 'unsituated'. As such, the feminist movement helped to place art back into the larger social context, and to raise questions about *its* roles, particularly its moral and political ones.

III. Radical moralism and autonomism

In Chapter 3, we looked at David Hume's theory of taste, in which he argues that the critic's job is to distance himself from his own sentimentality, to overcome his own prejudices and to become, as much as possible, a 'man in general' – a view closely related to Kant's disinterestedness. However, Hume argues that such an ideal judge cannot and should not free himself from moral assessment of art: '[W]here vicious manners are described, without being marked with the proper characters of blame and disapprobation; this must be allowed to disfigure the poem, and to be a real deformity. I cannot, nor is it proper I should, enter into such sentiments.'[13] Put another way, the ideal distance from one's own prejudices and sentimentality is not one that places him outside of morality – the 'man in general' is a *moral* person, and an ideal critic should not put morality to the side in artistic assessment.

Hume offers no specifics on what constitutes proper morality, arguing only that one cannot judge a work to be good which is morally blame-worthy. In *What Is Art?*, Leo Tolstoy suggests that 'In every age, and in every human society, there exists a religious sense, common to that whole society, of what is good and what is bad, and it is this religious conception that decides the value of feelings transmitted by art.'[14] Tolstoy's notion of religion in this context is a broad one. He suggests that each society has, tying it together, an understanding of the meaning of life – the highest good to which that society aims, whether or not any individual member of that society recognizes it. This, he says, is the society's 'religious perception'. The society of Socrates, Plato and Aristotle, Tolstoy argues, found meaning in happiness, and so works were praised insofar as they reflected this perspective, and condemned where they reflected its opposite. The religious perception of *our* time, he argues, revolves around a sense of universal brotherhood, a perspective he takes to be at the core of Christianity. Indeed, Tolstoy argues that this *is* the purpose of human life, and not merely one of a given society. On this basis, then, good art will be that which fosters feelings of brotherhood among men, and bad art that which runs counter to such feelings, in particular, he argues, by promoting elitism or social division. Good art should be esteemed and encouraged, while bad art should be stamped out. Into this latter camp, Tolstoy places the plays of the ancient Greeks and Shakespeare, all the works of Beethoven and Bach, and even his own great novels, *Anna Karenina* and *War and Peace*. In failing to promote the fraternity of mankind, such works simply fail to be good art, regardless of whatever aesthetic excellence might be found in them. On Tolstoy's view, in other words, the moral faults of a work defeat or negate its other merits, and a work's artistic value always depends directly and invariably on its moral value – a position now known as *moralism*.

Of course, we needn't take Tolstoy's *particular* ethical stance to be moralists. We could be moralists simply by claiming that for a work to be good art it must promote a positive ethical position, or denounce negative ones. We could be as specific or unspecific as we like about the ethical principles involved and still earn the title of 'moralists'.

The flip side to moralism is *autonomism*, the view that works of art stand outside moral evaluation – that to judge a work on moral grounds is to fail to judge it on artistic ones. And if Tolstoy is the poster-child for extreme or 'radical' moralism, his opposite is Clive Bell, whom we discussed in detail in Chapter 1. Bell argues that art as a *whole* is an unqualified good in the moral sense. He suggests that for a thing to be good in this sense is for it to be a means to good states of mind. Art, he argues, leads more directly to such states of mind than does any other human activity. So art, taken as a whole, is a moral good. It is worth remembering at this point that, as a consequence of Bell's definition of art, there is simply no such thing as *bad* art: art is that which gives rise to aesthetic emotion – most certainly, on his view, a good state of mind. And, by definition, the only thing that gives rise to aesthetic emotion is significant form. In sum, the only appropriate basis for a thing's being morally good is that it is a means to good states of mind. Aesthetic emotion is a good state of mind. Something gives rise to aesthetic emotion just in case it has significant form. All art has significant form. So all art is morally good – indeed, Bell argues, the *highest* moral good. As all art is of the highest moral good, nothing about an individual work can make it morally *better*. And as all art is of the highest moral good, nothing about it can make it worse – if it fails to achieve this moral good, it will be because it fails to bring about the aesthetic emotion, and if it fails to do this, it simply fails to be art. So, on Bell's view, while it is appropriate to judge art as a whole on moral standards, to judge any *particular* work on such standards is to fail to judge it *as a work of art*. Looking for moral *content* in a work, or for morality in its origin, has, on Bell's theory, nothing to do with its being art, and so nothing to do with its artistic value. To *use* art for moral purposes, then – say, in moral education – would run against its very nature as art.

However, just as we need not adhere to Tolstoy's particular view to be moralists, we need not hold to Bell's questionable views on the nature of art or morality to be autonomists. Although many autonomists, like Bell, contend that art as a kind is inherently valuable in the moral sense, in general autonomism is characterized by the view that only a work's formal qualities are germane to its artistic value. This is the view, for instance, of Monroe Beardsley, who (as we discussed in Chapter 3) argues that artistic value depends solely on aesthetic value, which depends only on a work's unity, intensity and complexity. On this view, there is simply no room for moral matters in the art-value equation. And, given his anti-intentionalist view (discussed in Chapter 2) separating the work from the life of the author, radical autonomism is a natural fit for Beardsley. This is, of course, an extreme position, as is Tolstoy's moralism, each making artistic evaluation an all-or-nothing affair. The radical moralist contends that not only does moral content contribute invariably to artistic value, but it outweighs all other considerations in artistic evaluation. The radical autonomist insists that moral considerations are inconsistent, beside the point or otherwise out of place when it comes to artistic value. But each of these positions seems at odds with our typical critical practices. Consider, first, the signature paintings of Agnes Martin. Martin is usually classified as a minimalist painter (though she considered herself an abstract expressionist), best known for her grid paintings: six-foot by six-foot square canvases covered in a system of minute, subtly drawn grids. Although her paintings are generally described as 'quiet' and Taoist, they lack what we would normally call content: they do not represent anything; they do not tell a story. Rather, the paintings affect the viewer with their soft, almost monochromatic hues and regular, systematic structure. To attempt to morally evaluate Martin's 1964 painting *Red Bird* is to look for something that just isn't there. So do we want to say that *Red Bird* is a failure as an artwork, as radical moralism would seem to require? This seems misguided.

Now consider a work like Moisés Kaufman's 2000 play *The Laramie Project*, an exploration of reactions to the 1998 murder of Matthew Shepard in Laramie, Wyoming. Shepard was gay, and his murder was widely denounced as a hate crime. The play is constructed on the basis of transcribed interviews with actual Laramie residents, and focuses in on each resident's perspective. It is an emotionally charged play, and is performed around the world, particularly in schools where it is often used to teach about prejudice and tolerance. Unsurprisingly, perhaps, performances have met with no little amount of controversy. Now, this seems precisely the sort of work that seeks to promote the brotherhood of mankind recommended by Tolstoy. However, if radical autonomists are right, any evaluation of the work that takes account of its moral dimensions is not an artistic evaluation. But, we have to ask, how can one even hope to *understand* the play unless one understands – and, indeed, perhaps participates in experiencing – the moral horror upon which it is built?

IV. Moderate moralism and autonomism

Last chapter, we looked at David Novitz's proposed solution to the paradox of fiction. Central to Novitz's argument is that any proper understanding of a work of fiction requires that one puts oneself in a position to be appropriately moved by its characters. *The Laramie Project* is non-fiction, of course, so the paradox does not apply to it. However, it seems reasonable to say that, like a fiction, a complete understanding of Kaufman's play requires emotional involvement. And, picking up on this notion, Noël Carroll notes that *some* of the emotions necessary to understanding a work have an essential moral dimension.[15] To watch *The Laramie Project* without a sense of moral horror is simply inappropriate to that work – it is to miss something central and critical to the play. And so, to *evaluate* the play without an understanding of moral perspectives appropriate to it is to fail to properly or fully evaluate it. Moreover, Carroll argues, by engaging us on a moral level, such works allow us to *practise* our moral abilities, helping us to clarify and enlarge our moral understanding, so the work *is* an appropriate tool in moral education. Some have argued for a similar view on Aristotle's behalf – that the whole point of cathartic engagement with tragedy was to allow us to safely practise becoming good people: to build good character and make good decisions by learning to feel emotion correctly.[16] Certainly, *The Laramie Project* is not an isolated work in this regard. Carroll argues that 'it is vastly improbable that there could be any substantial narrative of human affairs, especially a narrative artwork, that did not rely upon activating the moral powers of readers, viewers and listeners'.[17] What Carroll does not argue, however, is that this applies to *all* artworks – it does seem beside the point to an evaluation of *Red Bird* – rather, Carroll restricts his claim to narrative works. And so, arguing that morality is imperative to *some* but not *all* artistic evaluation, Carroll dubs himself a 'moderate moralist', to distinguish his position from a radical view like Tolstoy's.

Another moderate moralist is Berys Gaut, who calls his view 'ethicism'.[18] Gaut argues that an artwork's aesthetic value can depend on the attitudes manifested by that work. If those attitudes are reprehensible, this invariably counts against the work's aesthetic merit; if they are commendable, this counts towards it. Gaut contends that a work manifests an attitude by prescribing a certain response to the events it describes or depicts. Certainly, comedies prescribe humorous responses and horrors prescribe fear. Stories may prescribe empathy towards their characters, derision towards villains, admiration towards heroes. But, of course, not every work succeeds. Comedies fail by being unfunny, horrors by being unfrightening, thrillers by being unthrilling. Where we have reason not to respond as the work prescribes, the work fails aesthetically. An unfunny comedy is a bad comedy. Now, to return to the matter at hand, some of the responses prescribed by a work may be morally charged. And when a work prescribes an *immoral* response, Gaut argues, we *always* have reason not to respond as it prescribes. And since we have reason not to respond as prescribed, this counts against that work's aesthetic value. Conversely, where a work prescribes a positive ethical response, this is always an aesthetic merit. So, for example, when we are shown the gang rape of Sarah Tobias in the film *The Accused*, our prescribed horrified response counts towards the work's aesthetic merit. However, had the film been designed to elicit approval of the rape, say by being salacious, the work would have suffered aesthetically because it would have (in this way) suffered ethically.

Now, consider a film like Leni Riefenstahl's *Triumph of the Will*. Released in 1935 and commissioned by Adolf Hitler, the film chronicles a four-day Nazi Party Congress in an effort to promote the Nazi philosophy. The entire purpose of the film is to elicit approval of the Nazi regime – undoubtedly a moral and thus aesthetic failing on Gaut's view. However, Riefenstahl introduced a number of revolutionary techniques in both cinematography and music, making *Triumph of the Will* the most widely renowned propaganda film ever made. That the film is so well regarded, Gaut would point out, is not evidence against his view. As a moderate moralist, Gaut does not argue that the morality of a work outweighs all other aesthetic considerations – only that it invariably counts *against* its aesthetic merit. And as a moderate moralist position, the central position of ethicism does not apply to all works. If a work doesn't manifest an attitude, Gaut's ethicism simply does not apply to it. Lacking content, it would certainly be difficult to argue that Martin's *Red Bird* manifests *any* attitudes, and the same will be true for any number of works.

It is worth noting that Gaut's argument seems to depend upon a realist view about both aesthetic and moral characteristics. We discussed realism about aesthetic properties in Chapter 3, being the view that if something is, for example, beautiful, this is because of something *objective* in the thing – and while we might disagree about whether or not the object is in fact beautiful, and we might disagree about what would make it so, a claim that the object is beautiful is either true or false. A realist perspective on moral properties works the same way: persons or actions or events are good, evil, praiseworthy or blameworthy objectively – there is something about them that *makes* this the case, and our disagreements over whether or not something is evil does not alter the fact of the matter. On Gaut's view, that a work is immoral – that it prescribes an immoral response in its audience – invariably contributes negatively to its aesthetic value. However, if either moral or aesthetic characteristics are relativistic, whether or not the work is moral or immoral, beautiful or ugly, will always be an open question. Susan Feagin, whose view on tragedy we discussed in the previous chapter, offers a perspective on moral and aesthetic assessment which, while similar to Gaut's, avoids the problem of realism about either sort of characteristic.

Recall that, on Feagin's view, we can distinguish between 'direct responses' and 'meta-responses'. With tragedy, Feagin argues, we have a direct response to the events portrayed, and this will often (given the nature of tragedy) be negative in character. If it is a good tragedy, we will respond with pity, fear and terror. However, complicated creatures that we are, we also respond to our own responses – these are our meta-responses. And, assuming we are well balanced, we *approve* of our negative responses to the events portrayed in the tragedy. This relationship between direct and meta-responses, Feagin suggests, can also help us to make sense of immoral works of art: a judgement that a work is immoral is a judgement about the relationship between one's own ethical convictions and something about the work. Specifically, an immoral work would be one that manipulates our responses such that we respond favourably to something we believe to be immoral (or unfavourably to something we believe moral). A work may get us to root for the murderer in *Halloween* or *Silence of the Lambs*, for example. In Feagin's terms, an immoral work is one that produces a positive direct response to which our meta-response is negative. Looking back, we are sickened or perhaps simply disappointed that we were so manipulated. We might still recognize the artist's ability to get us to feel positively towards something we would otherwise find abhorrent, but, given our disapproving meta-response, nevertheless reach a negative verdict on the work's artistic value. Notice that nothing about Feagin's position assumes a realist view on either moral or aesthetic characteristics – rather, the question is about whether you would *judge* a work to be morally defective and, as a result, aesthetically defective.

It might be asked, if the matter is as simple as a direct relationship between moral and aesthetic values – whether or not we are committed to a realist perspective – why does it feel so uncomfortable to simply pronounce *Triumph of the Will* a great work of art? On Gaut's view, the work's moral character is simply a factor in assessing its aesthetic nature. Undoubtedly, the work prescribes what most of us would call an immoral response: approval of the Nazi philosophy. And so, Gaut would argue, this contributes negatively to the work's aesthetic value – simply not enough to overcome its overall aesthetic greatness. If the matter is so simple as this, why should we feel uncomfortable in making a blanket statement about its greatness? On Feagin's view, if the work *did*, despite our better nature, manage to get us to respond positively to the propagandist message we would otherwise abhor, we should judge the work to be aesthetically defective – but perhaps not defective *enough* that we call the work an overall aesthetic failure. So why not simply end the matter there and call it a great work of art? The reason, it would seem, is that we would not want to leave anyone with the mistaken impression that we in any way *approve* of the message of the film.

James Anderson and Jeffrey Dean might argue that the tension inherent in saying '*Triumph of the Will* is a great work of art' arises because the statement as such does not *distinguish* between our aesthetic assessment of the work and our moral assessment of it.[19] When we say *Triumph of the Will* is a great film, we mean this *specifically* aesthetically, and *not at all* morally. In general, while conceding that it may be appropriate to judge a work on moral grounds, Anderson and Dean argue that to do so is *not* to judge that work on aesthetic grounds. It is, rather, a distinct sort of assessment, and the two have nothing to do with each other. As such, Anderson and Dean defend a position of 'moderate autonomism'. The view is an autonomist position in that, on it, a work's moral qualities (whether positive or negative) do not contribute to its aesthetic ones. It is a moderate view in that, unlike Bell's radical autonomism, it does not hold that moral assessment is inappropriate to particular artworks. Indeed, Anderson and Dean suggest that the fact that we can judge a work both aesthetically and ethically may explain the sort of conflict we feel in judging a work like *Triumph of the Will*.

Anderson and Dean do not dispute that full engagement with a work may require moral understanding on the part of the audience, nor do they disagree with Gaut that a work's prescribing an inappropriate response in its audience is an aesthetic failing of the work, as when a comedy is unfunny or a thriller unthrilling. Where they suggest the moderate moralist fails is in establishing the *connection* between moral assessment and aesthetic assessment. They write:

> While it is true that we have a cognitive (not to mention ethical) interest in not having persons believe that bad people or actions are good, it does not follow that we do not have an *aesthetic* interest in seeing bad people or actions represented *as if* they were good. Indeed, our curiosity about seeing one thing represented as another is a hallmark of aesthetic interest.[20]

Thomas Harris's Hannibal Lecter, Bram Stoker's Count Dracula, and Quentin Tarantino's Vic and Vincent Vega would all be horrible people in our world. But they are *not* in our world, and much of the value of *Silence of the Lambs*, *Dracula*, *Reservoir Dogs* and *Pulp Fiction* seems to *rely* on these characters being portrayed in an appealing way. That we enjoy such stories does not make us immoral, nor does it mean we are amoral – rather, Anderson and Dean contend, it illustrates a gap between our moral and aesthetic judgements.

That a work prescribes a morally reprehensible attitude does not thus entail an aesthetic defect. However, Anderson and Dean certainly do not want to contend that it entails an aesthetic merit either. Rather, they argue, the two are conceptually distinct arenas of assessment. However, that aesthetic and moral assessment are conceptually distinct does not mean they will not come into conflict. Indeed, that the two are distinct may help to *explain* a number of cases of conflict. On that note, let us return to the difficult case that opened this chapter – Marco Evaristti's *Helena* – and see how it comes out on the views we have considered.

On the radical moralist position, ethical considerations are primary in the evaluation of art. Evaristti claims that the very point of *Helena* is to show a basic division of mankind into 'idiots', 'voyeurs' and 'moralists'. On this basis, the work certainly seems to run counter to fostering the 'brotherhood of mankind', Tolstoy's contended basis to morality, and so would be an immoral work on Tolstoy's view. Of course, not all radical moralists need ascribe to Tolstoy's particular perspective on morality, and the possible bases to morality are numerous. Rather than attempting to catalogue all of these views, let us turn to radical autonomism.

On Bell's radical autonomist position, all works of art are of the highest moral good, so the only question is whether *Helena* qualifies as a work of art. For Bell, something is art just in case it has significant form, and all and only things with significant form give rise to aesthetic emotion. Bell tells us little about how to recognize significant form except from the aesthetic emotion it gives rise to, and he tells us even less about how to recognize aesthetic emotion. However, given Bell's view, if a goldfish cannot give rise to significant form, and a blender is unlikely to, it seems questionable at best that a combination of these will do so. Ultimately, whether we subscribe to Bell's particular version of radical autonomism, or some other variety of it, while *Helena* might be immoral, it won't be as art.

Turning from the radical views to their moderate variants, let us first consider moderate moralism. Carroll restricts his version of the view to narrative works, and *Helena* does not easily qualify as one. So let us instead look at Gaut's version. As noted, Gaut's ethicism depends upon a realist view of both ethical and moral properties. Suppose, then, for the sake of argument that the wanton mulching of live goldfish is in fact wrong. *Helena* certainly *invites* the viewer to participate in killing goldfish, but does it *prescribe* a view about doing so, whether positive or negative? Not clearly. Indeed, the point of the work seems to be to prompt its audience to consider its own moral choices. So on Gaut's theory, the work appears to come out neither moral nor immoral. And, as such, the ethics of goldfish-mulching will be a non-factor so far as aesthetic considerations go. On Feagin's theory, if you believe that mulching goldfish is wrong, but you were convinced by the work to mulch one anyway, you might reasonably judge the work immoral. Of course, if you had no moral qualms about goldfish-mulching, or if the work did not make you feel positively about such an activity, there is no moral problem here.

As moderate autonomists, Anderson and Dean argue that moral evaluation of *Helena* as a work of art is reasonable, but that this does not contribute to the work's aesthetic value. Rather, they argue, the two sorts of value are in separate arenas. It may complicate matters that *Helena* involves audience *participation* – in particular, participation in a morally questionable action. And unlike watching *Reservoir Dogs*, *Helena*'s audience is not permitted the luxury of not engaging with the work on a moral level – for even the voyeur is making a moral choice, Evaristti would contend. But, Anderson and Dean would likely reply, this is just to say that the work, the artist or the participants may be judged ethically, and the pair do not dispute this. Rather, they merely contend that whether the work is morally good says nothing about whether it is aesthetically good.

V. Arts funding and censorship

Today, many governments include organizations dedicated to funding and promoting the arts. New Zealand has Creative New Zealand, the United States has the National Endowment for the Arts, and the United Kingdom has an array of separate arts councils for its composite countries and territories. In 2000, the International Federation of Arts Councils and Culture Agencies was formed as a global network of such national bodies, and today includes member agencies from over seventy countries. Although most countries also have any number of private, non-profit bodies dedicated to the same end, those run as government organizations sit in a unique position. While private organizations depend upon voluntary donations, government arts councils draw their budgets from tax revenue. As a result, such organizations tend to draw contention from time to time.

America's National Endowment for the Arts, in particular, has been called to task for funding a number of controversial works. In 1989, the Corcoran Museum of Art in Washington, DC abandoned plans to host an NEA-supported showing of photographs by Robert Mapplethorpe, known for his black-and-white – and often homoerotic – portraits of nude men. Many of Mapplethorpe's criticized works unabashedly depict scenes of sexual bondage and sadomasochism, one of his most famous (or infamous) being a self-portrait in which the handle of a bullwhip is depicted inserted into his anus. The decision to cancel the show followed in the wake of controversy over Andres Serrano's 1987 photograph *Piss Christ*, a depiction of a plastic crucifix bathed in light while submerged in a glass of Serrano's urine. Although Serrano was not directly funded by the NEA, the photograph was in a series by Serrano given a $15,000 award by the Southeast Center for Contemporary Art, with the cash prize partially funded by the NEA. Following the Mapplethorpe show's cancellation, the Corcoran was criticized by artists, civil liberties activists and gay advocates for having censored Mapplethorpe's works. That same year, Senator Jesse Helms put forward an amendment to the federal budget for arts endowment to deny federal funding used to 'promote, disseminate, or produce indecent or obscene materials, including but not limited to depictions of sadomasochism, homoeroticism, the exploitation of children, or individuals engaged in sex acts'.[21]

Helms's amendment was denied, but it raises interesting questions about art and ethics, and in particular about censorship. When the Corcoran cancelled its Mapplethorpe show, was it censoring Mapplethorpe? If Helms's amendment had gone through, would it have been censoring artistic depictions of sexual acts? Is censorship per se morally wrong? Are 'obscene' artworks morally wrong? Can censorship ever be morally good? Traditionally understood, censorship consists in the suppression of an individual's or group's expressions or ideas. But did the Corcoran actually *suppress* Mapplethorpe's work? Couldn't his work have simply been displayed elsewhere? And would the Helms amendment have *censored* works of a sexual nature? If passed, it would have kept the NEA from *funding* such art, but is my refusal to pay you for your art thus a *censorship* of your ideas and expressions?

Mary Devereaux argues that Helms and his supporters, while failing to get the amendment passed, nevertheless succeeded in creating a *climate* in which artists and those who patronize the arts came under hostile suspicion and scrutiny on moral rather than artistic grounds.[22] No longer, Devereaux notes, can artists expect the public to operate under an 'art for art's sake' perspective, to recognize a barrier of artistic autonomy. And artists whose works challenge our moral foundations, she argues, should not expect to have a chance at public funding. This, Devereaux notes, is largely a consequence of the feminist movement. Challenging the view that art spoke from a universal and enlightened perspective, we now question the context, history and origins of a work, and not merely its formal aspects. However, this openness on our part is a double-edged sword. While enriching our understanding and experience of art, and allowing art to arouse controversy and public interest, in doing so, it also opens art to political interference. Put simply, if art can have moral content, whether positive or negative, then it seems to open itself to moral – and thus political – interference. And even if we *could* return to a view in which art was seen in purely formal (and so non-ethical) terms, would we *want* to?

Devereaux suggests that art should be given a 'protected space'. This is a sort of autonomy, but not the sort of autonomy that implies that art has no moral content or context. Rather, she suggests, it is the sort of autonomy that demands freedom from outside interference. She writes: 'By "protected space" I mean the principle of granting artists control over both their subject matter and means of expression. It is this figurative space, that is, the space in which artists can work without outside interference, which the literal space of the museum and gallery concretely embody.'[23] This is not to say that artists should return to the idea of artist-as-genius, blameless beings who live beyond the reach of our judgement. Rather, Devereaux argues, we should recognize artists as playing a variety of special social roles: that of social critic, of reformer, of revolutionary and even as defender of the status quo.

Devereaux does not suggest, however, that such a protected space demands government funding, nor that failure to fund any art created in such a space constitutes censorship. Artist Richard Serra argues that the problem is not in the funding or not funding of art, but rather in the *selective* funding of art.[24] The government can choose to use or not use tax revenue for art funding, he argues, but as soon as it *does* fund the arts, it must fund *all* the arts. We might, in essence, think of government funding as a form of political interference: to fund work A and not work B is to give A a larger audience and to allow it to flourish. It is like planting two trees next to each other and only watering one of them. Before long, the watered plant will grow tall enough so that its leaves will block the other plant from the sun, and so the unwatered plant will wither away. To fund some works to the exclusion of others is, Serra argues, to *suppress*, and so to censor, the unfunded works.

Noël Carroll notes that we could attempt to justify government funding of the arts on the grounds that art performs a moralizing function.[25] That is, the moral well-being of a populace and the moral order of society seem to fall within the legitimate concerns of any state government. This being the case, if art, say, increases moral sympathies, helps to develop moral understanding and in general makes for a more moral society, a government might be *obligated* to fund such art. Carroll notes that there are, however, a number of problems with this line of thinking. First, there is the empirical question of whether art can *indeed* perform this function. Certainly, some of the views discussed in this chapter have at least *leaned* in this direction, but to justify the spending of tax revenue for this end would likely require some actual study of the moralizing effects of art. Second, while *some* art might perform this function, certainly not *all* art is likely to. It is difficult to see, for instance, how Martin's *Red Bird* could play such a role. And so, works like *Red Bird*, which did not perform this function, and any works that sought to instil moral divisiveness would have to be denied funding. And while this would certainly appeal to Tolstoy, for non-adherents to radical moralism, this argument is problematic.

Similarly, Carroll notes, it might be suggested that mankind has an *aesthetic need*, and that we might consider this a public health matter. As public health is a legitimate area of government concern, if beauty contributes to the well-being of a populace, then the government could be said to have an obligation to use tax revenue to this end. As such, we might have another compelling argument for government arts funding. The problem with such an argument is that, just as not all art is meant to be moralizing, not all art is meant to be beautiful. Some art is not at all concerned with beauty. Some art is decidedly *anti-aesthetic*. Some art is downright disturbing. So, while we *could* perhaps justify government funding of the arts on this basis, again it would only justify the funding of select kinds of art. And this, Serra might argue, would be to suppress those works that fell outside the government's area of concern (and, perhaps, specific take on beauty). As we have seen throughout this chapter and throughout this book, art is not a static thing. It changes as artists reconsider their role in society. It changes with the advent of new technologies. It changes when Marcel Duchamp attempts to turn an ordinary urinal into art, or perhaps when Marco Evaristti invites his audience to mulch goldfish in blenders. As Carroll argues, to attempt to justify government support for the arts either on the grounds that art has a moralizing effect, or on the grounds that the public has an aesthetic need that art can fulfil, 'may indeed disturb the structure of artistic production and perhaps destroy the art world as we know it'.[26]

Richard Shusterman argues that censorship need not always be a bad thing.[27] Indeed, he suggests, certain forms of censorship could be beneficial. Certainly, Plato argued that art censorship would be a good thing for the public, and this seems to have been the motivation behind Senator Helms's amendment, but Shusterman makes a different argument: he suggests that censorship of a particular kind could be beneficial to *art for art's sake*. And this, Shusterman argues, does not conflict with the sort of autonomy of art that Devereaux recommends. The sort of censorship Shusterman has in mind is 'aesthetic censorship': censorship of works on the basis that they are objectionable on aesthetic grounds. If all works, regardless of aesthetic merit, are allowed to equally claim our attention, Shusterman suggests, bad works will gain as much opportunity for a foothold on the public and artistic consciousness as good works. And while this might be *egalitarian*, Shusterman argues that it will be bad for *art*. Imagine if you *had* to eat an equal amount of bad and good food – what effect would this have on your taste? And, it might be suggested, *most* art is bad art (or, at best, mediocre art). So imagine that you had to suffer through a hundred or a thousand bad meals for every bit of good food you got to taste. Such overexposure to bad art, Shusterman argues, would likely divert and drain your attention from the relatively few works of real aesthetic worth, and generally dull our ability to appreciate the good. Given that, unlike eating, you don't *have* to consume art … *would* you? As artists build on the work that came before them, would *they* have the fortitude to carry on? The fact is, Shusterman notes, there will always be controlling influences in what art gets served to the public at large. Certain social, political and religious groups will always try to suppress some works while attempting to fortify others. Any number of works fail to make it to the public for economic reasons. Not every book, film or song is likely to turn a profit, and publishers are understandably hesitant to put the money into works that will not make them money. Opera companies and other large-scale productions can be *enormously* expensive, and often simply cannot survive without government funding. If the production of art must be regulated and restricted – and, Shusterman notes, this seems inevitable – isn't it better for *art* if such restrictions are made on aesthetic considerations rather than by the whims of the free market and at the hands of lobbying groups?

It should be noted, Shusterman does not go so far as to actually *recommend* we follow this argument. He notes that such claims are very likely to conflict with other factors – in particular moral ones. So this leaves a question: would it be *morally* wrong to suppress bad art so that good art could flourish, if, as it stands, some art *has* to be suppressed? On Bell's radical autonomism, this could be the best thing to happen to society, morally speaking: if art serves the ultimate moral good, then promotion of good art might be the most moral thing we could do. The same would seemingly be true for Tolstoy's radical moralism, though here the moral question will be necessarily prior to the aesthetic one. For the moderate moralist, the ethical question will be inextricably intertwined with the aesthetic question, and so aesthetic censorship will almost inevitably be censorship on ethical grounds as well. For the moderate autonomist, we would have to ask whether what we value aesthetically outweighs what we value morally, and this remains an open question.

Chapter summary

Throughout this chapter, we have surveyed many of the ways that the fields of ethics and aesthetics have clashed and intertwined, both historically and theoretically. We looked at some of the history of philosophy, focusing on how moral and aesthetic questions have been alternatively woven together and teased apart, both in terms of our concepts of 'beauty' and 'good' and in our faculties for recognizing and assessing these qualities. We considered how theories in the eighteenth century served to ground the movement of aestheticism, which in turn spurned both the Romantic and New Critical views on interpretation. And we looked at how the feminist movement served to undermine both of these schools of thought. Next, we looked at a number of views on how moral matters interact with aesthetic and artistic matters, including the radical moralism of Leo Tolstoy, the radical autonomism of Clive Bell, versions of moderate moralism proposed by Noël Carroll and Berys Gaut and a theory of moderate autonomism suggested by James Anderson and Jeffrey Dean. Finally, we considered questions of government funding and censorship of the arts, with arguments presented by Mary Devereaux, Richard Serra, Noël Carroll and Richard Shusterman.

Historical timeline

	c. 360 BCE	Plato, *Republic*
	c. 350 BCE	Aristotle, *Poetics*
	1711	Anthony Ashley Cooper, 3rd Earl of Shaftesbury, *Characteristics of Men, Manners, Opinions, Times*
	1725	Francis Hutcheson, *An Inquiry into the Original of Our Ideas of Beauty and Virtue*
	1746	Charles Batteux, *Les Beaux-Arts réduits à un même principe*
	1757	David Hume, 'On the Standard of Taste'
	1790	Immanuel Kant, *The Critique of Judgment*
Leo Tolstoy, *War and Peace*	1869	
	1873	Walter Pater, *Studies in the History of the Renaissance*
Leo Tolstoy, *Anna Karenina*	1878	
	1896	Leo Tolstoy, *What is Art?*
Bram Stoker, *Dracula*	1897	
	1913	Clive Bell, *Art*
Leni Riefenstahl, *Triumph of the Will*	1935	
Agnes Martin, *Red Bird*	1964	
Carl Andre, *144 Lead Square*	1969	
	1973	Valie Export, 'Woman's Art'

John Carpenter, *Halloween* Robert Mapplethorpe, *Untitled (Self-Portrait)*	1978	
	1983	Susan Feagin, 'The Pleasures of Tragedy'
	1984	Richard Shusterman, 'Aesthetic Censorship: Censoring Art for Art's Sake'
Andres Serrano, *Piss Christ*	1987	Noël Carroll, 'Can Government Funding of the Arts be Justified Theoretically?'
Jonathan Kaplan, *The Accused* Thomas Harris, *Silence of the Lambs*	1988	
	1989	Christine Battersby, *Gender and Genius: Towards a Feminist Aesthetics*
Felix Gonzales-Torres, *'Untitled' (Throat)*	1991	Richard Serra, 'Art and Censorship'
Quentin Tarantino, *Reservoir Dogs*	1992	
	1993	Noël Carroll, 'Moderate Moralism' Mary Devereaux, 'Protected Space: Politics, Censorship, and the Arts'
Quentin Tarantino, *Pulp Fiction*	1994	
	1998	Berys Gaut, 'The Ethical Criticism of Art' James C. Anderson and Jeffrey T. Dean, 'Moderate Autonomism'
Moisés Kaufman, *The Laramie Project* Marco Evaristti, *Helena*	2000	
	2008	Anne Eaton, 'Feminist Aesthetics'

Key terms and concepts

- Aesthetic Censorship (p. 182)
- Aestheticism (p. 167)
- Art for Art's Sake (p. 167)
- Autonomism, Moderate (p. 176)
- Autonomism, Radical (p. 171)
- Censorship (p. 164)
- Disinterestedness (p. 166)
- Ethicism (p. 174)
- Feminism (p. 168)
- Fine Art (p. 166)
- Genius (p. 166)
- Internal Sense (p. 166)
- Moralism, Moderate (p. 173)
- Moralism, Radical (p. 171)
- Moral Sense (p. 166)
- Situatedness (p. 169)
- Taste (p. 166)

Further reading

Essays outlining a number of the views we have considered in this chapter are collected in David E. W. Fenner's *Ethics and the Arts: An Anthology* (Garland Reference Library of Social Science, 1995), and the anthology as a whole delves into a number of related areas of interest, including authenticity and artistic property. Berys Gaut gives an extended inquiry into his view of ethicism in *Art, Emotion and Ethics* (Oxford University Press, 2007) that is well worth reading. The views of Plato, Hutcheson, Kant and Tolstoy are particularly worth reading in their original contexts, and their respective works are available in a great many editions. Views by Carroll, Gaut and Devereaux are collected in Jerrold Levinson's *Aesthetics and Ethics: Essays at the Intersection* (Cambridge University Press, 2001), along with a terrific selection of papers on the fundamental questions raised in this chapter. Trying to even more finely split the difference between moralism and autonomism is Matthew Kieran, who has proposed a view he calls 'most moderate moralism', outlined in his 2001 article, 'In Defence of the Ethical Evaluation of Narrative Art' (*British Journal of Aesthetics* 54: 337–51).

A collection of further essays of interest on the topic is offered in José Luis Bermúdez and Sebastian Gardner's *Art and Morality* (Routledge, 2006), and Elisabeth Schellekens provides an inquiry into the topic that is both insightful and entertaining in *Aesthetics and Morality* (Continuum, 2008).

Unresolved questions

1 The moderate autonomist position distinguishes sharply between aesthetic value and moral value. If these *are* distinct arenas of judgement, how could we reconcile them when they clash, for example, in issues of funding or censorship?

2 Berys Gaut presents a view that assumes realism about both moral and aesthetic properties, while Susan Feagin offers a similar view that assumes neither. If we were realists about moral properties but not aesthetic ones, or vice versa, what sorts of accounts of their interaction might this give rise to? Is there compelling reason to consider these sorts of views?

3 Something none of the views we have considered is, if immoral actions are required to *create* a given work of art, does that make the resulting work immoral?

4 If *Helena* is alternatively either protected from moral scrutiny as a work of art or susceptible to ethical evaluation as a work, does this protection or responsibility extend to the audience participant?

7

Art, Aesthetics and Identity

I. *The Good Earth* (1932) and *The Good Earth* (1937)

In 1932, drawing on her experiences growing up as the child of missionaries, Pearl S. Buck published her novel *The Good Earth*, the sprawling story of a Chinese farmer, his new wife and their family in early twentieth-century revolutionary China. The novel was an enormous commercial and critical success, topping the bestseller's list for the next two years and earning Buck the Pulitzer Prize in 1932. Six years later, she was awarded the Nobel Prize in Literature.

In her 1938 Nobel Lecture, Buck discusses the nature of the Chinese novel, which, she says, shaped her as a writer. However, the indigenous Chinese novel was not considered a form of art, Buck submits – at least not by the Chinese. Art was the domain of literary scholars, and the Chinese novelist wrote for the common people, not the scholar:

> [T]o farmers he must talk of their land, and to old men he must speak of peace, and to old women he must tell of their children, and to young men

Figure 7.1 Still from *The Good Earth* (1937), directed by Sidney Franklin.

and women he must speak of each other. He must be satisfied if the common people hear him gladly. At least, so I have been taught in China.[1]

Buck grew up in a multicultural, bilingual world, equally influenced by her English-speaking American family and her Chinese friends and neighbours. Although Buck was a white American, *The Good Earth* was written for the common people of China from the position of an author intimately familiar with their lives.

Earlier in 1938, Luise Rainer won the Academy Award for her role as O-Lan in Sidney Franklin's film adaptation of *The Good Earth*. The movie was, like Buck's novel, an enormous success. It was also an enormous undertaking. Producer Irving Thalberg had originally planned to film the whole of the movie in China, casting only Chinese and Chinese-American actors (one of the conditions that the Chinese government imposed before allowing the movie to be filmed there).[2] After an extensive search, however, Thalberg concluded that an exclusively Chinese cast was not possible. The decision was made instead to shoot primarily on location in Los Angeles, and to cast veteran Ukranian-American actor Paul Muni in the lead role of Wang Lung. The role of Wang's wife was given to German actress Luise Rainer. Anna May Wong, probably the most popular Chinese-American actress of the time, was offered the role of Wang's mistress, Lotus. Wong was incensed, offended that she was asked to play 'the only unsympathetic role' in the film, while the leads were played by white actors in make-up.[3] Part of the difficulty that the filmmakers found themselves in was that, having already cast a white actor at the male lead, casting a Chinese actress opposite him risked censorship for depicting *miscegenation* – interracial marriage – still illegal in several American states at the time, and explicitly outlawed by the film industry's content guidelines, the Motion Pictures Production Code.[4]

Although blackface – in which white actors are made up to play black characters – is largely a practice of the past, 'yellowface' has had surprising endurance.[5] Mickey Rooney's caricatured portrayal of Mr Yunishi in 1961's *Breakfast at Tiffany's* has long been the subject of scathing criticism, but Marlon Brando, Peter Sellers and Leonard Nimoy have all been made up to play Asian roles.[6] And, in 1983, white actress Linda Hunt won the Oscar for Best Supporting Actress for her portrayal of Chinese-Australian Billy Kwan in *The Year of Living Dangerously*.

In more recent years, the convention of yellowface has been largely (though not entirely) replaced with another controversial practice: what critics call 'whitewashing' – generally, the casting of white actors to play traditionally non-white roles (usually without being made up to appear non-white). In Marvel's 2016 superhero movie *Doctor Strange*, for example, the part of the Ancient One is played by Tilda Swinton. In the film, the Ancient One is a Celtic sorcerer, and so it may not be surprising that the actress playing her is white. But in the comics upon which the movie is based, the Ancient One is Tibetan. The 2017 film *Ghost in the Shell* is also based on a comic-book series, and similarly features a white performer (Scarlett Johansson) playing the role of what is an Asian character in the source material (Motoko Kusanagi). The controversy surrounding these casting decisions was undoubtedly heightened by the fact that their announcement came shortly after the 2016 Academy Awards, which itself drew controversy for being the second year in a row in which every nominated actor was white. Indeed, although Luise Rainer won the Academy Award for her role as O-Lan in *The Good Earth*, and Linda Hunt won the Oscar for her role in *The Year of Living Dangerously*, no actor of actual Chinese descent has *ever* been nominated for an Academy Award.

The central concern with whitewashing (and one of the problems with yellowface) is that Asian characters – as well as those of other ethnicities – are already sorely underrepresented in major films.[7] So, when a pre-established character of an underrepresented group (especially a fairly major character in the source material) is played by a white actor or replaced with a white character, the problem is only further perpetuated.

In the case of *Ghost in the Shell*, in order to justify the cost of making the film – a sci-fi special effects extravaganza – the producers needed a big star to headline, and it might be suggested that there simply aren't any Asian or Asian American actresses big enough to fit the bill. As actor and activist George Takei suggests, there isn't a single Asian American 'whose name you can take to the bank and get a project financed'.[8] But that, in itself, is telling. Graeme McMillan writes:

> A Kikuchi (who is four years older than Johansson) – or a similar Asian-American actress – couldn't have debuted as the daughter of John Ritter and Sean Connery, as Johansson did in her early films … She couldn't have effectively played an outsider in Tokyo in *Lost in Translation*, which catapulted her to stardom, or a Dutch painter's muse in *Girl With a Pearl Earring* … She couldn't have played a London magician's assistant in *The Prestige* or Mary Boleyn in *The Other Boleyn Girl*. And most of all, she never, ever would have been cast as the Black Widow in the Marvel Cinematic Universe.
>
> So how does an Asian actor become famous enough to play an Asian character?[9]

II. Artistic exclusion

McMillan is suggesting that Johansson's casting in *Ghost in the Shell* is not a singular event of whitewashing – an action we could simply attribute to the choice of one casting director or film producer – but is instead a symptom of a larger *system* of exclusion. A 2016 study of 109 current movies and 305 television and streaming series found that fully half of the films and series had no speaking or named Asian characters at all, and only a little more than 1 per cent had an Asian performer in a lead role.[10] The underrepresentation of minority actors and characters in major films is often blamed on a persistent belief that white audiences are unwilling to pay to see stories about non-white characters. Indeed, producers of the *Pokémon* television show reportedly had the eyes of one animated character redrawn because 'American test audiences felt he looked too Asian'.[11]

Bruce Lee famously entered the American public consciousness in 1966 playing the role of Kato in the short-lived TV action series *The Green Hornet*. According to an often-cited story, after working with executives at ABC and Warner Bros to develop a show about a Chinese martial arts master travelling the Wild West – which would eventually become the series *Kung Fu* – Lee was deemed 'too Asian' for the role, and white actor David Carradine was chosen instead. The story can be traced back to a 1975 memoir written by Lee's widow, Linda Lee Cadwell, and may well be apocryphal, but it captures a sentiment generally shared by Asian Americans in the film industry. Although it may seem ridiculous today that Bruce Lee could ever have been deemed 'too Asian' to play a Chinese kung fu master, being Asian remains a quantifiable barrier to working in Hollywood.

Things are not substantially better for black actors. Although George Takei names Denzel Washington as one of 'a whole host' of African Americans whose name could get a film financed, the disastrous 2014 leak of Sony corporate emails included one by an unnamed producer, sent to Sony's chairman, suggesting that Washington's being cast in the lead role in *The Equalizer* (2014) was the reason for the film's meagre revenues. 'I believe that the international motion picture audience is racist,' the producer writes; 'in general, pictures with an African-American lead don't play well overseas'.[12] A general belief that audiences do not want to watch movies about black characters (whether a true belief or not) may help to explain the lack of such characters on screen: although there *are* black headliners in Hollywood – Denzel Washington among them – the 2016 study mentioned above found that only 14.3 per cent of lead roles, and only 12.2 per cent of the characters overall, were black.

Black filmmaking has a long tradition in America, going back to the Lincoln Motion Picture Company. Founded in 1916 in response to D. W. Griffith's *Birth of a Nation* – a wildly successful 1913 movie, now infamous for its romantic depiction of the Ku Klux Klan and racist, demeaning portrait of African Americans – the all-black company produced a series of what were called 'race films', movies centred on the stories of realistic black characters. Mainstream movies with black protagonists were effectively unknown in the first half of the twentieth century, and black actors in American films were generally relegated to stereotyped roles as slaves, servants and villains. Studios like Lincoln worked to fill that vacuum, but usually only made a few films before folding (Lincoln only managed to produce five). In 1941, Hattie McDaniel became the first black performer to win an Academy Award, taking the Best Supporting Actress Oscar for her role as Mammy, the house servant in *Gone With the Wind*. Although the film was a critical and commercial success – earning back ten times its budget and winning eight of its record-setting thirteen Academy Award nominations – it has been widely criticized as historically revisionist in its glorification of slavery and depiction of African Americans. Shortly after the movie's release, filmmaker Carlton Moss complained in an open letter to the film's producer: 'Whereas "The Birth of a Nation" was a frontal attack on American history and the Negro people, "Gone with the Wind," arriving twenty years later, is a rear attack on the same.'[13] The film may have secured the first-ever black Oscar, but in doing so it further cemented and perpetuated a black stereotype.

Paul C. Taylor writes:

> Hollywood studios now embrace 'black' movies in a way that would have seemed unthinkable not that many years ago. But what counts as a black movie tends to be bound up with stereotypical characters and formulaic, whitely plots. And the black characters cannot be *too* black, especially if they are women, which is to say that leading ladies must be able to pass the brown paper bag test.[14]

A movie might be thought 'too black' because it has too many black actors (or actors whose skin is too dark), because it has black actors in too-prominent roles or because it revolves around a plot perceived to be too endemic to the black community. Making a film 'too black', Taylor says, 'threatens, or is thought to threaten, its marketability across populations.'[15] George Lucas's *Red Tails*, then, would have been the perfect storm: a film about the Tuskegee Airmen – a group of African American Second World War fighter pilots – featuring no major roles for white actors. Lucas worked on the film for twenty-three years, reporting that the film's unusually long development was due to an inability to interest the major studios in backing a film with no major white roles. Studios, he reports, wouldn't touch the film, saying: 'We don't know how to market a movie like this.' Ultimately Lucas financed the 2012 picture himself.[16]

The 'brown paper bag test' that Taylor mentions was a test infamously used in some American cities to determine who would be permitted into a party, a club or a church: if your skin was darker than a standard brown paper bag, you were left out on the street. Of course, black and Asian actors aren't the only ones who have been left out on the street. The 2016 study discussed above found that the characters in only 5 per cent of the 414 works studied were anywhere near the racial and ethnic proportions of the US population. And, of the 11,194 speaking characters identified in the study, only 158 were identifiably gay, male characters, only forty-nine were lesbians, seventeen were bisexual and seven were transgender: in total, some 2 per cent – and, even among these LGBT characters, the majority were white males.[17] Indeed, in general, male speaking roles outweighed female speaking roles two to one.

In 1985, comics creator Alison Bechdel published an instalment of her alternative strip, *Dykes to Watch Out For*, about two women discussing a 'rule' that one of them follows in picking a movie to watch. The rule, which gained attention in the 2010s, has come to be known as the *Bechdel Test*.[18] To pass the Bechdel Test, a movie must (1) have at least two (named) women in it (2) who talk to each other (3) about something other than a man. This may not sound like a terribly high bar, but as of 2016, 42.2 per cent of the 6,866 movies analysed at bechdeltest.com fail to reach that bar.

Although film and television are perhaps the easiest art forms to study in this regard – on-screen characters being fairly easily observed and counted – underrepresentation is a historical problem across the arts. In Chapter 6, we briefly discussed Linda Nochlin's famous 1971 essay, 'Why Have There Been No Great Women Artists?', in which she suggests that the field of art history is effectively the field of white, Western, male art. This is not simply, she contends, because we are ignoring the body of great female and non-white artists here in the West, but rather because there is no such body:

> The fact, dear sisters, is that there *are* no women equivalents for Michelangelo or Rembrandt, Delacroix or Cézanne, Picasso or Matisse, or even, in very recent times, for de Kooning or Warhol, any more than there are Black American equivalents for the same ... The miracle is, in fact, that so many of both have managed to achieve so much sheer excellence, in those bailiwicks of white masculine prerogative like science, politics or the arts.[19]

The history of Western art, Nochlin notes, is a history of exclusion. It is not that women or black artists lack (or ever have lacked) that special quality of genius. The issue is not a matter of genetics or biology, but of social institutions and education. Traditionally, students of the fine arts progressed through a fairly rigid academic programme, beginning with copying the drawings of the masters, to drawing from famous sculptures, to finally drawing from living models. But living models were traditionally in the nude, a subject (and object) considered inappropriate for women. As late as 1893, Nochlin notes, women were not admitted to life drawing at the Royal Academy of London – and when they eventually were, models had to be 'partially draped'. Thus deprived of training in nude models, women aspiring to be painters were generally restricted to 'minor' genres of portraiture, landscape or still life, from which 'great' artists generally did not arise. Those excluded from the academy altogether would be relegated to the traditionally even-less-serious 'decorative arts' of quilting, pottery and needlework.

Nearly half a century earlier, in a 1926 speech before the National Association for the Advancement of Colored People (NAACP), W. E. B. Du Bois made a strikingly similar observation:

> There is in New York tonight a black woman molding clay by herself in a little bare room, because there is not a single school of sculpture in New York where she is welcome. Surely there are doors she might burst through, but when God makes a sculptor He does not always make the pushing sort of person who beats his way through doors thrust in his face. This girl is working her hands off to get out of this country so that she can get some sort of training …
>
> We have, to be sure, a few recognized and successful Negro artists; but they are not all those fit to survive or even a good minority. They are but the remnants of that ability and genius among us whom the accidents of education and opportunity have raised on the tidal waves of chance. We black folk are not altogether peculiar in this. After all, in the world at large, it is only the accident, the remnant, that gets the chance to make the most of itself; but if this is true of the white world it is infinitely more true of the colored world.[20]

One of the women artists whom Nochlin mentions (but thus implies is no Michelangelo, Picasso or Warhol) is author Virginia Woolf. Perhaps ironically, then, Woolf herself made a similar observation about the exclusion of women from the arts in her narrative essay *A Room of One's Own*. Published in 1929, the title of Woolf's essay points to the idea that in order for a woman to write, she must have money and a room of her own – one with a lock and key. She must also have an education – a luxury denied most women in history (and a great many today). And if, by some miracle, she had these things, she could not expect to be published, at least not under her own name. Woolf writes: 'I would venture to guess that Anon, who wrote so many poems without signing them, was often a woman.'[21] Jane Austen's first novel, *Sense and Sensibility* was published anonymously; her second novel, *Pride and Prejudice*, carried the by-line 'By the author of "Sense and Sensibility"'. George Eliot, of course, was not christened with a man's name. Charlotte Brontë published under the pseudonym of Currer Bell, her sister Emily under the name Ellis Bell. And Mary Shelley's *Frankenstein* was first published anonymously in 1818, though word seems to have got out that its author was a woman. One reviewer wrote:

> The writer of it is, we understand, a female; this is an aggravation of that which is the prevailing fault of the novel; but if our authoress can forget the

gentleness of her sex, it is no reason why we should; and we shall therefore dismiss the novel without further comment.[22]

It was only towards the end of the nineteenth and beginning of the twentieth century that women authors were more generally taken seriously as writers, and on their own merits.

Although the institutional barriers that once categorically denied or limited access to the artworld on the basis of sex, gender, race or ethnicity have largely crumbled, the arts continue to be dominated by white, male artists. This may point at something deeper – something behind the art, in our more fundamental ideas of beauty.

III. Aesthetic exclusion

Carolyn Korsmeyer suggests that the problem may partly be grounded in a long-standing distinction traditionally separating the arts from the non-arts, and the aesthetic from the non-aesthetic. With few exceptions, all of the central arts focus attention on the visual or auditory aspects of experience: on seeing or hearing the work. The prioritization of seeing and hearing over the other senses goes back at least as far as Plato, who offers in his *Hippias Major* (as we have noted already in previous chapters) a definition of 'beauty' as 'the pleasant which comes through the senses of hearing and sight'.[23] Aristotle suggests that while the animal kingdom in general enjoys pleasures derived from touch, taste and smell, humans alone seem able to appreciate the cognitive and intellectual pleasures of sight and sound.[24] In his thirteenth-century treatise, the *Summa Theologica*, St Thomas Aquinas follows Aristotle in suggesting that sight and hearing are the primary 'aesthetic' senses because they are the most closely associated with the mind or intellect.[25] And this is echoed some 200 years later by Marsilio Ficino, who suggests that smell, taste and touch can only sense what is nearby, and so are essentially material, while sight and hearing (like the mind) can sense what is more remote, and so are more closely related to the soul. Beauty, like the soul, is incorporeal, and so is not to be found through those senses tied to matter.[26] Where the arts have generally appealed to the 'higher', 'intellectual' senses of sight and hearing, the 'lower' senses of smell, taste and touch have been the domain of perfumes, food, drink and clothing – the sensual and the domestic. Historically, the rational has been chiefly regarded as the domain of the male, and the emotional that of the female. And so, Korsmeyer suggests, the traditional hierarchy of senses reveals a:

marked gender dimension, for the higher senses turn out to be those the exercise of which develops 'masculine' traits and virtues. Here we see at work a conception of philosophy itself that has precluded serious attention to taste and to the other bodily senses, in part because they have been lumped into a category of 'the feminine' that traditionally has never contained much of interest to philosophers.[27]

Insofar as aesthetic judgement is treated as a remote, intellectual exercise, and the senses of taste, touch and smell are more strongly sensuous and emotional, on this understanding the aesthetic will be the domain of the masculine. In focusing on the visual and auditory, tying art to reason, art criticism limits the conditions for its experience and appreciation (and so its audience). Feminist art critic Joanna Frueh writes:

> Art criticism, like other disciplines that privilege the intellect, is generally deprived of the spontaneous knowing of intuition – of knowledge derived from the senses and experience as well as the mind … Knowing is being alive, wholly, not just intellectually.[28]

That is, Frueh suggests, knowing is not simply the domain of the traditionally masculine intellect, but should also be understood to include the sensuous and the emotional – the traditional domain of the feminine. So long as aesthetic knowing is tied to the intellect (and the intellect in turn is tied to the visual and the auditory), we should not be surprised to find the artworld dominated by men.

This prioritization of the intellect in aesthetic judgement is most closely tied to the views of Hume and Kant, who together set the direction for much of Western aesthetics over the next two centuries. But, Monique Roelofs suggests, there are further difficulties to be found here. In Chapter 3, we discussed Hume's view that the ideal judge must become someone who is, as much as possible, a 'man in general', free from any bias or prejudice in his evaluation of art. Following him, Kant similarly contends that in order to be 'pure', our aesthetic judgements must be disinterested, disconnected from any goals or concepts had by the judge: without anything peculiar about the judge infecting the process, and working on the assumption that any other similarly disinterested judge will have the same faculties of judgement, we are then justified in believing that our aesthetic evaluations will hold universally. Kant's view is that pure aesthetic judgements are made solely on the feelings that arise in appropriately positioned judges. However, it would seem that Kant does not actually believe that every person has these same basic faculties required for an appreciation of beauty. Blacks in particular – Kant contends – 'have by nature no feeling that rises above the trifling'.[29] Presumably, then, a black man would be incapable of the sort of feeling involved in a pure experience of beauty, and because this deficiency is in him by nature, there is (unlike the white man) nothing he can do about it. (Things do not fare much better for members of other races in Kant's estimation.)[30] It would seem that when Kant speaks about the faculties shared by everyone, he means 'all white men', not 'all humans'.[31] Kant points to an earlier essay of Hume, who writes: 'I am apt to suspect the negroes to be naturally inferior to the whites'.[32] A talented black man, Hume submits, is on par with the parrot that learns a few words of English: uncivilized and naturally inferior. '[T]here is reason to think,' Hume contends, 'that all the nations, which live beyond the polar circles or between the tropics, are inferior to the rest of the species, and are incapable of all the higher attainments of the human mind.'[33] Hume pronounces the ideal judge to be a 'man in general', but it would seem that the man in general *is a white man*.[34]

As Roelofs summarizes the matter, the theories of Kant and Hume 'render the aesthetic white'[35]. Now, we could simply reject as empirically false the contentions of Hume and Kant that non-whites, or non-males, will lack the necessary faculties to assess beauty on their own accounts. Although he is famous for advancing a view of empiricism, Hume is doing little more than armchair anthropology here, and despite what he writes here and in other essays on the races of the world, Kant is known for having never travelled more than a hundred miles outside his hometown of Königsberg. Kant's view on race comes from much earlier in his career than his more developed view on aesthetic judgement, and we might hope that he has matured in his views. Pauline Kleingeld notes that, by the time Kant has worked out his aesthetic theory, the topic of race has almost entirely disappeared from his writing, and he appears to have abandoned the view that there is anything like a hierarchy among the races, or any natural differences between them in character.[36] Certainly, to accept Hume's view, or Kant's, on aesthetic judgement, we do not need to accept any views they might hold about the natural faculties of the races. Nevertheless, Taylor writes, '[t]he objective gaze is the whitely gaze'.[37]

With 'whitely gaze', Taylor is playing off the term *male gaze*, coined by film theorist Laura Mulvey to describe the dominantly heterosexual male perspective in cinema.[38] The term describes the viewpoint of the filmmaker, but also that of the characters and, relatedly, what the viewer is required to adopt in order to watch and understand the work. Watching a film, Mulvey argues, usually requires the viewer to *identify* with the default heterosexual male perspective – most pointedly by sexually objectifying the female subjects of that gaze – and resisting that perspective will (more often than not) conflict with the film itself. Worse, this male, heterosexual viewpoint is treated as the *norm*. Similarly, Taylor argues, 'whitely' ways of seeing, which require the viewer to adopt the hegemonic perspective (which notably disregards and demeans non-white people) have become the social default – a viewpoint so standard in what is expected of audiences that we have come to regard it as the universal, objective viewpoint – exactly what the views of Hume and Kant would seem to prescribe. As Peggy Brand notes, however, '[t]he general consensus' among scholars 'is that there is no disinterested gazer of visual images, only one whose gaze is saturated with interest'.[39] Rather than seeking to eliminate the personal and unique from aesthetic experience, we might ask, why not revel in those differences in our appreciation of art?

Tobin Siebers observes that attempts to exclude women and those of other races from aesthetic assessment have largely been made on groundless claims that women, blacks, Asians and others lack some requisite ability – either physical or mental – and so are *inferior*. That is, at the basis of all such disqualification is some difference treated as a natural defect, weakness or inferiority: a *disability*. 'Disability,' Siebers says, 'is the master trope of human disqualification.'[40] Mental disabilities in particular are selected as disqualifiers for both the creation and appreciation of art. Traditionally, the appreciation of beauty is treated as a matter of refined and disinterested *taste*, and the creation of art a matter of innate *genius*. Siebers writes:

> The appreciation of the work of art is a topic well rehearsed in the history of aesthetics, but rarely is it considered from the vantage point of the disabled mind – no doubt because the spectacle of the mentally disabled person, rising with emotion before the shining work of art, disrupts the long-standing belief that pronouncements of taste depend on a form of intelligence as autonomous and imaginative as the art object itself.[41]

David Hume describes the desirable *delicacy of taste* as a disposition to be calmly affected by beauty, and distinguishes it from the undesirable *delicacy of passion* – an inclination to be overcome by violent passions in the face of prosperity or misfortune.[42] The disabled mind may be unable to achieve the delicacy Hume contends is proper or necessary to the appreciation of beauty. And, Siebers notes, as the notion of aesthetic judgement has long been focused on an image of the detached judge, the whole of aesthetic value – of beauty – has been couched in a narrow understanding of perfection and harmony, of formal integrity and perfect health. The field of *disability aesthetics*, Siebers suggests, 'embraces beauty that seems by traditional standards to be broken, and yet is not less beautiful, but more so, as a result'.[43] On what grounds can we claim that a cracked vase is less beautiful than an intact one? To suggest that the unbroken vessel is more beautiful *because* it is unbroken rather puts the cart before the horse. Indeed, Siebers notes, modern and contemporary art have embraced the 'broken beauty' of disability, treating disability as an aesthetic value in itself – its own sort of beauty.

For the 'broken beauty' of disability in modern art, we might think of Picasso's iconic depictions of the human form. Or we might think of Frida Kahlo, who was born with congenital spina bifida, contracted polio when she was 6 years old and was seriously injured in a bus collision when she was 18. Kahlo endured a lifetime of operations, chronic pain and fatigue, and these are unabashedly depicted in her art – mostly self-portraits. Anita Silvers writes: 'Art has a positive transfigurative – almost a redemptive – effect on configurations we otherwise would apprehend as being ugly … Art can make impairment powerful.'[44] In general, Siebers writes, twentieth- and twenty-first-century art is pervaded by representations of traumatic injury, psychological alienation, a 'love affair with misshapen and twisted bodies' and the 'stunning variety of human forms'.[45]

Feminist art and black aesthetics have in turn worked to throw off inherited presumptions about the nature of art and artistic beauty, and the dominance of the white, male gaze as the objective standard. Rejecting the art/craft distinction that often left women out of the artworld, feminist art has embraced an approach to art that is more tactile, often working with materials and methods traditionally deemed 'craft' by the artworld at large. Works like Judy Chicago's groundbreaking installation *The Dinner Party* further employ imagery and narratives that serve to deconstruct or replace the male gaze and to build a community among women. Black aesthetics has similarly – and perhaps more explicitly – rejected the notion of 'art' that opened this book, pointing instead to African cultures and African American practices that do not reflect the same art/non-art distinctions that developed in European society in the eighteenth century. In general, black aesthetics works 'to expose the whitely pretensions to universality and neutrality that deny black perspectives',[46] and to study how those perspectives inform black art and black communities.

IV. Authenticity and appropriation

The black aesthetic, Taylor argues, was never a disinterested matter. Quite the opposite. Consider, for example, the genre of blues music, which developed in African American communities in the Mississippi Delta and East Texas in the late nineteenth and early twentieth centuries before spreading north, then nationwide, then worldwide. At its core, Taylor argues, the blues is a *racial project* – it is a 'cultural space within which the meaning of race is articulated'.[47] That is, Taylor argues, the blues is very much *about* being black – both for the performer and for the audience. More specifically, the blues is about life as an African American – 'a member of an oppressed and downwardly constituted social category, subject to racialized hostile misfortune'.[48] The blues is about being a member of this particular disenfranchised American community – and this, Taylor says, is true of both performer and audience. The audience of a blues performance was not supposed to become (to borrow again Hume's term) a 'man in general', was not supposed to be disinterested – but was rather expected to be *very* interested. The blues singer spoke to the audience as a member of that same community. As such, Taylor suggests, a white blues musician like Eric Clapton or Eva Cassidy can't play the blues – not because a white musician is incapable of learning the chord progressions of blues guitar, or of singing the specialized notes known as 'blues notes', but because playing the blues is not simply a matter of plucking guitar strings in the right way, or of singing the right words to the right melody. Playing the blues involves speaking as a member of a community. One way to think of this is that the blues involves a certain sort of call-and-response structure, evolving out of musical expression in Sub-Saharan African cultures, which required the engagement and involvement of the audience in the perfor-mance. The problem for the white blues musician, Taylor argues, is that the audience would not accept such a singer as speaking from their communal perspective – would not respond to that singer as a member of their community. As such, Taylor agrees with critic Ralph Gleason, who says that 'the blues is black man's music, and whites diminish it at best or steal it at worst. In any case, they have no moral right to use it.'[49]

Joel Rudinow argues that if the blues is an essentially racial project, then it is an evolving one – and one that could (or should) allow for a white blues performer. If the question is not a matter of musical ability, then to say that one can or cannot play the blues would seem to be a matter of *authenticity* – of whether the performer can legitimately claim the necessary relation to the original source of the blues. However, Rudinow notes, most contemporary black Americans have no more direct access to the experience of living as a black American on the Mississippi Delta during the 1920s than does the average contemporary white American. It may be, Rudinow suggests, that what's essential is membership in the community that evolved from those communities of beleaguered black sharecroppers in the American Deep South who originally developed the blues. And it may very well be that a black American blues musician today could claim a better connection to those earlier communities than could the average white musician. But, Rudinow contends, there is nothing here that would disbar a white musician *in principle* from being initiated into the requisite community.[50] In Rudinow's view, the blues is probably better described as a *cultural* project than an essentially racial one.

James O. Young suggests that, insofar as Eric Clapton's own culture is not the culture in which the blues originated, and insofar as he takes the blues for his own use, he is committing an act of *cultural appropriation*.[51] Specifically, Young suggests, Clapton's appropriation is a kind of *style appropriation*: the taking of a stylistic form endemic to (or born out of) a culture of which one is not a member. Insofar as the blues is a stylistically peculiar genre, characterized by cyclical chord progression – particularly what are called 12-bar blues or 8-bar blues – stanza structure, melody and duration, it is a form that any sufficiently talented musician could learn and adopt. Although better known for his rock music, there is little doubt that Clapton has adopted and mastered the form of the blues. (As blues legend Buddy Guy says of him, 'Eric's got it.')[52] But, as a white Englishman, Clapton seems personally far removed from the African American culture in which the blues originated.

Style appropriation is not restricted to musical styles, of course. We might think of the stylistic 'tribal' tattoos inspired by the Māori of New Zealand, or of colourful Mexican 'sugar skull' designs, or of the complex mandalas from Indian Buddhists. Each of these stylistic forms has been adopted by Westerners who cannot reasonably claim membership in the cultures from which those styles originated. Related to style appropriation is what Young calls *motif appropriation*, where an artist is *influenced* by the works of another culture, but without their new works being in the same *style*. Here, Young identifies Picasso's *Les Demoiselles d'Avignon*, which is clearly influenced by West African mask carving – particularly the masks of the Fang people of the Bantu – but without being in precisely the same style.

Jazz has similarly appropriated motifs from African music, merging these traditional forms into new jazz styles.

Taylor might argue that Clapton's blues appropriation more properly belongs to another category identified by Young: *subject* or *voice appropriation*. With this form of appropriation, one *depicts* another's culture, but does so as an outsider rather than an insider. If Clapton cannot claim membership in the community that can legitimately play the blues, then he can only ever do so as an outsider. Of particular concern with subject appropriation is that the outsider may be taken to be speaking *as* an insider – to be speaking with an authentic voice he cannot have.

The central worry about cultural appropriation is that it represents yet another form of colonization and subordination – in this case, of African Americans. In his 1963 book *Blues People*, Amiri Baraka argues that white musicians co-opted black music – specifically blues and jazz – by transforming it from an African American cultural practice to an American *art form*. If an art form is something defined by its form – say, its chord progressions and specialized notes – then it is something that anyone could learn. But the *blues*, Baraka writes, 'means a Negro experience, it is the one music the Negro made that could not be transferred into a more general significance than the one the Negro gave it initially'.[53] The white musician could understand the blues as a musical form, but not as an attitude or world-view.

Related to subject or voice appropriation is Young's category of *content appropriation*: the reuse of an idea first expressed in the work of an artist from another culture.[54] Here, Young identifies the work of poet Robert Bringhurst as appropriating the traditional stories of the Haida people of Canada's west coast. Also fitting into this category might be the flag of New Mexico, which uses the ancient, iconic red sun symbol of the indigenous Zia people, or the logo for the 2010 Winter Olympics in Vancouver, British Columbia, which centrally depicts an inuksuk, a traditional cultural symbol of the Inuit and other native Arctic peoples.

We might also think of Disney's 1992 film *Aladdin*, adapted from the story of Aladdin and his magic lamp in *The One Thousand and One Nights*, a collection of Middle Eastern and South Asian stories tracing back to the eighth century, and possibly much, much earlier. But, in fact, the story of Aladdin was added to the growing collection in the eighteenth century by French scholar Antoine Galland, and appears to have no original version in Arabic.[55] In other words, Galland seems to have invented a story about Middle Eastern or Asian culture – an act of *subject* appropriation, not *content* appropriation. Disney would appear to be appropriating content from eighteenth-century French culture, not an earlier, more distant one. A similar pattern can be found with Disney's 1967 and 2016 adaptations of *The Jungle Book* (1894) by English author Rudyard Kipling. Is it permissible for us to tell stories originating in nineteenth-century England or eighteenth-century France? Does it matter if *those* stories were works of subject appropriation? In general, we might ask, what exactly is wrong with telling the stories of – or depicting – another culture? What's wrong with using the styles and motifs of another culture's art? So far as it goes, Young argues, there *isn't* anything wrong with using the stories, image, styles or motifs of another culture. The problem arises when that act of taking causes *harm* or *profound offence*, and not all such acts will do so.

In general, a harm is a setback to one's interests, so an act of cultural appropriation will constitute a cultural harm if it brings about a setback to the interests of a culture. If blues music belongs to the black American community, and a white musician like Eric Clapton or Eva Cassidy profits from his or her appropriation of that music, Young submits, then that would qualify as a harm – as a form of theft. Similar harm would be caused if culturally appropriative products by outsiders – say, through cheaper mass production – pushed insiders' works out of the market. But harm can come in other forms as well. Subject appropriation that misrepresents its subjects – say, by introducing or perpetuating a stereotype – may certainly be harmful to a community. This is the complaint often levied against Kipling and Disney. Content and style appropriation may likewise misrepresent the works of a culture, and so diminish the dignity of that culture in the eyes of others. Worse, Young suggests, is that insiders might come to see *themselves* through the distorted lenses of outsiders' eyes. The acute worry is that those insiders might treat the flawed appropriative works of outsiders as authentic, imitating these and beginning a downward spiral to assimilation – the absorption of that culture into the larger, dominant culture.

However, Young argues, a representation by an outsider is not necessarily a *misrepresentation*. Indeed, an outsider may offer an accurate or fresh perspective, while an insider may misrepresent or poorly represent her own culture. The insider may just as easily cause as much harm as the outsider – more, in fact, since the insider's work (even if flawed) is more likely to be treated as authentic and accurate. And although Young identifies cultural assimilation as the single greatest threat to minority cultures, the danger, he argues, does not arise from the cultural appropriation, but from the insiders' failing to protect themselves against appropriation. 'Insiders,' Young argues, 'bear the primary responsibility for the perpetuation of their culture.'[56] And the introduction of appropriated works into the market may as easily open new markets for works of minority cultures as choke them out of those markets. A harm may be a wrong by definition, but cultural appropriation is not itself harmful by definition on Young's view.

The other way an act of cultural appropriation could be wrong, Young suggests, is by being profoundly offensive. This will occur when the appropriation is an affront to the culture it is taken from, striking at the core values or very identity of that culture. Young offers as examples the 2005 cartoon depictions of Muhammad in the Danish newspaper *Jyllands-Posten*, which offended a great many Muslims, and George Southwell's *Labour* mural, installed in the British Columbia Legislature in 1935, which degradingly depicts First Nations people as 'conquered and subservient'.[57] Amiri Baraka would probably put white blues music in the category of things profoundly offensive to African American identity. In general, Young submits:

> One ought not to cause widespread profound offence, especially not to members of a culture that has already suffered serious harms and affronts, and especially not if one can make a living in a way that is not the source of offence.[58]

However, Young argues, we need to distinguish between *reasonable* offence and *unreasonable* offence. Although drawing that line precisely may well be impossible, Young suggests that 'Old Hollywood Westerns that represent Indians as cruel and duplicitous are certainly the source of reasonable offence.'[59] But, Young suggests, we cannot simply say that because an act is profoundly offensive, it is thus wrong. It may be that the social value of the offensive work outweighs the offence itself, or it may be that the act of censoring that work would be morally worse than the work itself.

Returning to the discussion of the blues that opened this section, several music critics and musicologists have raised the case of white harmonica player Paul Butterfield, who started hanging out in the blues clubs of Chicago in 1957. Often the only white person in the club, Butterfield would sit in on sessions whenever he could. Before long, he was apprenticing with blues harmonica masters Little Walker and Junior Wells. Steve Huey writes:

> It's impossible to underestimate the importance of the doors Butterfield opened: before he came to prominence, white American musicians treated the blues with cautious respect, afraid of coming off as inauthentic. Not only did Butterfield clear the way for white musicians to build upon blues tradition (instead of merely replicating it), but his storming sound was a

major catalyst in bringing electric Chicago blues to white audiences who'd previously considered acoustic Delta blues the only really genuine article.[60]

Butterfield, Huey suggests, played the blues *authentically*, despite being white. But was Butterfield also *appropriating* the blues? Jeannette Bicknell suggests: 'The kind of authenticity under discussion – fidelity to a tradition – makes sense only within a social group to whom the concept is important and who can be in a position to pronounce on questions surrounding it.'[61] Ultimately, Bicknell argues, whether someone is playing the blues *authentically* is up to the blues community at large. Clapton and Cassidy have been widely praised by blues musicians and critics alike. Butterfield was *invited* into the blues community and trained by its master musicians. Can you appropriate what is given to you? Of course, one might ask whether Little Walker or Junior Wells had the *power* to invite Butterfield into the blues community – to give him the stage. If not, we might ask, who *would* have that power? Who gets to act on behalf of a culture? In general, Bicknell suggests that authenticity is a matter for both the performer *and* the audience, and that playing or listening authentically involves adopting an attitude of *moral deference* by focusing 'on the pain of others, both historically and currently'.[62] More generally, Bicknell adds:

> Adopting an attitude of moral deference – finding out which songs might be important to which audiences, thinking about why certain material has the significance that it does, and what kind of performance best honors this significance – will increase our sensitivity as listeners. If we listen well enough it will also increase our moral sensitivity more generally, and such a result could only be to the good.[63]

V. Our bodies, ourselves

Given the discussion of identity, exclusion and diversity that has pervaded this chapter, it would be negligent to leave out discussion of the aesthetics of the human body. Despite its central place in ordinary talk of beauty,[64] the human body has received little special attention by philosophers until quite recently. Philosophers studying beauty have tended to suggest that what makes the human body beautiful is the same thing that made anything else beautiful – proportion, harmony or variety, for example. So, for these philosophers, human beauty is no different from the beauty of a flower, a painting or a song. But, Sherri Irvin writes:

A crucial thing about bodies is that they are not detachable from the persons whose bodies they are. The body is deeply intertwined with one's identity and sense of self, and aesthetic consideration of bodies thus raises acute ethical questions. Notoriously, the aesthetic assessment of bodies can perpetuate a variety of forms of oppression.[65]

And so, the aesthetics of the human body raises special concerns regarding identity, exclusion and diversity.

In his 1757 treatise *A Philosophical Inquiry into the Origin of Our Ideas of the Sublime and Beautiful* – in a section titled 'Darkness Terrible in its Own Nature' – Edmund Burke suggests we have a natural fear of darkness, and so a natural fear of black bodies. Burke recalls third-hand the story of a boy, blind since birth, who has had his cataracts removed: 'the first time the boy saw a black object, it gave him great uneasiness; and … some time after, upon accidentally seeing a negro woman, he was struck with great horror at the sight'.[66] Burke uses the story as purported evidence that the white fear of black bodies is simply innate and natural: the boy had no associations with black persons, so the fear must simply have been fear of darkness. Two and a half centuries later, things have not changed much. George Yancy suggests that, under the whitely gaze, the black body is criminal, dangerous. 'Like the night,' Yancy writes, 'I am to be avoided. After all, peril lurks in the dark.'[67] As he notes, 'yellow bodies', 'brown bodies' and 'red bodies' have been similarly criminalized under the whitely gaze. At several points in history, for example, white Westerners have spread what Kaiser Wilhelm II of Germany called 'the Yellow Peril' – a xenophobic fear of the 'rising tide' of Asians. Today, the brown bodies of Middle Easterners and Hispanics are probably as criminalized under the whitely gaze as the black body. Conversely, Yancy suggests, the white body has carried the presumption of innocence and purity, or at least neutrality. Worse, the white body has become the *universal* body under its own gaze – the only body *not* defined in terms of its race, the default.

Curiously, a little later in his treatise, Burke writes: 'Black bodies, reflecting none, or but a few rays, with regard to sight are but as so many vacant spaces dispersed among the objects we view.'[68] Burke is writing about 'bodies' in a very broad sense to include all physical objects, but human bodies will be among these. Whether he means to or not, Burke reflects something curious about the black human body under the whitely gaze: when it isn't threatening, it's invisible. Invisibility has become the standard term since Ralph Ellison borrowed the title of an H. G. Wells story for his own 1952 novel, *Invisible Man*. Ellison's novel opens:

I am an invisible man. No, I am not a spook like those who haunt Edgar Allan Poe, nor am I one of your Hollywood-movie ectoplasms. I am a man of substance, of flesh and bone, fiber and liquids – and I might even be said to possess a mind. I am invisible, understand, simply because people refuse to see me … The invisibility to which I refer occurs because of a peculiar disposition of the eyes of those with whom I come into contact. A matter of the construction of their *inner* eyes, those eyes with which they look through their physical eyes upon reality.[69]

The invisibilizing of black bodies, Taylor suggests, manifests several forms of denial or disregard towards black persons. Physically, the history of racial segregation and ghettoization has placed visual minorities outside the view and contact of whites. And where those minorities – and blacks in particular – are integrated into white society, they are often relegated to positions of low social standing, further reinforcing their invisibility. In movies, Taylor notes, black characters largely serve as vehicles for developing white characters and driving white plots, disappearing into the background when they aren't needed.[70] Even when the film is ostensibly *about* black characters, Taylor notes – as in *Mississippi Burning*, Alan Parker's 1988 movie about the disappearance of three civil rights workers in Jessup County, Mississippi – the black characters effectively become set dressing, an interchangeable mass of victims. Taylor calls this 'the purest form of invizibilization'.[71]

It isn't only the black body that is rendered invisible by the whitely gaze, of course. David Haekwon Kim says: 'I believe the invisibility of Asian-Americans in our culture has been so deep and enduring that Asian-Americans themselves are often ambivalent about how they would like to see themselves portrayed and perhaps even uncomfortable about being portrayed at all.'[72] By contrast, then, Tobin Siebers notes, the disabled body is *hypervisible* – at least when appearing on the stage or screen. In the traditional mindset, the disability becomes 'a distraction at the very least, an obstacle at most', Siebers writes.[73] According to Sigmund Freud, the portrayal of physical and mental disability cannot be converted into aesthetic pleasure for the audience, but summons a feeling of suffering that bars the audience's identification with the characters.[74] Simply put, the spectacle of disability stands between the audience and the art. Perhaps, you say, you can think of disability portrayed to great effect on the stage or screen. You might point at Daniel Day Lewis's Oscar-winning performance in *My Left Foot*, depicting Christy Brown's real-life struggle with cerebral palsy. Or you might point at Dustin Hoffman's Oscar-winning perfor-mance as Raymond Babbitt, an autistic savant, in *Rain Man*. But now note that neither of these Oscar winners has the disabilities they portrayed in their respective movies. Can you think instead of a role played by a visibly disabled performer, but where the character portrayed does not have that disability? Although we will accept normally abled actors playing characters with superabilities – Gal Gadot as Wonder Woman, Mike Colter as Luke Cage, anyone as Sherlock Holmes – we have serious difficulties accepting a disabled actor in a normally abled role. Of course, Siebers notes, when the visibly disabled person is not on the stage or the screen, but on the street, that person is rendered invisible: 'There is no disability so obvious that it cannot go unnoticed.'[75]

Perhaps no body is more maligned than the fat body. Anne Eaton writes that:

> distaste for fat bodies lies at the center of what I shall call our *collective taste in bodies*; that is, the set of aesthetic preferences for particular body-types that dominates the prevailing forms of cultural expression in our society today.[76]

We live, Eaton says, 'in a fat-hating world' where fatness is 'routinely portrayed as a paradigm of unattractiveness, especially for women'.[77] Disgust with the fat body is often treated as a perfectly natural or evolutionarily developed response, or else it is justified on the basis that fat bodies are unhealthy bodies. To dispel the 'health objection', Eaton points to recent studies showing that, short of class 2 obesity (where body mass index exceeds 35.0), the effects of fatness on health – morbidity or mortality – are negligible or grossly exaggerated. And, Eaton notes, in any event, we don't aesthetically discriminate against other bodies whose state does represent a significant health risk, like those with breast implants, anorexia nervosa or tanned skin. In general, taste for bodies would seem to be strongly subject to social pressures, as historically and culturally variable as many of our other preferences. Eaton points by way of example at the celebrated paintings of Peter Paul Rubens, whose name has been adjectivized as 'Rubenesque': 'of, relating to, or suggestive of the painter Rubens or his works; *especially*: plump or rounded usually in a pleasing or attractive way'.[78]

In his *Crito* of 1752, Joseph Spence (under the pen name Harry Beaumont) writes that 'some may delight themselves in a black Skin, and others in a white; some in a gentle natural Rosiness of Complexion, others in a high, exalted, artificial Red; some Nations, in Waists disproportionably large; and another in Waists as disproportionably small. In short, the most opposite Things imaginable may each be looked upon as beautiful, in whole different Countries; or by different People, in the same Country.'[79] (Not all eighteenth-century Western philosophers held as problematic views on the aesthetics of race as Burke, Hume and Kant.) What one finds beautiful in the human body, Spence suggests, is a matter of *custom* or *fancy* – of social standards and personal preference. The difficulty is that custom, arbitrary though it may be, nevertheless normalizes and exalts certain bodies over others. Even knowing all of this – and that the customary preferences normalized in our society serve to marginalize those who do not fit the mould – Eaton notes, our preferences for bodies resist rational persuasion, and may often conflict with our other strongly-held attitudes and commitments. We may know that it is at best arbitrary and at worst *wrong* to prefer one kind of body to another, but knowing that may have little effect on our preferences. Instead, Eaton suggests, we need to engage in the practice of what she calls 'bending taste', particularly in the direction of fat acceptance: we need to 'produce and widely promote vivid, imaginatively engaging, and artistically interesting representations that *celebrate* fat bodies and encourage us to see them as likeable and attractive'.[80]

Chapter summary

This chapter has focused on a number of topics that might broadly be categorized as issues of race, gender and disability, of inclusion and exclusion, or of diversity in art and aesthetics. We opened with a discussion of exclusion from the arts, particularly through whitewashing and the institutional exclusion of women. We then looked at how the history of philosophy and the arts has similarly excluded non-whites, women and the disabled from the domain of aesthetic judgement, and how new movements have pushed back at this exclusion by embracing difference. We considered issues of authenticity and various forms of cultural appropriation, and then finally focused on the aesthetics of the human body.

Historical timeline

	c. 390 BCE	Plato, *Hippias Major*
	c. 350 BCE	Aristotle, *Eudemian Ethics*
Various, *The One Thousand and One Nights*	c. 800	
	c. 1274	St Thomas Aquinas, *Summa Theologica*
	1469	Marsilio Ficino, *Commentarium in Convivium Platonis, de Amore*
	1742	David Hume, 'Of the Delicacy of Taste and Passion'
	1748	David Hume, 'Of National Characters'
	1752	Joseph Spence, *Crito: or a Dialogue on Beauty*
	1757	David Hume, 'Of the Standard of Taste'
		Edmund Burke, *A Philosophical Inquiry into the Origin of Our Ideas of the Sublime and Beautiful*
	1764	Immanuel Kant, 'Observations of the Feeling of the Beautiful and Sublime'
	1790	Immanuel Kant, *The Critique of Judgment*
Jane Austen, *Sense and Sensibility*	1811	
Jane Austen, *Pride and Prejudice*	1813	
Mary Shelley, *Frankenstein*	1818	
Rudyard Kipling, *The Jungle Book*	1894	
Pablo Picasso, *Les Demoiselles d'Avignon*	1907	
D. W. Griffith, *The Birth of a Nation*	1913	
	1926	W. E. B. Du Bois, 'Criteria for Negro Art'
	1929	Virginia Woolf, *A Room of One's Own*

Pearl S. Buck, *The Good Earth*	1932	
George Southwell, *Labour*	1935	
Sidney Franklin, *The Good Earth*	1937	
Victor Fleming, *Gone With the Wind*	1939	
Blake Edwards, *Breakfast at Tiffany's*	1961	
	1963	Amiri Baraka, *Blues People: Negro Music in White America*
Various, *The Green Hornet*	1966–7	
Wolfgang Reitherman, *The Jungle Book*	1967	
	1971	Linda Nochlin, 'Why Have There Been No Great Women Artists?'
Various, *Kung Fu*	1972–5	
Judy Chicago, *The Dinner Party*	1974-79	
	1975	Laura Mulvey, 'Visual Pleasure and Narrative Cinema'
Peter Weir, *The Year of Living Dangerously*	1982	
Alison Bechdel, *Dykes to Watch Out For*	1983–2008	
Barry Levinson, *Rain Man* Alan Parker, *Mississippi Burning*	1988	Joanna Frueh, 'Towards a Feminist Theory of Art Criticism'
Jim Sheridan, *My Left Foot*	1989	
Ron Clements and John Musker, *Aladdin*	1992	
	1994	Joel Rudinow, 'Race, Ethnicity, Expressive Authenticity: Can White People Sing the Blues?'
	1995	Paul C. Taylor, '... So Black and Blue: Response to Rudinow'
	1999	Carolyn Korsmeyer, *Making Sense of Taste: Food and Philosophy*
	2000	Anita Silvers, 'From the Crooked Timber of Humanity, Beautiful Things Can Be Made'
	2007	Pauline Kleingeld, 'Kant's Second Thoughts on Race'

	2008	James O. Young, *Cultural Appropriation and the Arts*
		George Yancy, *Black Bodies, White Gazes*
	2009	Jeanette Bicknell, 'Reflections on "John Henry"'
	2010	Tobin Siebers, *Disability Aesthetics*
George Lucas, *Red Tails*	2012	
Antoine Fuqua, *The Equalizer*	2014	Monique Roelofs, *The Cultural Promise of the Aesthetic*
Scott Derrickson, *Doctor Strange*	2016	Paul C. Taylor, *Black is Beautiful: A Philosophy of Black Aesthetics*
Jon Favreau, *The Jungle Book*		Sherri Irvin, *Body Aesthetics*
		A. W. Eaton, 'Taste in Bodies and Fat Oppression'
		Tobin Siebers, 'In/Visible: Disability on the Stage'
Rupert Sanders, *Ghost in the Shell*	2017	

Key terms and concepts

- Authenticity (p. 203)
- Bechdel Test (p. 195)
- Bending Taste (p. 211)
- Black Aesthetics (p. 201)
- Blackface and Yellowface (p. 191)
- Content Appropriation (p. 204)
- Cultural Appropriation (p. 203)
- Cultural Assimilation (p. 205)
- Delicacy of Passion (p. 200)
- Delicacy of Taste (p. 200)
- Disability Aesthetics (p. 201)
- Feminist Art (p. 201)
- Harm (p. 205)
- 'Higher' and 'Lower' Senses (p. 197)
- Invisibilization (p. 209)
- Male Gaze (p. 199)
- Moral Deference (p. 207)

- Motif Appropriation (p. 203)
- Profound Offence (p. 205)
- Reasonable vs Unreasonable Offence (p. 206)
- Style Appropriation (p. 203)
- Subject or Voice Appropriation (p. 204)
- Whitely Gaze (p. 199)
- Whitewashing (p. 191)

Further reading

The topics filling this chapter – on race, gender, disability and the aesthetics of the human body – have been surprisingly overlooked by analytic aestheticians and philosophers of art until quite recently. As such, most of the sources discussed in this chapter fall into three groups: (1) philosophical writing of the last two decades; (2) philosophical writing of the eighteenth century; and (3) non-philosophical writing. For reasons that may be obvious after reading this chapter, most of the writing from the second category does not get reprinted much these days. But material in the first category is burgeoning, and well worth taking time to comb through. Paul C. Taylor's 2016 book, *Black is Beautiful* (Blackwell), is particularly rewarding. I would also recommend James O. Young's *Cultural Appropriation and the Arts* (Blackwell, 2008), Carolyn Korsmeyer's *Making Sense of Taste* (Cornell University Press, 1999) and *Gender and Aesthetics* (Routledge, 2004) and Tobin Siebers's *Disability Aesthetics* (University of Michigan Press, 2010). Two excellent collections of essays are *The Ethics of Cultural Appropriation* (Blackwell, 2009), edited by James O. Young and Conrad G. Brunk, and Sherri Irvin's *Body Aesthetics* (Oxford University Press, 2016). The category of non-philosophical writing is extensive, and will take a long time to wade through. I would particularly recommend the writing of W. E. B. Du Bois and Amiri Baraka, and – as a starting place – Hilary Robinson's robust collection, *Feminism Art Theory: An Anthology 1968–2014* (2nd edn, Wiley, 2015).

Unresolved questions

1 In the opening section of this chapter, we learned about Tilda Swinton's casting as the Ancient One in *Doctor Strange* – traditionally the character of a Tibetan man. In fact, the original character of the

Ancient One in the *Doctor Strange* comics is a tired stereotype of the wise, old Asian mystic, which some would argue is itself racist. However, the character of the Ancient One is integral to Doctor Strange's origin story. So, if you were going to make a *Doctor Strange* movie, is it better to cast an Asian man in the problematically stereotypical role, or to do what the filmmakers did and move about as far from that stereotype as possible by reinventing the Ancient One as a Celtic woman?

2 In the discussion of cultural appropriation, a suggestion was made that such appropriation might qualify as theft of cultural property. This suggestion is modelled on the idea of intellectual property – like copyright – but can a *culture* own something in the same way that a person or even a corporation can own something?

3 Certainly, the film adaptation of *The Good Earth* would qualify as a case of subject appropriation on Young's account, but would the same be true for Pearl S. Buck's novel? Buck actually grew up in China in the early twentieth century, but as the child of missionaries. Is she an insider or an outsider of the relevant culture? Would the answer help us to determine whether Buck has done anything *wrong*?

4 James O. Young suggests that even where an act of cultural appropriation is harmful or profoundly offensive, its wrongness may be outweighed by other factors. How would we determine when such an outweighing has occurred? Just *how* wrong *is* the wrongness of cultural appropriation?

8

Aesthetics Without Art

Chapter Outline

I. Mr Blobby

Everyone wants to be the best at something. The blobfish is the best at being ugly.

The blobfish is unofficially the World's Ugliest Animal, a dubious honour granted in 2013 by the Ugly Animal Preservation Society, which adopted the blobfish as its official mascot in an effort to raise the profile 'of some of Mother Nature's more aesthetically challenged children'.[1]

The US National Oceanic and Atmospheric Administration (NOAA) describes the blobfish (*Psychrolutid microporos*) as looking cartoonishly 'like a big, blobby tadpole, just a mass of pale, jelly-like flesh with puffy, loose skin, a big nose, and beady staring eyes'.[2] It probably doesn't help that the blobfish officially belongs to a group of fishes called 'fatheads'. Typically about a foot long, the bubblegum-pink blobfish has soft bones and a gelatinous body, allowing it to withstand the pressures 1,000 metres below the ocean's surface. There, it floats along, just above the sea floor, presumably eating whatever particles of organic matter happen to float into its big, sad

Figure 8.1 'Mr Blobby'. Photograph by Kerryn Parkinson.

mouth. In fact, scientists aren't sure *what* the blobfish normally eats – we've had little opportunity to study it in nature – but it has hardly a muscle in its body, so it isn't chasing down prey.

The blobfish first entered public consciousness thanks largely to the portrait of the blobfish you see here, which exploded on social media after being taken by marine ecologist Kerryn Parkinson. Affectionately named 'Mr Blobby', the 285mm specimen was caught off the coast of New Zealand in 2003 by the crew of the RV *Tangoroa*, a deep-water scientific research vessel, named for the Māori god of the sea. Parkinson's job aboard ship was to photograph all of the unique specimens caught by the team's deep-sea nets. Parkinson photographed a lot of fish that trip, but it was Mr Blobby's portrait – and his recognition by the Ugly Animal Preservation Society – that made him the 'poster-blob for the grotesque'.[3]

The Ugly Animal Preservation Society is actually comedian and biologist Simon Watt, who tours his Ugly Animal Roadshow to schools, theatres and festivals to promote conservation and the beauty of nature's 'unloved wonders'. The blobfish beat out ten competitors for the 'Ugliest Animal' crown, including the pubic louse, the kakapo (a rotund, flightless parrot) and the etymologically unfortunate *Tematobius coleus* ('scrotum frog'), better known as the (still etymologically unfortunate) Titicaca water frog.

Certainly, nobody is going to call Mr Blobby a 'pretty' fish. He doesn't have the brilliant colours of the angelfish or clownfish. He doesn't have the betta's resplendent fins or even the common goldfish's glistening scales. He's basically a fleshy, finned blob. But against what standard do we judge Mr Blobby's beauty? Against what standard *should* we compare it? What are the appropriate features of natural objects – like fish – for aesthetic evaluation? Are natural objects even suitable subjects for aesthetic assessment?

II. On beauty and nature

Most of this book has been dedicated to philosophical questions about art, and indeed such questions have dominated aesthetics for more than a century. But this was not always the case. As outlined in Chapter 3, the ancient Greek philosopher Pythagoras believed that beauty arose from mathematical harmony, order and regularity. In this way, Pythagoras and his followers did not distinguish between the beauty of nature and the beauty of art (or the beauty of anything else, for that matter). Beauty, the Pythagoreans believed, was simply an objective principle of the universe. Plato followed the Pythagoreans' lead, concluding in the *Laws* that beauty arises from the proper arrangement of parts, grounded in proportion, harmony and order. In the *Poetics*, Aristotle added scale to the principles of beauty:

> [A]n animal, or indeed anything which has parts, must, to be beautiful, not only have these parts in the right order but must also be of a definite size. Beauty is a matter of size and order. An extraordinarily small animal would not be beautiful, nor an extraordinarily large one … [A]s bodies and animals must have a size that can be easily perceived as a whole, so plots must have a length which can easily be remembered.[4]

Although art offered, for the ancient Greeks, problems of its own, so far as beauty was concerned, there was no principled distinction between art and nature: the same rules applied to both. During the second and first century BCE, Hellenistic philosophers known as the Stoics took this line of thought a step further, suggesting that the world as a whole was beautiful, regarding nature as both art and artist, the universe as the most perfect work of art.

During the medieval period, Christian philosophers worked to meld the philosophical principles of the classical period with the tenets of Christianity. And although this was not always an easy fit, in this notion of the Stoics', they found a foothold. God, they believed, created the world and created it perfectly – so how could it fail to be beautiful? Although we are not always sensitive to its beauty, the thinking went, God's purpose gave the world beauty. This notion of universal beauty, known as *pankalia*, particularly gripped the late fourth-century St Augustine, who described the world as a beautiful poem.[5] However, he notes, we are not always *aware* of the world's beauty, for we are *within* the world. And just as one cannot expect to perceive the beauty of a poem from a single word or a single line, we should not expect to be able to perceive the beauty of the world from where we happen to stand at any given time. We will perceive beauty, Augustine suggests, in the shape of a flower or the song of a bird, but it may not be immediately apparent in all natural things. We may fail to stand back far enough to see a thing's place in the beauty of the world, or we may fail to look closely enough, overlooking the harmony, symmetry or unity of that which we take to be ugly. Although we can safely assume he had never seen one, Augustine may as well have been referring specifically to the blobfish. Augustine's drawing together of classical and Christian principles would dominate Western thinking on natural beauty for a millennium. God was seen as an artist and the world as his masterpiece. The world was beautiful because it was God's creation, and so, it was thought, reflected *his* beauty.

In the modern period, God largely dropped out of the equation, but nature remained the standard against which the beauty of art was compared. As such, artists sought to imbue their works with beauty by looking first to nature. However, this approach developed along two lines. Some thinkers of the period held to the view that the beauty of art was directly derivative of the beauty of nature and obtained through direct imitation. The sixteenth-century Italian poet Torquato Tasso writes:

> Beauty is a work of nature that consists in a certain proportion of parts, as well as appropriate size and lovely grace of coloring … If works of nature are this way in themselves, works of art, which imitate nature, must also be this way in themselves … [I]f the proportion of the parts is beautiful in itself, this same thing will be beautiful in itself when the painter or sculptor imitates it; and if the natural object be praiseworthy, the artificial object based on it will be praiseworthy.[6]

Others held that nature, in some circumstances, produced less-than-beautiful objects – or, as some put it, objects unsuitable for portrayal in art – allowing the artist to actually *improve* upon the beauty of nature, either by selecting and portraying the most beautiful objects that nature has to offer, or by determining the *principles* that underlie the beauty of nature, and working directly from these. The seventeenth-century biographer Giovan Pietro Bellori writes:

> [E]ven though nature intends always to make its effects excellent, nevertheless, owing to the inequality of matter, forms are altered, and human beauty in particular is confounded, as we see in the innumerable deformities and disproportions that there are in us. For this reason noble painters and sculptors, imitating that first maker, also form in their minds an example of higher beauty, and by contemplating that, they emend nature without fault of color or of line.[7]

The idea of 'emending' nature was applied not only to sculpture and painting, but also gave rise to the popularity of landscape gardening, today better known as landscape architecture. Prior to the eighteenth century, gardens of royal and governmental properties were largely designed according to mathematical principles of beauty, resulting in highly contrived and geometrically arranged gardens. In the eighteenth century, however, the practice of landscape design turned to the 'English garden' style, an idealized version of wild nature, with properties looking on the one hand natural and accidentally placed, and, on the other hand, polished. One of the founders of the style, William Kent, was even said to have planted dead trees in his creation of Kensington gardens to 'heighten the allusion to natural woods'.[8]

Immanuel Kant, whose aesthetic theory we explored in Chapter 3, argued that a pure aesthetic judgement must be disinterested – that it must be made without concern for the object's purpose or place in the world. Although Kant allows that nature may very well *be* structured with purpose, he argues that this should not direct our aesthetic judgement of it:

> because then we would have to learn from nature what to consider beautiful, and a judgment of taste would be subject to aesthetic principles. In fact, however, what counts in judging beauty is not what nature is, not even what purpose it [has] for us, but how we receive it.[9]

So far, it would seem, judgements of beauty in art and nature are not so different. However, unlike art, Kant contends, nature gives rise to a *direct interest* – an interest disconnected from any purpose. This is not an interest we *bring* to the object of appreciation, but rather one we *gain* from it. In the beauty of nature, Kant says, we find a lawful harmony which pleasurably arouses the reason and intellect. This feeling, Kant suggests, is akin to moral judgement. With art, however, we recognize that it is contrived, intentionally aimed at our liking. And so, while it may give rise to an interest, this interest will always be directed at its underlying cause, its purpose or its artefactuality, rather than itself, and so will be *indirect*.

Nature, Kant contends, can also give rise to feelings of the *sublime* – what we might think of as a pronounced *awe*: where something is sublime, it is quite literally *awesome*. We have this feeling when something is so large or powerful as to overwhelm the imagination. Consider the feeling had when standing before the Rocky Mountains or Alps, when viewing the endlessness of the Sahara desert or Australian outback, or simply when watching an approaching thundercloud overtake the landscape. The sublime, Kant says, is not to be sought in art, nor even in natural things, but only in the vastness and unboundedness of 'crude nature'. This feeling, he notes, is at one and the same time both positive and negative. It is negative in the sense of inadequacy or powerlessness that it gives rise to, threatening to overwhelm the self and the imagination. But, Kant says, provided we are viewing such vistas from a safe vantage point, we find the ability in ourselves to *resist* being overwhelmed. And so, as the imagination is expanded, we find the experience pleasurable as well. In this, Kant argues, we find an awareness that we are not mere natural organisms, but that we stand outside nature – that we *transcend* it. Specifically, he suggests, we find that however overwhelming nature may seem, it is nothing compared with the awesomeness of man's reason and intellect. Our humanity, Kant suggests, is what is *truly* sublime. Although not a matter of beauty, judgements of the sublime are, Kant says, nevertheless aesthetic.

A fellow German, Georg Wilhelm Friedrich Hegel's work was greatly influenced by Kant, and in many ways Hegel agreed with him.[10] However, where Kant argues that the aesthetics of nature outstrip that of art, Hegel takes the opposite view. Hegel does not go so far as to say that nature is *not* beautiful, but, he argues, its beauty is the beauty of particular appearance. Conversely, the beauty of art is the product of the human mind. Rather than being grounded in particular appearance, Hegel contends, art reveals and accentuates what is universal. Although it takes particular form, art points beyond itself – art has content and meaning. Unlike articles of nature, Hegel suggests, a work of art is apprehended on a mental or spiritual plane. As such, he argues, '[E]verything spiritual is better than anything natural. At any rate, no existence in nature is able, like art, to represent divine ideals.'[11] Where the beauty of nature arises from its sensuous apprehension, the beauty of art is made for apprehension by both the senses *and* the mind: the artist *shapes* the sensuous to the spiritual.

With regard to the beauty of art and nature, then, the views of Kant and Hegel are diametrically opposed. And while the general philosophical influence of each is incalculable, following Hegel, philosophical interest in the beauty of nature dwindled, with 'aesthetics' thereafter largely becoming synonymous with the 'philosophy of art'. This is perhaps not entirely surprising as it was in the eighteenth century that the notion of 'fine art' coalesced, and brought with it a general burgeoning interest in the philo-sophical problems of art. Issues of natural beauty, meanwhile, were put to the side, where they would gather dust for a century.

III. Natural aesthetics

In 1966, Ronald W. Hepburn published his article 'Contemporary Aesthetics and the Neglect of Natural Beauty', and in the process dusted off decades of neglect by philosophers.[12] The myopic approach of aestheticians, Hepburn suggests, arose in part because of a prevailing view that natural beauty did not lend itself to the sorts of general accounts of aesthetic excellence pursued by philosophers. How, for instance, were we meant to discuss the 'interpretation' of nature? How could nature be 'expressive'? Artworks had become the aesthetic object *par excellence*, and nature – viewed as an aesthetic outlier – fell by the wayside. However, in focusing so specifically on art, Hepburn impassionedly argues, philosophers had done a great disservice to aesthetics, because natural aesthetics has a great deal to offer to the field. Like artworks, Hepburn notes, we can focus in on particular natural objects – but unlike artworks, nature typically surrounds the observer on all sides. The appreciator is a *part* of the object of appreciation; she is *within* nature. And while the institutions of art have contrived all manner of ways of framing artworks – both literally and figuratively – nature does not present us with natural frames. Where frames might be said to *bind* or *complete* artworks, the 'framelessness' of nature offers an openness and adventurousness to aesthetic appreciation not found in art. As such, Hepburn argues, nature is not only aesthetically interesting, but provides a host of issues hitherto overlooked in aesthetics.

Hepburn's article served as a call to arms to aestheticians, and, since its publication, issues of natural aesthetics have garnered exponentially growing interest by philosophers. Following Hepburn's line of thinking, Allen Carlson argues that the ways we traditionally approach art will not serve as models for appreciating the beauty of nature.[13] The problem with treating a natural object as one would, say, a sculpture, is that removing the natural object from its environment (whether physically or, figuratively, by focusing on the object to the exclusion of its environment) *distorts* the object of appreciation. In Mr Blobby's case, this is literally true. His particularly sad look in his portrait is due in part to the fact that the photograph was taken at sea level, where the pressure is about 1 per cent of what it is a kilometre below the surface, where Mr Blobby lived. Pulled from the sea floor, he essentially deflated (you probably wouldn't look too pretty in Mr Blobby's natural environment either). But Hepburn's point is broader than this: the natural setting of a tree or hedgehog or blobfish is *relevant* to its aesthetic appreciation in a way that where you place a sculpture in a gallery or home usually is not. Moreover, some clear natural candidates for aesthetic appreciation simply cannot be appreciated in this way. What would it mean to treat a sunset, forest or mountain vista as one would a sculpture?

So, it might be thought that it is more appropriate to appreciate nature as a *scene*, and certainly many of us do appreciate nature this way. In his seminal 1894 essay 'A Near View of the High Sierra', John Muir tells of meeting a pair of aspiring painters while hiking through the California mountains.[14] As Muir guides them through the forest, the painters are disappointed, saying: 'All this is huge and sublime, but we see nothing as yet at all available for effective pictures. Art is long, and art is limited, you know; and here are foregrounds, middle-grounds, backgrounds, all alike; bare rock-waves, woods, groves, diminutive flecks of meadow, and strips of glittering water.'[15] While Muir marvelled at the environment around him, the painters were seeking 'the picturesque' – the sort of beauty found, literally, 'in the manner of a picture'. This aesthetic notion had developed in popularity not surprisingly at about the same time that the English garden style had overtaken landscape design. A natural scene was seen as beautiful for the same reasons that a painting of a natural scene was beautiful – indeed, on this sort of view, the beauty of a natural scene could be established according to how well suited it was for depiction in a painting. The mistake with this model of assessing natural beauty, Carlson suggests, is essentially the same as that for the object-based model: it falsifies the object of appreciation. He argues that 'what must be kept in mind is that the environment is not a scene, not a representation, not static, and not two dimensional'.[16] So to appreciate it as if it were is to *fail* to appreciate it: if *that* is what you are appreciating, you aren't appreciating nature. Instead, Carlson and others argue, if we are to appreciate nature aesthetically, it must be appreciated *on its own terms*.

In Chapter 3, we looked at an argument by Kendall Walton that the aesthetic properties that a work of art actually has are those that are found in it when it is perceived in the correct art category. If one assesses a modern abstract expressionist painting as if it were a fourteenth-century Flemish landscape, for instance, one will simply be *wrong* in one's assessment. Determining the correct category, Walton argues, depends upon certain knowledge of the work, its context of creation, and its creator. Carlson argues that something similar applies to aesthetic assessment in nature, but that the appropriate knowledge is *scientific* knowledge – a position known as 'scientific cognitivism'. Just as the art historian and art critic are best equipped to aesthetically appreciate art, Carlson argues, so those best qualified to aesthetically appreciate nature will be the naturalist and the ecologist. Correctly appreciating the grace of a rorqual whale, for example, requires knowledge that the animal is a marine mammal and not a fish. As a fish, the creature would seem lumbering and perhaps a bit on the clumsy side; as a mammal, the whale is graceful and majestic. St Augustine had noted that when we are inappropriately positioned, we can fail to notice the order, harmony and beauty of a thing. If we realize, however, that Mr Blobby's general blobbiness (and everything that comes with it) is the result of his adaptation as a bottom feeder, we will be able to better appreciate him for the thing that he is. The blobfish's jelly-like structure not only allows it to survive the pressures of the deep sea; it is also of precisely the right density to let it float just above the sea floor with no effort on its part. The blobfish is essentially the self-sustaining Roomba of the sea. Its physiology is in harmony with its functions, which are in turn in harmony with its environment. The ultimate result of scientific cognitivism, Carlson argues, inevitably leads to *positive aesthetics*: that, when viewed properly (i.e. in light of scientific knowledge), wild nature is *always* going to be aesthetically good. This is because, while artworks and their categories are created, natural things are discovered, and scientists thereafter create categories that best suit these things. Because the natural categories are designed to suit natural objects and not the other way around, when viewed through the lens of scientific knowledge, natural objects will always be viewed correctly, and will always be perfectly suited to their categories.

While admitting that scientific cognitivism is intriguing, several philosophers have raised questions about the theory. Robert Stecker, for example, asks *what* scientific knowledge is relevant?[17] Is the chemical composition of a flower germane to its beauty? How about the blood composition of the blobfish? Unfortunately, Stecker suggests, scientific cognitivism provides no means of determining which scientific knowledge is relevant to the aesthetic appreciation of nature and which is not. Yuriko Saito suggests in reply that the method for determining which knowledge is relevant is a fairly simple one: scientific knowledge is relevant to aesthetic assessment if such knowledge bears on our perceptual experience of nature.[18] If knowledge of the flower's chemical composition or the blobfish's blood composition impacts our perceptual experience of it, it is relevant; if not, not. (As it happens, the blood of deep-sea fish *is* surprisingly fascinating, and ties directly into function – and thus, perhaps, to aesthetic appreciation.)

Emily Brady argues that while scientific knowledge may be *sufficient* for appreciating the aesthetic qualities of nature, it isn't *necessary*.[19] That is, Brady argues, we may be able to appreciate many aesthetic qualities of nature without such scientific knowledge. Do we need to know about oceanography to appreciate the aesthetic qualities of waves pounding against the surf, or about geology to appreciate the awe and majesty of Muir's Sierra Nevada? Certainly, humans were capable of appreciating such beauty long before we had knowledge of oceanography or geology, and children continue to do so without such knowledge. It might be said, however, that just as a child *could* aesthetically assess, say, Agnes Martin's *Red Bird* without knowing anything about abstract expressionism or minimalism, perhaps even arriving at the same assessment as someone with encyclopaedic knowledge of art history, it does not mean that the work has been *correctly* assessed. Likewise, that we are able to appreciate the beauty of the surf or sublimity of a mountain range does not mean that we are assessing it properly. The matter, it might be said, is as much about the *method* of assessment as it is about the *result*.

The Ugly Animal Preservation Society operates on the guiding premise that 'the panda gets too much attention'.[20] It is no accident that the official logo of the World Wildlife Fund is an adorable panda. The cuter the animal, or the more we have a sentimental bond with it, the more likely the animal is to receive attention from us – even from scientists – and, as such, the more likely we are to direct our funding to its preservation.[21] 'People have always shouted "Save the Whale", says Simon Watt, 'but until now no one has stood up for the gob-faced squid or the hundreds of species that go extinct every day.' (The gob-faced squid, incidentally, is the nickname of *Promachoteuthis sulcus*, a species of cephalopod known from a single specimen caught in 2007, and famous for its mouth, which appears to have human-like teeth.) And, as with the big-eyed panda, we tend to worry more about the conservation of an idyllic stream than we do a fetid swamp. Our standard view of nature is still inclined towards the picturesque and to promoting whatever best suits us. This predisposition tends to have very negative consequences: swamps get drained, species die off and the unpredicted effects on nature can be disastrous. But, as Sheila Lintott puts it, scientific interest supports aesthetic interest, and aesthetic interest tends to breed ethical interest.[22] There is a growing philosophical and popular interest in environmental ethics, and Lintott and others suggest that aesthetics can in this way support our ethical interests in the environment: when we appreciate things aesthetically, we want to protect them, and scientific cognitivism promotes aesthetic appreciation.[23]

The media attention that the blobfish has garnered is having an interesting effect: the wider Mr Blobby's fame – the more the public becomes familiar with him – the lesser his apparent revulsion. Some would say that he is so ugly, he's cute.[24] Today, thanks to Mr Blobby's celebrity, you can buy huggable plush blobfish, fluffy blobfish slippers and blobfish games for your smartphone. Blobfish show up on children's cartoons and in all manner of crafts for sale on the internet. Despite persistent rumours to the contrary, the blobfish is not endangered, but many of its competitors for the 'Ugliest Animal' crown are in trouble.[25] The kakapo is critically endangered, due largely to human intrusion in its environment. The Titicaca water frog, which only lives in Lake Titicaca, is critically endangered as well – again, thanks to humans. Indeed, changes in human grooming fashions seem to be causing unexpected problems for the pubic louse. Simon Watt hopes that bringing attention to the unique features of nature's less conventionally adorable creatures will foster a more general appreciation for biodiversity.

Where 'cognitivism' – in our case, *scientific* cognitivism – suggests that aesthetic appreciation depends upon some particular beliefs or knowledge, there are also 'non-cognitivist' theories for the aesthetic appreciation of nature, which suggest that the appropriate appreciation may depend upon something else. Noël Carroll, for one, argues that it is appropriate to appreciate nature *emotionally*.[26] Carroll does not claim that this is the *only* legitimate method for such appreciation; only that we should not discount it. In experiencing some natural environment, Carroll notes, our attention may be drawn to a tree, a clearing or a waterfall, and arouse an emotional response. The awe that one feels when one looks at the Grand Canyon and the quiet comfort that one feels in attending to a willow tree swaying in the breeze are, Carroll argues, *appropriate* emotional responses. A feeling of fear aroused by the willow tree or anger at the canyon would, conversely, be *inappropriate*. Appropriate arousal, Carroll notes, need not be grounded in anything like scientific knowledge, but neither need we think of it as a religious or mystical experience. Rather, the 'arousal model' is simply a traditional and legitimate approach to the aesthetic experience of nature that scientific cognitivism cannot account for.

Emily Brady argues that, removing the guidance of any artist's intention, aesthetic appreciation essentially comes down to perception and imagination, not knowledge.[27] As such, Brady is in many ways returning to the principles of aesthetic appreciation outlined by Kant. In perceptually attending to the elements of a natural object or environment, one's imagination is aroused, allowing for free contemplation of the object. One is free to imaginatively compare the object of contemplation with other objects one has experienced, to discover order and variety, to place the object in a narrative, and even to imagine what it is like to *be* that thing. You might imagine being, for instance, the blobfish – feeling that pendulous mass as you are suspended balloon-like just above the sea floor. Such imaginative aesthetic experiences, Brady suggests, allow for aesthetic *revelation* – the realization of aesthetic *truths*. However, for such appreciation to be appropriate, it must be both disinterested and of proper depth. As Brady puts it, we must 'imagine well'.

IV. Environmental aesthetics

As noted above, one important difference between the aesthetic appreciation of art and that of nature is that with nature we are typically *surrounded* by the object of appreciation. And so, while Carlson discusses the aesthetic appreciation of particular natural objects, he centrally argues for an 'environmental model' of natural aesthetics. In simply taking a walk through the woods, one not only *sees* the trees, the rocks and the dirt; one also *hears* the rustling of leaves and creaking of branches, one *feels* the humid air and the cool breeze, one *smells* the pine and the moss. In contrast to the experience of a painting, an art installation or even a play, the sensory experience of nature is irreducibly rich. Certainly, we *can* focus on particular features of the environment, but while we are expected to ignore, say, the fellow theatre patron rustling in the next seat, there is no element of the natural environment that we are *supposed* to ignore, aesthetically speaking – not even ourselves. Ordinarily, perhaps, we do not look at our immediate environment in a predominantly aesthetic way. Rather, we treat it as the *background* to those things we focus on. Carlson argues that the aesthetic appreciation of the environment requires shifting it from the background of the aesthetic experience to the foreground.

Arnold Berleant suggests on this basis that the appropriate model of environmental appreciation is one of *immersion* – what he calls an 'aesthetics of engagement'.[28] However, where Carlson's approach is a cognitivist one, Berleant's is decidedly non-cognitivist. He writes:

> Unlike many arts in which one or two senses dominate our direct sensory experience with the other receptors joining in by imaginative association, environment activates the entire range of our sensory capacities. I not only see, hear, touch, and smell the place I move through: I grasp them with my feet and hands, I taste them in the air I draw in, I even adjust the way I hold and balance my body to the contours of the land and the texture of the ground under my feet.[29]

On Berleant's view, as an experience, these distinct sensations are all engaged together – they are all aspects of one's immersion in one's environment. And, Berleant suggests, they are experienced along with the memories and associations of the perceiver. When you walk through the woods, along a beach or across a field, you are an active participant and not merely a passive observer. You are a *part* of your environment: it reacts to you just as you react to it.

Originally, environmental aesthetics largely focused on the natural environment – what some have called 'wilderness aesthetics' – but in recent years, philosophers have expanded their interests to take in other sorts of environment. One step removed from the natural environments of the forest, beach and mountain are such environments as agricultural landscapes, the rural countryside and other forms of what we might think of as artefactualized nature: environments that, while shaped by man, are largely constructed of natural elements. Existing as they do in what Carlson calls 'the never-never land between nature and art',[30] these sorts of environments tend to complicate matters. Although Berleant's immersion model seems to apply as easily to a cornfield, park or vegetable garden as to primeval nature, one cannot as easily apply the scientific cognitivist's positive aesthetics view, as we are no longer dealing with raw nature. However, as most cornfields and vegetable gardens are not primarily constructed *as* objects for aesthetic appreciation, most models of art evaluation will not easily apply either.

Carlson argues that non-wilderness environments – 'human environments' – must be aesthetically assessed analogously to how we treat natural environments – as ecosystems – but with an understanding that these are to some degree *designed* ecosystems.[31] Ecosystems are held together by their various parts performing their interrelated functions. No one part performs its function in isolation; rather, each thing in the system impacts other things in it. As such, one cannot appreciate any given thing in isolation. Rather, one must appreciate that thing as a part of a greater *unity*. And this is no less true in aesthetic appreciation than in any other form of evaluation. Carlson notes that the fate of an ecosystem hangs on the success or failure of functional fit. In 1859, for example, rabbits were introduced to Australia, apparently by an English immigrant, Thomas Austin, who missed hunting them. However, Austin's initial dozen rabbits quickly began reproducing, and, finding the Australian outback to their liking, spread across the country. The population grew from a dozen to millions within a decade, forever altering the many ecosystems that they invaded. An ecosystem can either adapt to changes or be eradicated. And this issue of functional fit applies just as much to human environments as it does to wholly natural ones. The layout of a farm, the arrangement of roads, even the arrangement of plants in a park, can all have enormous impact on the functioning of their respective ecosystems. And form, Carlson argues, tends to follow function. When functional fit is achieved, he suggests, 'there is an ambience of everything being and looking right or appropriate, an ambience of the environments looking as they should'.[32] When there isn't, things seem … off. Although this line of thinking has a quasi-mystical feel, and risks running into the problems of Clive Bell's 'significant form', Carlson suggests that the beauty of a farmstead, garden or other such human environment depends upon how well the elements of the environment serve their individual and collective functions, and, given the sorts of ecosystems we are dealing with, the degree to which they are productive and sustainable.

Unlike the forests and other natural environments we discussed earlier, when it comes to an environment like a farmstead or a rural landscape, most of us experience it in one of two ways – either by driving past it on a road or by working in it – and both of these forms of experience have been explored philosophically. Hepburn had argued that nature does not, like a landscape painting, come with a frame. But driving through a landscape comes with frames all its own. The first and most obvious frame is the window through which we observe the scene. But, as well, the view from the highway is foregrounded by the guardrail, the shining asphalt of the road, and the whizzing lines painted upon it. It is likely interrupted by road signs and utility poles. The scene is not static like a painting; rather, the deep background moves slowly as the foreground flies past in a blur. There is, as well, the vibration of the seat, the hum of the motor as the car itself trundles along and perhaps the cool air of the air conditioning. The experience is, in a sense, a new form of the eighteenth-century picturesque. Malcolm Andrews notes:

> The speed, smoothness, and facility of Autoroute journeys through the landscape enhance the sense of our being increasingly distanced from the past, and strengthen the sense of a 'lost myth' that picturesque tourists for over two centuries have associated with landscape and antiquity. Progress, of which the Autoroute is one of the great symbols, is by definition a pulling away from the past: in the process we are alienated from the direct experience of natural landscape, of living and working with it and in it, of traveling over its uneven surface.[33]

Of course, not all of us are so far removed from the land. The farmer undoubtedly experiences it in a different way than the rest of us do. Pauline von Bonsdorff writes: 'The bourgeois aesthetics of the rural landscape, being the result of sight-seeing, short stays, and purchasing power, creates a quite different kind of space from year-round farming practices and activities: stepping, touching, digging, hitting, carrying, swinging, tearing, pulling, pushing, toeing, breaking, killing, slaughtering.'[34] The farmer does not have the privilege of forming a picturesque aesthetic perspective on the rural landscape – she is too busy getting her hands dirty. The farmer does not get to sit back and allow her imagination to flow freely. She is not disinterested. Rather, she experiences her environment by cultivating it, through repeated, coordinated movements developed as skills over years. She is, in many ways, like a dancer performing movements for no one but herself. If you have ever run long distances, or mowed expansive lawns, and taken the time to appreciate the feel of your muscles and movements, you have probably experienced a sense of the proprioception (awareness of body position and balance) and kinesthesia (awareness of body movement) that the agricultural labourer feels. More than this, von Bonsdorff notes, the farmer develops a sensitivity to, and engagement with, the rotation of the seasons, with each season calling for its own form of repetitive work.

Of course, most of us are not farmers, and many of us have never set foot on a farm. Indeed, currently, some 60 per cent of the world's population consists of city dwellers, nearly double that of 1950.[35] This is where most of us live, work and play. And urban environments present aesthetic questions all their own. If natural wilderness is at one end of the scale, then cities are at the other extreme, with any natural elements relegated to designed parks, manicured lawns and the occasional bit of wild fauna. Urban environments are dominated by buildings, roads and other constructed elements. So in many ways, like artworks, cities are artefactual: they are things intentionally made by mankind. But, unlike artworks, on the large scale, cities are mostly accidental. Certainly, many cities were designed on grid systems, including such diverse locales as Kyoto, Japan, Mexico City and Barcelona, Spain. But, unless we are flying over it, we don't typically *see* the city's grid. Rather, we walk or drive the streets, and we see homes, office buildings, shops and churches. We see the crisscrossing wires overhead, the traffic lights, benches and rubbish bins. No unifying mind decided where each building should go, how each shopfront should look, what colour each door should be painted. So with little left of the natural to rely on, and no single mind to look to for intention, how are we to assess a city aesthetically?

Carlson treats urban environments as human environments in the extreme – in particular, environments of commerce, industry and residence. And, Carlson contends, such an environment is not in principle unlike any other ecosystem, with the same principles of aesthetic assessment at play. Even more than a farmstead, a city is composed of functional elements: from the zoning of urban areas to the placement of a city bench, functional considerations are everywhere at both the large and small scale. This is perhaps most clearly the case in city areas like railways and harbours, but is equally true in old neighbourhoods, local market areas and other pockets of the city. When functional fit is achieved in all these areas, Carlson contends, it will look right: 'It appears as if the whole were the result of "natural" processes akin to the ecological and evolutionary forces that shape natural environments.'[36] It will be almost as if the city came together despite itself.

In his essay 'Cultivating an Urban Aesthetic', Arnold Berleant suggests that there is more to the aesthetic appreciation of urban environments than look: there is an awareness of 'past and place' – a sense of human continuity.[37] Any city, Berleant notes, is shaped over time, with its inter-mixing styles reflecting its social patterns and regional cultures – it is a living museum. We cannot walk through a city without recognizing its social history, with particular locations being tied to particular people and events. A city can be both stimulating and oppressive, and can threaten to overwhelm anyone aesthetically, especially a city's visitors. Berleant's theory, remember, is an aesthetics of *immersion* in the environment, and the city is perceived from within. Especially to visitors, cities threaten to overwhelm with sensation. We are aware of our own bodies, of the sights and most especially of the sounds. We are awash with the murmuring of crowds, the barking of dogs, the rumbling of vehicles and trains. We hear music from the open windows of cars and homes, the screeching tyres of cars and all manner of other sounds – which may all seem to be a general cacophony until one stops and pays attention. Perhaps most peculiar are natural sounds in this environment: think of the sound of wind whistling between office buildings, the sound of water pinging off cars and concrete, and the gurgling of impromptu streams forming in gutters. At the best of times, an urban environment is a harmonious one; at the worst, raucous.

In 'Urban Richness and the Art of Building', Pauline von Bonsdorff presents a view that pulls in elements from both Carlson and Berleant.[38] She suggests that, more than anything else, the city is a *habitat* of people (along with other various creatures). And its elements are mediated by our ideas of the human activities that they are involved in. A building, von Bonsdorff notes, is never just a building: it is a synagogue or an apartment complex or a school. It functions in some particular way. And, as elements of a habitat, we ask about their suitability. But, being a human environment, suitability pertains not only to physical needs, but also to cultural and spiritual ones. In other words, the aesthetics of an urban environment are not simply about spaces and buildings, but about how life is lived there. So it is a human creation not only in the physical sense, but also in virtue of the various networks and systems at play. These are the forces that serve to shape the city over time, von Bonsdorff suggests, in much the same way that weather and other natural forces impact the shape of nature. And these are all relevant factors in the aesthetic experience of the city.

V. Everyday aesthetics

With Hepburn's reintroduction of natural aesthetics, aestheticians have come a long way in broadening the field of study. Since the synonymy of 'aesthetics' and 'philosophy of art' was dismantled, the field has moved from studying the aesthetics of nature and natural environments, to such human environments as the farm and the rural landscape, and ultimately to the heart of the city. But, we can ask, if the study of aesthetics can be expanded to take in the forest, the farm and the urban centre, where else can it go? It would seem the answer is … everywhere. Both Carlson and Berleant have suggested that their respective views apply as much to our ordinary environments as to our extraordinary ones. Berleant notes that, although it is the more exotic and unfamiliar environments we visit that tend to stand out aesthetically, 'how we engage with the prosaic landscapes of home, work, local travel, and recreation is an important measure of the quality of our lives'.[39] After all, we spend most of our time in our more familiar environments – our homes, our schools, our workplaces. Why should their utter familiarity preclude their being aesthetic? Is there anything about them that is aesthetically *unique*?

Whether you are at home in your bedroom or living room, in a library, in a classroom, coffee shop, or somewhere else, take a moment and look at the room around you. How would you describe it? Is it neat or cluttered? Clean or dirty? How are you and those around you dressed? Are you tidy or dishevelled? Sloppy or polished? Tom Leddy suggests that these 'everyday surface aesthetic qualities' are not only parts of our aesthetic experiences of the world, but *important* parts.[40] In principle, Leddy notes, these terms are not different in kind from such standard aesthetic terms as 'balanced' or 'harmonious'. Like other aesthetic terms, they seem to apply in virtue of the form of the thing observed, depending upon that thing's non-aesthetic properties: the room is messy *because* there are socks balled up on the floor and books piled haphazardly on the table, or tidy *because* everything is in its place. And like other aesthetic properties, we may be more or less able to see the messiness and tidiness around us (many, it must be said, are not aware when their environments or themselves are a mess). However, unlike such standard aesthetic terms as 'balanced' and 'harmonious', we tend to reserve terms like 'dirty' and 'clean' for our non-art environments – and we have been taught to use them in this way since childhood. Although Leddy suggests that everyday surface aesthetic terms are conceptually simpler than 'balanced' and 'harmonious', Yuriko Saito contends that such terms *are* complex terms – but that their complexity comes from their context-dependence and pragmatic significance:

> There is nothing dirty about ketchup, unless it is on my shirt. Mud on our kitchen floor is dirty, but not outdoors on a rainy day or in a dwelling with a mud floor. A pile of clothes in the laundry basket or a cleaner's counter does not invoke the notion of mess, but the same thing in the middle of a living room floor would.[41]

So, on Saito's view, whether something is clean or dirty, messy or tidy, depends in large part upon the kind of environment we are considering.

In principle, this isn't so different from an artwork's aesthetic properties depending upon its proper comparison-category.

If the environment is a domestic one, Kevin Melchionne argues, applying such terms as 'messy' and 'tidy' is largely a matter of function and habit.[42] How you arrange the items in a room, whether furniture, appliances, books or knick-knacks, depends upon what that room is for and how you use it – things you may not fully understand until you have lived in that space for some time. A room, Melchionne suggests, is tidy when it is in line with our planned and habitual uses of the room; it is messy when it impedes such function. So, following Carlson's more general view about the aesthetics of human environments, we might say that form follows function in domestic environments as well, and that aesthetic assessment of such environments arises from consideration of their functional elements. Similarly, Saito notes, many of our positive and negative aesthetic assessments of our ordinary environments are made on the basis of *apparent* fit for function. A threadbare couch might work as well as a new couch, but we probably will not like it as much. And in many local jurisdictions, property owners may be fined or jailed if their property is deemed an 'eyesore' even where there is no apparent danger to anyone. That is, when things start to look old, we tend to appreciate them less, and we start to think about replacing them.

Saito suggests, however, that there is more at issue in such items than their apparent functionality. If we did in fact generally aesthetically devalue articles that looked old, it would seem very strange indeed that there is today such a thriving market for 'distressed' furniture and clothing. When I was working on the first edition of this text, I was in the process of trying to figure out how to get an enormous oak table from where it was stored in Canada to where I would be living in Pennsylvania. The table was once my grandfather's, was inherited by my mother and spent most of my life in my parents' garage, where it served as an all-purpose worktable. Over the decades, it had been gouged, it had been scratched and it had had paint and oil spilled across it. When I moved out of my parents' house, I refinished the table, but I could not entirely remove signs of its age: gouges were too deep, and oil and paint had penetrated so far into the wood that no amount of sanding could remove them. I love that table, not just because of its sturdiness, but *because* it looks old – because it has a history and it shows. Sometime after finishing the first edition of this book, the table did arrive in Pennsylvania, but its removable legs did not. I had to hire an artisan to make new legs to match the design and weathered look of the table, which is my writing desk today. Pauline von Bonsdorff suggests that the aesthetics of an urban environment depends in part upon the history of that place – how its present form arose from its past. On a similar basis, Saito suggests, 'the aesthetic experience of an aged object is derived from the associated thoughts and images concerning the object's origin, its historical development, its longevity, and events and activities that brought about changes'.[43] Appreciating the aged object, Saito notes, allows for free play of the imagination, one of the cornerstones of Kant's aesthetic theory.

Following this line of thought, Tom Leddy notes:

> Kant ties 'beauty' with the aesthetic pleasure we get from appreciation of good design and pleasing form. This kind of pleasure is surely not absent from the dinner party, the garden, or the use of tiles in the bathroom. Kant clearly includes such things as costumes and wallpaper under the category of beauty, rather than that of the agreeable. Since we would generally want to include these in the field of everyday aesthetics, Kant's distinction [between beauty and the agreeable] may not be useful for defining that field.[44]

Aesthetic terms like 'messy' and 'tidy' are not the only such terms generally reserved for non-art, Leddy notes. Such terms as 'fun' and 'nice', 'kitsch' (have another look at the cover of this book) and 'tasteful', though rarely applied to art, have centrally aesthetic applications. A style of dress can be fun, a walk can be nice and the decorations in your home can be kitschy or tasteful. While I might want your kitschy wall decorations in *my* home, or I might want to take *another* nice walk, none of this interest obviously disqualifies me from being able to simply appreciate their respective aesthetics.

As noted in Chapter 3 and discussed further in Chapter 7, aesthetic evaluation traditionally focuses on two senses: seeing and hearing. Like those before him, Kant divided the senses into 'higher' and 'lower' categories.[45] The highest senses, seeing and hearing, were given special treatment by Kant for being the most objective and the most directly associated with imagination. Being the most objective, he believed, seeing and hearing were best suited for universal claims of aesthetic value – taste – while the other senses were merely matters of subjective agreeableness. Better than touching, tasting and smelling, seeing and hearing were, Kant suggests, particularly well suited to the free play of the imagination. Problematically, much of our aesthetic interaction with non-art involves what Kant would call the 'lower' senses, and philosophers have recently begun challenging the primacy of sight and sound in aesthetics. Emily Brady questions claims that the 'lowest' of the senses, taste and smell, lack the appropriate discriminatory powers for aesthetic judgements. Connoisseurship of many sorts, she notes, focuses specifically on these senses. Wine tastings, whisky tastings and cigar tastings are designed around developing discriminations of taste and smell:

> In this sort of appreciation discrimination is clearly taking place. But we do not have to turn smells and tastes into a high art in order to find cases where judgments are made. Our everyday life is infused with this kind of appreciation, in appreciating our daily route to work, in choosing the best ingredients for tonight's dinner, and so on. We find one aroma pleasant, another unpleasant, one taste interesting, another uninteresting.[46]

Clearly, these are not simply chemical discriminations, but aesthetic ones as well. Moreover, Brady notes, taste and smell may be even more closely tied to emotion than sight and sound. Certainly, smell has often been closely associated with memory, and research suggests that humans are capable of relaying chemical pheromones olfactorily, affecting behaviour in subtle ways.[47] The primary olfactory cortex (the part of the brain that processes smells) is separated from the amygdale (which deals with expression and the experience of emotion) by only two synapses, making for a very potent relationship. Psychologists Rachel S. Herz and Trygg Engen note: 'No other sensory system makes this kind of direct and intense contact with the neural substrates of emotion and memory, which may explain why odor-evoked memories are unusually emotionally potent.'[48] So there is certainly *something* going on here.

The fine arts have traditionally focused almost exclusively on sensations of sight and sound, but with the renewed interest in environmental and everyday aesthetics, the 'lower' senses have come to take an important place. They help to orient us in our environments, to provide value and meaning to our experiences, to invoke memories and emotions and to allow for the free play of the imagination. What a painting by Cézanne smells like, or a sculpture by Rodin tastes like, might be ridiculous questions, but the taste of soup and the smell of a perfume or new car seem critically important to our aesthetic appreciation of our everyday lives. With environmental and everyday aesthetics now taking in the senses that aesthetics had for so long dismissed, is there no end to the sort of input that should be taken to be 'aesthetic'? Environmental aesthetics had already pointed to kinesthesia and proprioception – those senses involved in bodily position and movement – as valuable elements in the aesthetic experience of our surroundings. What's left?

In her article 'Scratching an Itch', Sherri Irvin argues that both itches and scratches should be included in the domain of the aesthetic.[49] Itches, of course, come in all varieties. There are mild itches and intense ones, itches of long duration and itches that pass in a moment. And there are itches that you barely notice are there until you think about them, and which then absolutely *need* to be scratched. The fact that we have few linguistic resources available to describe an itch doesn't make them any less a part of our phenomenal experiences. More than this, though, Irvin argues that one can have *aesthetic* experiences of itches and scratches. Even if not all scratches are positive experiences, and even if every itch is a negative experience, we are at least *capable* of attending to such experiences and evaluating them for their own sake. We can contemplate how an itch grabs our attention, how one itch can draw our attention to other bodily discomforts, and how it can distract us from them. Determining exactly what qualifies as 'aesthetic' is a difficult project, and there is a great deal of disagreement about the matter, but these means of attending to itches and scratches seem paradigmatically aesthetic. That there does not seem to be a distinct *object* that one is attending to when one is attending to an itch, Irvin suggests, does not pose a problem. One can have an experience *about* one's itch- or scratch-experience. The latter is what is called a *somatic* experience – an experience of one's own body; the former is an aesthetic experience.

Looking to Carlson's cognitivist view, Irvin suggests that if appropriate aesthetic appreciation must be cognitively informed, somatic experiences are perfectly apt for aesthetic appreciation: 'It is possible to develop a sophisticated awareness not only of the phenomena themselves, but also of the way in which they are produced by and indicative of complex physical and psychological processes.'[50] If one is more swayed by a non-cognitivist view like Carroll's arousal model, which requires no sophisticated under-standing of the underlying processes, then itches, scratches and other somatic experiences raise no particular problems here either. Certainly, the qualities of itch- and scratch-experiences seem not exhausted by knowledge of how they arise and the role they play in one's bodily functions.

Everyone has itches, and everyone scratches them. But this, Irvin argues, does not mean they must be mundanely experienced:

Such commonplace moments of everyday experience are richly replete with qualities that we tend to neglect as we physically or psychologically multitask, giving our full attention to nothing. These qualities of somatic

experience are available to everyone, cost nothing, and require no environmental degradation or natural resource depletion to produce. They are
already here at every moment, and accessing them requires only attention.[51]

It takes only the right sort of attention to turn an otherwise forgettable
experience into an appreciable one. Just as Carlson had argued that the
aesthetic appreciation of the environment requires shifting it from the
background of the aesthetic experience to the foreground, so too does the
aesthetic appreciation of our own somatic experiences require only bringing
them to the foreground and attending to them in the right way. The
aesthetic, it might be said, is all around you – and occasionally inside you.

Chapter summary

This chapter has focused on emerging subjects of aesthetic inquiry. Although
art and nature were intertwined subjects of aesthetic inquiry since antiquity,
this changed in the eighteenth century with Immanuel Kant's prioritization
of natural over artistic beauty. A generation later, G. W. F. Hegel reversed
Kant's arrangement, ranking the importance of artistic beauty over that
of the natural. With the rise of the fine arts, interest in natural aesthetics
waned in philosophy until the publication of R. W. Hepburn's influential
article, 'Contemporary Aesthetics and the Neglect of Natural Beauty'. We
have looked at how Hepburn's article renewed philosophical interest in
natural aesthetics, giving rise to the scientific cognitivism and positive
aesthetics of Allen Carlson and competing views proposed by Noël Carroll,
Emily Brady and Arnold Berleant. We discussed how natural aesthetics
gave rise to aesthetic interest in the natural environment, to interest in
agricultural and rural environments and to interest in urban aesthetics.
Finally, we considered a number of ways in which aesthetic theories have
been applied to our ordinary lives, including our ordinary domestic spaces,
the things we smell and taste, and ultimately to … well … our itches and
scratches.

Historical timeline

	c. 360 BCE	Plato, *Laws*
	c. 350 BCE	Aristotle, *Poetics*
	389	St Augustine, *De musica*
	c. 426	St Augustine, *De civitate Dei*
	1587	Torquato Tasso, *Discorsi dell'arte poetica*
	1672	Givan Pietro Bellori, *The Lives of the Modern Painters, Sculptors and Architects*
	1790	Immanuel Kant, *The Critique of Judgment*
	1798	Immanuel Kant, *Anthropology from a Pragmatic Point of View*
	1835	G. W. F. Hegel, *Lectures on Aesthetics*
John Muir, 'A Near View of the High Sierra'	1894	
Agnes Martin, *Red Bird*	1964	
	1966	R. W. Hepburn, 'Contemporary Aesthetics and the Neglect of Natural Beauty'
	1970	Kendall Walton, 'Categories of Art'
	1979	Allen Carlson, 'Appreciation and the Natural Environment'
	1986	Arnold Berleant, 'Cultivating an Urban Aesthetic'
	1992	Arnold Berleant, *The Aesthetics of the Environment*
	1993	Noël Carroll, 'On Being Moved by Nature: Between Religion and Natural History'
	1995	Tom Leddy, 'Everyday Surface Aesthetic Qualities: "Neat," "Messy," "Clean," "Dirty"'
	1997	Arnold Berleant, *Living in the Landscape*
		Robert Stecker, 'The Correct and the Appropriate in the Appreciation of Nature'

1998	Emily Brady, 'Imagination and the Aesthetic Appreciation of Nature'
	Kevin Melchionne, 'Living in Glass Houses'
	Yuriko Saito, 'Appreciating Nature on Its Own Terms'
	Yuriko Saito, 'The Aesthetics of Unscenic Nature'
2000	Allen Carlson, *Aesthetics and the Environment*
	Pauline von Bonsdorff, 'Urban Richness and the Art of Building'
2001	Allen Carlson, 'On Aesthetically Appreciating Human Environments'
2005	Pauline von Bonsdorff, 'Agriculture, Aesthetic Appreciation and the Worlds of Nature'
	Emily Brady, 'Sniffing and Savoring'
	Tom Leddy, 'The Nature of Everyday Aesthetics'
2006	Sheila Lintott, 'Toward Eco-Friendly Aesthetics'
2007	Malcolm Andrews, 'The View from the Road and the Picturesque'
	Yuriko Saito, *Everyday Aesthetics*
2008	Sherri Irvin, 'Scratching an Itch'
2009	Allen Carlson, *Nature & Landscape*

Key terms and concepts

- Aesthetics of Engagement (p. 229)
- Agreeableness (p. 236)
- Arousal Model (p. 228)
- Direct and Indirect Interest (p. 221)
- Environmental Model (p. 228)
- Everyday Surface Aesthetic Qualities (p. 234)
- 'Higher' and 'Lower' Senses (p. 236)
- Human Environments (p. 230)
- Kinesthesia (p. 231)
- Landscape Gardening (p. 221)
- Non-Cognitivism (p. 227)
- Pankalia (p. 220)
- The Picturesque (p. 224)
- Positive Aesthetics (p. 225)
- Proprioception (p. 231)
- Scientific Cognitivism (p. 225)
- Somatic Experience (p. 238)
- Sublime (p. 222)

Further reading

As mentioned at the beginning of this chapter, the topics of natural, environmental and everyday aesthetics are drawing a great deal of interest from aestheticians, and it seems like there is more material available every day. Certainly most of the contemporary work done on natural and environmental aesthetics is due primarily to two philosophers: Allen Carlson and Arnold Berleant. Each has written several books and essays on the subject, and together they edited *The Aesthetics of Human Environments* (Broadview Press, 2007), which includes articles on a number of the views discussed throughout this chapter. Another excellent collection of articles on environmental aesthetics is Allen Carlson and Sheila Lintott's *Nature, Aesthetics, and Environmentalism* (Columbia University Press, 2008), which also features essays by both historical naturalists and contemporary environmentalists. With regard to everyday aesthetics, I would strongly recommend Carolyn Korsmeyer's *Making Sense of Taste: Food and Philosophy* (Cornell University Press, 1999) and Yuriko Saito's *Everyday Aesthetics* (Oxford University

Press, 2007). Beyond the specific topics discussed in this chapter, philosophers have also looked to such diverse subjects as the aesthetics of sport, of weather and of food – and a terrific anthology including essays on these and other topics is *The Aesthetics of Everyday Life*, edited by Andrew Light and Jonathan M. Smith (Columbia University Press, 2005).

Unresolved questions

1 How is the experience of the sublime like or unlike the experience of tragedy or horror, discussed in Chapter 5? Might they be two sorts of the very same thing?

2 Essayist Ralph Waldo Emerson once wrote: 'Even the corpse has its own beauty.' Allen Carlson's view can account for this, but given his theory on the aesthetics of human environments, can he account for the growing aesthetic interest in *urban* decay?

3 Is there *any* aspect of human experience that is not open to aesthetic assessment? Can we have aesthetic experiences of purely *imaginary* experiences? What does this tell us about aesthetic inquiry?

4 Should we expect that aesthetic assessment should operate the same way for art, for nature and for everything in between? If so, how?

Notes

Preface

1   Margalit Fox, 'Don Featherstone, Inventor of the Pink Flamingo (in Plastic), Dies at 79', *New York Times*, 23 June 2015, http://www.nytimes.com/2015/06/24/business/don-featherstone-inventor-of-the-pink-flamingo-in-plastic-dies-at-79.html (accessed 17 March 2016).
2   Charlyne Varkonyi Schaub, 'Flying into the Sunset', *Victoria Advocate*, 26 October 2006, E1.

Chapter 1: Defining Art

1   In recent years, this oft-told story has been challenged. Most damning, perhaps, is the apparent fact that J. L. Mott Iron Works neither made nor sold this particular model of urinal at the time. Most controversial is a letter that Duchamp wrote to his sister (on 11 April 1917, two days after the Society rejected *Fountain*), saying that 'one of my female friends under a masculine pseudonym, Richard Mutt, sent in a porcelain urinal as a sculpture'. In *The Blind Man*, Duchamp talks of Richard Mutt as if Mutt is someone other than himself, and indeed, he would not claim credit from *Fountain* for many years. So who might this 'female friend' be? Art historians' best guess is that it is 'Baroness' Elsa von Freytag-Loringhoven, an enigmatic poet, artist and performer friend of Duchamp's. Like Duchamp, Freytag-Loringhoven worked with ready-mades, and the work seems directly in line with her sense of humour. Unlike Duchamp, she died in poverty, largely forgotten. For more, see Irene Gammel (2002), *Baroness Elsa: Gender, Dada, and Everyday Modernity* (Cambridge, MA: MIT Press) and Chapter 2 of John Higgs (2015), *Stranger Than We Can Imagine: An Alternative History of the 20th Century*. London: Weidenfeld & Nicolson.
2   Immanuel Kant (1790/1987), *The Critique of Judgment*, trans. Werner S. Pluhar (Indianapolis, IN: Hackett), §§44–54.
3   Ibid., §44.

4   It wasn't until well into the twentieth century that photography was accepted as an art form. Indeed, Alfred Stieglitz, who took the photograph of *Fountain* reproduced at the beginning of this chapter, spent much of his life advocating for photography as a fine art.

5   H. W. Janson (1969), *History of Art: A Survey of the Major Visual Arts from the Dawn of History to the Present Day* (New York: Harry N. Abrams, Inc.), 492.

6   The term 'Post-Impressionism' was coined by art critic Roger Fry, who would go on to defend a formalist view of art, following the theory of Clive Bell (see next section).

7   Laurie Schneider Adams (2002), *Art Across Time, Second Edition. Volume II: The Fourteenth Century to the Present* (New York: McGraw-Hill), 839.

8   Representational theories of art have not been abandoned entirely. For instance, see Noël Carroll's 'neo-representational theory of art' in Carroll (1999), *Philosophy of Art: A Contemporary Introduction* (London: Routledge), 26–33. And while representation is no longer standardly seen as essential to art, it continues to draw serious interest as an aspect of art. See, for example, Chapter 6 of M. C. Beardsley (1958), *Aesthetics: Problems in the Philosophy of Criticism* (Indianapolis, IN: Hackett); Peter Kivy (1984), *Sound and Semblance* (Princeton, NJ: Princeton University Press); and Kendall Walton (1990), *Mimesis as Make-Believe: On the Foundations of the Representational Arts* (Cambridge, MA: Harvard University Press).

9   Clive Bell (1913/2006), *Art* (Rockville, MD: IndyPublish).

10   Bell refers to the painting as 'Paddington Station'.

11   R. G. Collingwood (1938/74), *The Principles of Art* (Oxford: Oxford University Press).

12   Ibid., 24.

13   Ibid., 122.

14   Henri Matisse (1931/2003), 'Notes of a Painter', in *Art in Theory: 1900–2000*, ed. C. Harrison and P. Wood (Oxford: Blackwell), 70.

15   M. C. Beardsley (1983), 'An Aesthetic Definition of Art', in *What is Art?*, ed. H. Curtler (New York: Haven Publications), 58.

16   Oswald Hanfling (1995), 'Art, Artifact and Function', *Philosophical Investigations* 18 (1): 37.

17   George Schlesinger (1979), 'Aesthetic Experience and the Definition of Art', *British Journal of Aesthetics* 19 (2): 175.

18   Richard Lind (1992), 'The Aesthetic Essence of Art', *Journal of Aesthetics and Art Criticism* 50 (2): 124.

19   Beardsley (1958), 527.

20   Paul Ziff (1953), 'The Task of Defining a Work of Art'. *Philosophical Review* 62 (1).

21   M. Weitz (1956), 'The Role of Theory in Aesthetics', *Journal of Aesthetics and Art Criticism* 15 (1).

22   Arthur Danto (1964), 'The Artworld', *Journal of Philosophy* 61 (19): 580.

23   George Dickie (1974), *Art and Aesthetic* (Ithaca, NY: Cornell University Press); ibid. (1984/97), *The Art Circle: A Theory of Art* (Evanston, IL: Chicago Spectrum Press).

24   Dickie (1974), 36

25   Dickie (1984/97), 80–2.

26   Jerrold Levinson (1979), 'Defining Art Historically'. *British Journal of Aesthetics* 19 (3).

27   See Robert Stecker (2010), *Aesthetics and the Philosophy of Art: An Introduction*, 2nd edn (New York: Rowman & Littlefield), 114–16; see also Stecker (1997c), *Artworks: Definition, Meaning, Value* (University Park, PA: Pennsylvania State University Press). Something cannot be an artwork at a time before it is created, Stecker notes.

28   Stecker (2010), 116.

Chapter 2: Interpretation and Intention

1   Gary Graff and Daniel Durchholz (2000), *Musichound Rock: The Essential Album Guide* (London: Omnibus Press), 1205.

2   *The Big Picture*, MTV, 18 May 1989.

3   *Morning Edition*, NPR, 28 December 2009.

4   *Fresh Air*, NPR, 31 October 2011.

5   See Robert Stecker (1993), 'Art Interpretation', *Journal of Aesthetics and Art Criticism* 52 (2).

6   Immanuel Kant (1790/1987), *The Critique of Judgment*, trans. Werner S. Pluhar (Indianapolis, IN: Hackett).

7   Eugène Delacroix (1824/1998), 'On Romanticism' (Journal Entries, 1822–4), in *Art in Theory: 1815–1900*, ed. C. Harrison, P. Wood and J. Gaiger (Oxford: Blackwell), 28.

8   Washington Allston (1850/1998), 'Art', in *Art in Theory: 1815–1900*, ed. C. Harrison, P. Wood, and J. Gaiger (Oxford: Blackwell), 93–4.

9   Partial transcript available at: http://www.the-leaky-cauldron. org/2007/10/20/j-k-rowling-at-carnegie-hall-reveals-dumbledore-is-gay-neville-marries-hannah-abbott-and-scores-more (accessed 17 March 2016).

10   Toronto Press Conference, Canadian Broadcast Corporation, 22 October 2007.

11   T. S. Eliot (1919/82), 'Tradition and the Individual Talent', *Perspecta* 19.

12   Ibid., 42.

13   Ibid., 39.

14   http://azpoetryautobiography.blogspot.com/2011/04/in-well-analysis.html (accessed 17 March 2016).

15   W. K. Wimsatt, Jr and Monroe C. Beardsley (1954), 'The Intentional Fallacy', in *The Verbal Icon: Studies in the Meaning of Poetry*, ed. W. K. Wimsatt, Jr. (Lexington, KY: University of Kentucky Press).

16   Personal correspondence with the author.

17   Elizabeth Gilbert (2003), 'Play It Like Your Hair's on Fire', in *Da Capo Best Music Writing*, ed. Matt Groening (New York: Da Capo), 92.

18   For an updated version of this anti-intentionalist view, see Monroe C. Beardsley (1982), 'Intentions and Interpretations: A Fallacy Revived', in *The Aesthetic Point of View: Selected Essays*, ed. M. J. Wreen and D. M. Callen (Ithaca, NY: Cornell University Press).

19   Roland Barthes (1967/77), 'The Death of the Author', in *Image, Music, Text*, ed. and trans. Stephen Heath (New York: Noonday).

20   Ibid., 143.

21   Ibid., 145.

22   Ibid., 148.

23   Michel Foucault (1969/77), 'What is an Author?', in *Language, Counter-Memory, Practice*, trans. Donald F. Bouchard and Sherry Simon, ed. Donald F. Bouchard (Ithaca, NY: Cornell University Press).

24   Roland Barthes (1977), 'From Work to Text', in *Image, Music, Text*, ed. and trans. Stephen Heath (New York: Noonday), 162.

25   See Stanley Fish (1980), *Is There a Text in This Class? The Authority of Interpretive Communities* (Cambridge, MA: Harvard University Press).

26   See Roman Ingarden (1979), *The Literary Work of Art: An Investigation on the Borderlines of Ontology* (Evanston, IL: Northwestern University Press), 246–54.

27   Michael Krausz (1993), *Rightness and Reasons: Interpretation in Cultural Practices* (Ithaca, NY: Cornell University Press).

28   Ibid., 121.

29   See Robert Stecker (1997a), 50.

30   E. D. Hirsch, Jr (1967), *Validity in Interpretation* (New Haven, CT: Yale University Press).

31   Ibid., 8.

32   Ibid., 18.

33   Noël Carroll (1992), 'Art, Intention, and Conversation', in *Intention and Interpretation*, ed. Gary Iseminger (Philadelphia, PA: Temple University Press).

34   Ibid., 118.

35 Ibid., 120.

36 Ibid., 124.

37 Daniel Nathan (1992), 'Irony, Metaphor, and the Problem of Intention', in *Intention and Interpretation*, ed. Gary Iseminger (Philadelphia, PA: Temple University Press), 199. See also Daniel Nathan (1982), 'Irony and the Author's Intentions', *British Journal of Aesthetics* 22 (3); and for a related view, see Alexander Nehamas (1981), 'The Postulated Author: Critical Monism as a Regulative Ideal', *Critical Inquiry* 8 (1) and (1986), 'What an Author Is', *Journal of Philosophy* 83 (11).

38 See Carroll's discussion of Andrew Greeley's novel *Ascent into Hell* in Carroll (1992), 99.

39 Jerrold Levinson's view is first presented in Levinson (1992), 'Intention and Interpretation: A Last Look', in *Intention and Interpretation*, ed. Gary Iseminger (Philadelphia, PA: Temple University Press), a paper slightly modified in Levinson (1996), 'Intention and Interpretation in Literature', in *The Pleasures of Aesthetics: Philosophical Essays* (Ithaca, NY: Cornell University Press).

40 Levinson (1996), 177.

41 William Tolhurst (1979), 'On What a Text Is and How It Means', *British Journal of Aesthetics* 19 (1): 11.

42 Berys Gaut (1993), 'Interpreting the Arts: The *Patchwork Theory*', *Journal of Aesthetics and Art Criticism* 51 (4).

Chapter 3: Aesthetic Properties and Evaluation

1 Strictly speaking, the black square in *Black Square* isn't actually a square: its height and width are a little bit off. Malevich had originally titled it *Quadrangle*, but apparently changed his mind.

2 K. S. Malevich (1978), *The Artist, Infinity, Suprematism – Unpublished Writings 1913–1933*, ed. Troels Anderson, ed. (Copenhagen: Borgen), 147

3 Alexander Benois, Review of the '0,10' exhibition, *The Word*, 9 January 1916. See discussion in Linda S. Boersma (1994), *0,10: The Last Futurist Exhibition of Painting* (Rotterdam: 010 Publishers).

4 For example, you can visit the website of Dr Stephen Marquardt at http://www.beautyanalysis.com (accessed 17 March 2016).

5 Historically, the most famous treatise attempting to establish the mathematical basis to beauty is Luca Pacioli's three-volume 1509 work, *De Divina Proportione* (*The Divine Proportion*). For more recent discussions on the matter, see for example Mario Livio's *The Golden Ratio*

(New York: Broadway Books, 2002), Bülent Atalay's *Math and the Mona Lisa* (Washington, DC: Smithsonian Books, 2004) and György Doczi's *The Power of Limits: Proportional Harmonies in Nature, Art, and Architecture* (Boulder, CO: Shambhala Publications, 1994).

6   Plato (c. 360 BCE/1963), *Laws*, in *The Collected Dialogues of Plato Including the Letters*, trans. A. E. Taylor, ed. Edith Hamilton and Huntington Cairns (Princeton, NJ: Princeton University Press), §§653e–655b.

7   Bonaventure (1259/1956), *The Journey of the Mind to God*, trans. Philotheus Boehner (Indianapolis, IN: Hackett), II.4–6.

8   Augustine (398/1876), *Confessions*, trans. J. G. Pilkington (Edinburgh: T&T Clark), X.XXXIV, 53.

9   Thomas Aquinas (c. 1274/1921), *Summa Theologica*, trans. Fathers of the English Dominican Province (London: Burns Oates & Washbourne Ltd), Q.39, A.8.

10 See Władysław Tatarkiewicz (2005), *History of Aesthetics in Three Volumes*, Vol. 3 (London: Continuum), 109.

11 Francis Hutcheson (1725/2008), *An Inquiry into the Original of Our Ideas of Beauty and Virtue*, ed. Wolfgang Leidhold (Indianapolis, IN: Liberty Fund Books).

12 Plato (c. 390 BCE /1963), *Hippias Major*, in *The Collected Dialogues of Plato Including the Letters*, trans. Benjamin Jowett, ed. Edith Hamilton and Huntington Cairns (Princeton, NJ: Princeton University Press), §298a–b.

13 David Hume (1757/1987a), 'Of the Standard of Taste', in *Essays, Moral, Political, and Literary*, ed. Eugene F. Miller (Indianapolis, IN: Liberty Fund Books).

14 Ibid., I.XXIII.8.

15 Kant (1790/1987).

16 Although this is true for judging a painting as *beautiful*, Kant concedes that judging a painting *as a painting* will require concepts – such as what makes something a good Cubist painting versus a good landscape – but these will be artistic concepts, not aesthetic ones.

17 Kant gets this notion from Shaftesbury.

18 Immanuel Kant (1790/1987), *The Critique of Judgment*, trans. Werner S. Pluhar (Indianapolis, IN: Hackett), §211.

19 Frank Sibley (1959), 'Aesthetic Concepts', *Philosophical Review* 68 (4).

20 Ibid. (1974), 'Particularity, Art and Evaluation', *Proceedings of the Aristotelian Society* 48 (Supplement).

21 Roger Scruton (1974), *Art and Imagination: A Study in the Philosophy of Mind* (London: Methuen).

22 Ibid., 54.

23   Philip Pettit (1983), 'The Possibility of Aesthetic Realism', in *Pleasure, Preference, and Value: Studies in Philosophical Aesthetics*, ed. E. Schaper (Cambridge: Cambridge University Press).

24   Arthur Danto (1964), 'The Artworld', *Journal of Philosophy* 61 (19): 580.

25   K. L. Walton (1970), 'Categories of Art', *Philosophical Review* 79 (3).

26   Jorge Luis Borges (1939/62), 'Pierre Menard, Author of Don Quixote', in *Ficciones*, trans. Anthony Bonner (New York: Grove Press), 51–3.

27   M. C. Beardsley (1983), 'An Aesthetic Definition of Art', in *What is Art?*, ed. H. Curtler (New York: Haven Publications), 58.

28   Ibid. (1958), *Aesthetics: Problems in the Philosophy of Criticism* (Indianapolis, IN: Hackett), 529; ibid. (1963), 'The Discrimination of Aesthetic Enjoyment', *British Journal of Aesthetics* 3 (4): 297.

29   See Beardsley (1963); ibid. (1969), 'Aesthetic Experience Regained', *Journal of Aesthetics and Art Criticism* 28 (1).

30   J. Feinberg (1994), 'Not With My Tax Money: The Problem of Justifying Government Subsidies for the Arts', *Public Affairs Quarterly* 8 (2).

31   Malcolm Budd (1995), *Values of Art: Pictures, Poetry, and Music* (London: Penguin).

32   Ibid., 7.

33   See Robert Stecker (1997c), *Artworks: Definition, Meaning, Value* (University Park, PA: Pennsylvania State University Press), 247–68.

34   Andrew Huddleston (2012), 'In Defense of Artistic Value', *Philosophical Quarterly* 62 (249): 713.

Chapter 4: The Ontology of Art

1   John Szarkowski (1971), *Walker Evans* (New York: Museum of Modern Art), 20.

2   Abigail Solomon-Godeau (1985/96), 'Winning the Game When the Rules Have Been Changed: Art Photography and Postmodernism', in *Illuminations: Women Writing on Photography from the 1850s to the Present*, ed. L. Heron and V. Williams (London: I.B. Tauris & Co.), 307–19, at 309.

3   See, e.g., Jerrold Levinson (1980b), 'What a Musical Work Is', *Journal of Philosophy* 77 (1): 8–9; Gregory Currie (1989), *An Ontology of Art* (New York: St. Martin's Press), 11–12; Robert Stecker (1997c), 26.

4   See D. Davies (2004), *Art as Performance* (Oxford: Blackwell), 18; ibid. (2009), 'The Primacy of Practice in the Ontology of Art', *Journal of Aesthetics and Art Criticism* 67 (2): 162.

5   Amie L. Thomasson (2004), 'The Ontology of Art', in *The Blackwell Guide to Aesthetics*, ed. P. Kivy (Oxford: Blackwell); ibid. (2005), 'The Ontology

of Art and Knowledge in Aesthetics', *Journal of Aesthetics and Art Criticism* 63 (2).

6   Richard Wollheim (1968), *Art and Its Objects* (New York: Harper & Row).

7   Ibid., 3.

8   Nelson Goodman (1976), *Languages of Art: An Approach to a Theory of Symbols*, 2nd edn (Indianapolis, IN: Hackett Publishing Company).

9   Jerrold Levinson (1980a), 'Autographic and Allographic Art Revisited', *Philosophical Studies* 38 (4).

10   C. S. Peirce (1906), 'Prolegomena to an Apology for Pragmaticism', *The Monist* 16.

11   Nicholas Wolterstorff (1980), *Works and Worlds of Art* (Oxford: Clarendon Press).

12   Julian Dodd makes a related suggestion that artworks are 'norm-types' in Dodd (2007), *Works of Music: An Essay in Ontology* (Oxford: Oxford University Press).

13   Julian Dodd (2000), 'Musical Works as Eternal Types', *British Journal of Aesthetics* 40 (4).

14   Peter Kivy (1983), 'Platonism in Music: A Kind of Defense', *Grazer Philosophische Studien* 19; ibid. (1987), 'Platonism in Music: Another Kind of Defense'. *Philosophical Quarterly* 24 (3).

15   Joseph Margolis (1977), 'The Ontological Peculiarity of Works of Art', *Journal of Aesthetics and Art Criticism* 36 (1).

16   Levinson (1980b).

17   Michael Krausz (1993), *Rightness and Reasons: Interpretation in Cultural Practices* (Ithaca, NY: Cornell University Press).

18   Robert Stecker offers criticisms of the various constructivist views in a number of places, most fully in Stecker (2003), *Interpretation and Construction* (Oxford: Blackwell).

19   Currie (1989). See also D. Davies (2007), *Aesthetics and Literature* (London: Continuum).

20   Jeanna Siegel (1988/91), 'After Sherrie Levine', in *Art Theory and Criticism: An Anthology of Formalist, Avant-Garde, Contextualist and Post-Modernist Thought*, ed. S. Everett (Jefferson, NC: McFarland & Co. Inc.), 264–72, at 266.

21   Simon Blond (2009), 'Creativity in Art: A Modernist Challenge to Postmodern Myths', in *Subjectivity, Creativity, and the Institution*, ed. C. Crouch (Boca Raton, FL: BrownWalker Press), 113–22, at 112.

Chapter 5: Emotions and the Arts

1   Mark Kermode (2003), *The Exorcist*, rev. 2nd edn (London: British Film Institute), 120.

2   Dave Karger, Rebecca Ascher-Walsh, Christ Nashawaty, Steve Daly and Daniel Fierman, 'The 25 scariest movies of all time', *Entertainment Weekly*, http://www.ew.com/article/1999/07/23/25-scariest-movies-all-time (accessed 17 March 2016).

3   Gene Siskel (1974), 'Crowds upset neighborhood: "Exorcist" also is disturbing outside theater', *Chicago Tribune*, 10 February.

4   Clarence Page (1974), '2 being restrained: 6 who saw "Exorcist" under care', *Chicago Tribune*, 18 January.

5   Claudia Cassidy (1974), 'On The Aisle: The Devil you say', *Chicago Tribune*, 7 April.

6   Mark Kermode (1998), *The Fear of God: 25 Years of 'The Exorcist'* (BBC documentary).

7   Benedetto Croce (1909/22), *Aesthetic: As Science of Expression and General Linguistic*, trans. Douglas Ainslie (New York: Noonday); Leo Tolstoy (1896/1959), *What Is Art?*, trans. Aylmer Maude (New York: Thomas Y. Crowell & Co.).

8   Croce refers to the relevant mental state in such cases as an 'intuition'.

9   This theory of Tolstoy's, outlined in his book *What Is Art?*, is intertwined with his views on ethics and religion. In addition to proper transmission of feelings, Tolstoy requires that a work's subject matter be of a certain dignified quality.

10 Guy Sircello (1972), *Mind & Art: An Essay on the Varieties of Expression* (Princeton, NJ: Princeton University Press).

11 Peter Kivy (1989), *Sound Sentiment* (Philadelphia, PA: Temple University Press).

12 See also Alan Tormey (1971), *The Concept of Expression: A Study in Philosophical Psychology and Aesthetics* (Princeton, NJ: Princeton University Press).

13 Ismay Barwell (1986), 'How Does Art Express Emotion', *Journal of Aesthetics and Art Criticism* 45 (2): 180. See also Robert Stecker (1984), 'Expression of Emotion in (Some of) the Arts', *Journal of Aesthetics and Art Criticism* 42 (4).

14 Alexander G. Schauss (1985), 'The Physiological Effect of Color on the Suppression of Human Aggression: Research on Baker-Miller Pink', *International Journal of Biosocial Research* 7 (2): 55–64.

15 See 'Seduction and Indifference' and 'Lamentations: Music, Madness, and Melancholia' in Oliver Sacks (2008), *Musicophilia: Tales of Music and the Brain: Revised and Expanded* (New York: Vintage Books).

16 Derek Matravers (1998), *Art and Emotion* (Oxford: Oxford University Press).

17 Plato (c. 380 BCE/1963), *Ion*, in *The Collected Dialogues of Plato Including the Letters*, trans. Lane Cooper, ed. Edith Hamilton and Huntington Cairns (Princeton, NJ: Princeton University Press), §535c.

18 Colin Radford (1975), 'How Can We Be Moved by the Fate of Anna Karenina?', *Proceedings of the Aristotelian Society* 49 (Supplement).

19 Eva Schaper (1978), 'Fiction and the Suspension of Disbelief', *British Journal of Aesthetics* 18 (1).

20 K. L. Walton (1978), 'Fearing Fictions', *Journal of Philosophy* 75 (1); ibid. (1990), *Mimesis as Make-Believe: On the Foundations of the Representational Arts* (Cambridge, MA: Harvard University Press).

21 David Novitz (1980), 'Fiction, Imagination and Emotion', *Journal of Aesthetics and Art Criticism* 38 (3).

22 Ibid., 287.

23 The Ancient Greeks are also responsible for the term 'tragedy', literally translated as 'goat song', though the reasons for the term remain the subject of some debate.

24 Sigmund Freud used the story to name the 'Oedipus complex'. Each of Aeschylus, Sophocles and Euripides had plays devoted to Oedipus.

25 David Hume (1757/1987b), 'Of Tragedy', in *Essays: Moral, Political, and Literary*, ed. Eugene F. Miller (Indianapolis, IN: Liberty Fund Books).

26 Hume argues that on occasion, the spectacle of tragedy may be *too* atrocious to be converted into pleasure. In these cases, we might think of the logs as being too much for the river to overcome.

27 Friedrich Nietzsche (1872/1999), *The Birth of Tragedy*, in *The Birth of Tragedy and Other Writings*, trans. Ronald Spiers, ed. Raymond Geuss and Ronald Spiers (Cambridge: Cambridge University Press).

28 Nietzsche argues that this is true in the works of Aeschylus and Sophocles, but that in the works of Euripides, tragedy begins a downward turn.

29 It is worth noting that this discussion of Nietzsche's view puts aside a great deal of Nietzsche's book for the sake of the problem at hand.

30 Susan Feagin (1983), 'The Pleasures of Tragedy', *American Philosophical Quarterly* 20 (1).

31 See John Morreall (1985), 'Enjoying Negative Emotions in Fiction', *Philosophy and Literature* 9 (1).

32 Marcia M. Eaton (1982), 'A Strange Kind of Sadness', *Journal of Aesthetics and Art Criticism* 41 (1): 59.

Chapter 6: Art and Morality

1   Dieter Buchhart and Anna Karina Hofbauer (2002), 'Sollen wir alle Menschen verklagen, die Meeresfrüchte essen?', *Kunstforum International* 162: 270–9.
2   http://news.bbc.co.uk/2/hi/3040891.stm (accessed 17 March 2016).
3   Plato (c. 360/1963), *Republic*, in *The Collected Dialogues of Plato Including the Letters*, trans. Paul Shorey, ed. Edith Hamilton and Huntington Cairns (Princeton, NJ: Princeton University Press).
4   Ibid., §607.
5   3rd Earl of Shaftesbury (Anthony Ashley Cooper) (1711/1999), *Characteristics of Men, Manners, Opinions, Times*, ed. Lawrence E. Klein (Cambridge: Cambridge University Press), 326.
6   Immanuel Kant (1790/1987), *The Critique of Judgment*, trans. Werner S. Pluhar (Indianapolis, IN: Hackett), §299.
7   Théophile Gautier (1848/1998), 'Art in 1848', in *Art in Theory: 1815–1900*, trans. Jonathan Murphy, ed. C. Harrison et al. (Oxford: Blackwell), 315.
8   Walter Pater (1873), *Studies in the History of the Renaissance* (London: Macmillan and Co.), 213.
9   Valie Export (1973/2003), 'Woman's Art', in *Art in Theory: 1900–2000*, trans. N. Walker, ed. C. Harrison and P. Wood (Oxford: Blackwell), 928
10   Christine Battersby (1989), *Gender and Genius: Towards a Feminist Aesthetics* (Bloomington, IN: The Women's Press).
11   Linda Nochlin (1971), 'Why Have There Been No Great Women Artists?', *ARTnews* (January).
12   A. W. Eaton (2008), 'Feminist Philosophy of Art', *Philosophy Compass* 3 (5): 883.
13   David Hume, (1757/1987a), 'Of the Standard of Taste'. in *Essays, Moral, Political, and Literary*, ed. Eugene F. Miller (Indianapolis, IN: Liberty Fund Books), §33.
14   Leo Tolstoy (1986/1899), *What Is Art?*, trans. Aylmer Maude (New York: Thomas Y. Crowell & Co.), 47.
15   Nöel Carroll (1993a), 'Moderate Moralism', *British Journal of Aesthetics* 36 (3).
16   See, e.g., Rishard Janko (1987), 'Introduction', in *Poetics* by Aristotle (Indianapolis, IN: Hackett).
17   Ibid., 228.
18   Berys Gaut (1998), 'The Ethical Criticism of Art', in *Aesthetics and Ethics: Essays at the Intersection*, ed. Jerrold Levinson (Cambridge: Cambridge University Press).

19   James C. Anderson and Jeffrey T. Dean (1998), 'Moderate Autonomism', *British Journal of Aesthetics* 38 (2).

20   Ibid., 163.

21   HR 2788, Helms Amendment No. 894, US Senate, 29 September 1989, *Congressional Record*, S12283.

22   Mary Devereaux (1993), 'Protected Space: Politics, Censorship, and the Arts', *Journal of Aesthetics and Art Criticism* 51 (2).

23   Ibid., 213.

24   Richard Serra (1991), 'Art and Censorship', *Critical Inquiry* 17 (3).

25   Nöel Carroll (1987), 'Can Government Funding of the Arts be Justified Theoretically?', *Journal of Aesthetic Education* 21 (1).

26   Ibid., 34.

27   Richard Shusterman (1984), 'Aesthetic Censorship: Censoring Art for Art's Sake', *Journal of Aesthetics and Art Criticism* 43 (2).

Chapter 7: Art, Aesthetics and Identity

1   http://www.nobelprize.org/nobel_prizes/literature/laureates/1938/buck-lecture.html (accessed 17 March 2016).

2   See Zhiwei Xiao (2002), 'Nationalism, Orientalism, and an Unequal Treatise of Ethnography: The Making of *The Good Earth*', in *The Chinese in America: A History from Gold Mountain to the New Millennium*, ed. S. Cassel (Walnut Creek, CA: Altamira), 279.

3   Sarah Berry (2004), 'Hollywood Exoticism: Cosmetics and Color in the 1930s', in *Stars: The Film Reader*, ed. L. Fischer and M. Landy (London: Routledge), 189

4   '"Good Earth" a Bad Casting Headache', *Variety*, 18 December 1935, 3.

5   It is less unusual for a white performer to play a white character who dons blackface in the story, as in *Soul Man* (1986), *Tropic Thunder* (2008) and *Dear White People* (2014).

6   Brando as Sakini in *The Teahouse of the August Moon* (1956), Nimoy as Ahman Fanakati in *Marco Polo* (1982) and Peter Sellers as Fu Manchu in *The Fiendish Plot of Dr. Fu Manchu* (1980), among other roles.

7   As such, casting a non-white actor to play the role of a traditionally white character (such as Samuel L. Jackson's being cast as Nick Fury in Marvel's *Avengers* movies) does not raise the same concerns.

8   Quoted in Ross Von Metzke, 'Takei to WB: Do the Right Thing', *The Advocate*, 18 April 2011, http://www.advocate.com/news/

news-features/2011/04/18/takei-wb-do-right-thing (accessed 18 April 2016).

9   Rebecca Sun and Graeme McMillan, 'Why did "Doctor Strange" and "Ghost in the Shell" Whitewash Their Asian Characters?', *Hollywood Reporter*, 15 April 2016, http://www.hollywoodreporter.com/heat-vision/doc-strange-whitewashing-shell-884385 (accessed 18 April 2016).

10 S. Smith, M. Choueiti and K. Pieper (2016), *Inclusion or Invisibility? Comprehensive Annenberg Report on Diversity in Entertainment* (Los Angeles: USC Annenberg School for Communication & Journalism).

11 Abé Mark Nornes (2007), *Cinema Babel: Translating Global Cinema* (Minneapolis, MN: University of Minnesota Press), 219.

12 Alan Duke, 'Denzel Blacklisted! Sony Execs Warned Not to Cast Washington In Big Flicks Because Black Leads "Don't Play Well" – Latest Shocking Email Leak', *Radar Online*, 17 December 2014, http://radaronline.com/exclusives/2014/12/sony-email-hack-denzel-washington-black-leads-international-audience-racist/ (accessed 17 March 2016).

13 9 January 1940

14 Paul C. Taylor (2016), *Black is Beautiful: A Philosophy of Black Aesthetics* (Oxford: Blackwell), 123.

15 Ibid., 65.

16 Playwright and director Lee Breuer similarly recounts having a play rejected by the Spoleto Festival in Charleston, South Carolina: 'I was told it was too politically hot, too feminist, too black, too integrated and, basically, bad for funding. Money is doing the talking now.' Gabrielle Cody and Lee Breuer (1989), 'Lee Breuer on Interculturalism', *Performing Arts Journal* 11 (3)/12 (1): 65.

17 In 2016, Jeffrey Tambor was awarded the Emmy for Outstanding Lead Actor in a Comedy Series for his role as trans woman Maura Pfefferman in the series *Transparent*. In his acceptance speech, calling out for better inclusion of transgender performers in film and television, Tambor lamented: 'To you people out there, you producers and you network owners and you agents and you creative sparks, please give transgender talent a chance ... I would not be unhappy were I the last cisgender male to play a female transgender [woman] on television. We have work to do.' Cavan Sieczkowski, 'Jeffrey Tambor Challenge Hollywood To Give Transgender Actors More Roles', *Huffington Post*, 18 September 2016, http://www.huffingtonpost.com/entry/jeffrey-tambor-transparent-best-actor_us_57df39c1e4b04a1497b51770 (accessed 18 September 2016).

18 Bechdel herself prefers to call it the Bechdel-Wallace test, citing a friend named Liz Wallace, to whom Bechdel attributes the test itself.

19 Linda Nochlin (1971), 'Why Have There Been No Great Women Artists?', *ARTnews*, January, 25.

20 W. E. B. Du Bois (1926), 'Criteria for Negro Art', *The Crisis* 32, paras 21 and 26.

21 Virginia Woolf (1929), *A Room of One's Own* (New York: Harcourt, Brace and Co.), 85.

22 Anon., Review of *Frankenstein; or the Modern Prometheus*, *The British Critic*, April 1818, repr. in *The New Critic, New Series*, Vol. IX (London: F. C. and J. Rivington, 1818), 432–8, at 438. Shelley's mother was early feminist philosopher Mary Wollstonecraft, best known for her work *A Vindication of the Rights of Woman*, arguing for the education rights of women. Her earlier work, a political pamphlet titled *A Vindication of the Rights of Men*, was published anonymously. When her name was attached to the second edition of the pamphlet, criticism came to be centred on her sex, her passion and her impertinence for writing outside a woman's domain.

23 Plato (c. 390 BCE/1963), *Greater Hippias*, in *The Collected Dialogues of Plato Including the Letters*, trans. Benjamin Jowett, ed. Edith Hamilton and Huntington Cairns (Princeton, NJ: Princeton University Press), 298a.

24 See, e.g., Aristotle (c. 350 BCE /1987), 'Eudemian Ethics', trans. M. J. Woods, in *A New Aristotle Reader*, ed. J. L. Ackrill (Princeton, NJ: Princeton University Press), §1215b31–36.

25 Thomas Aquinas (c. 1274/1921), *Summa Theologica*, trans. Fathers of the English Dominican Province (London: Burns Oates & Washbourne Ltd), I-a II-ae, Q. 27 A.1 ad 3.

26 Ficino outlines this view in his *Commentary on Plato's Symposium*, specifically his commentary on the Fifth Speech.

27 Carolyn Korsmeyer (1999), *Making Sense of Taste: Food and Philosophy* (Ithaca, NY: Cornell University Press), 5.

28 Joanna Frueh (1988), 'Towards a Feminist Theory of Art Criticism', in *Feminist Art Criticism: An Anthology*, ed. A. Raven, C. L. Langer and J. Frueh (Ann Arbor, MI: UMI Research Press), 160.

29 Immanuel Kant (1764/1960), *Observations on the Feeling of the Beautiful and Sublime*, trans. John T. Goldthwait (Berkeley, CA: University of California Press), 110

30 For example, 'The Japanese could in a way be regarded as the Englishmen of [Asia], but hardly in any other quality than their resoluteness – which degenerates into the utmost stubbornness – their valor, and disdain of death. For the rest, they display few signs of a finer feeling.' Kant (1764/1960), *Observations*, 110.

31 The same problem would seem to hold for Kant's views on moral judgement. See C. W. Mills (2005), 'Kant's *Untermenschen*', in *Race and Racism Philosophy*, ed. A. Valls (Ithaca, NY: Cornell University Press).

32 David Hume (1748/1875), 'Of National Characters', in *Essays: Moral, Political, and Literary*, Vol. 1 (London: Longmans, Green, and Co.), 252n.

33 Ibid., 252.

34 Roelofs suggests that other comments by Hume betray a view that women have only limited capacity for aesthetic judgement, though his comments are less clear than his views on race. See Monique Roelofs (2014), *The Cultural Promise of the Aesthetic* (London: Bloomsbury), 31–2.

35 Ibid., 53.

36 See Pauline Kleingeld (2007), 'Kant's Second Thoughts on Race', *Philosophical Quarterly* 57 (229).

37 Taylor (2016), *Black is Beautiful*, 40.

38 Laura Mulvey (1975), 'Visual Pleasure and Narrative Cinema', *Screen* 16 (3).

39 Peggy Zeglin Brand (1998), 'Disinterestedness and Political Art', in *Aesthetics: The Big Questions*, ed. C. Korsmeyer (Oxford: Blackwell), 160.

40 Tobin Siebers (2010), *Disability Aesthetics* (Ann Arbor, MI: University of Michigan Press), 27

41 Ibid., 15.

42 David Hume (1742/1987c), 'Of the Delicacy of Taste and Passion', in *Essays, Moral, Political, and Literary*, ed. Eugene F. Miller (Indianapolis, IN: Liberty Fund Books).

43 Ibid., 3.

44 Anita Silvers (2000), 'From the Crooked Timber of Humanity, Beautiful Things Can Be Made', in *Beauty Matters*, ed. P. Z. Brand (Bloomington, IN: Indiana University Press), 206, 215.

45 Siebers (2010), *Disability Aesthetics*, 4.

46 Taylor (2016), *Black is Beautiful*, 61.

47 Ibid. (1995), '…So Black and Blue: Response to Rudinow', *Journal of Aesthetics and Art Criticism* 53 (3): 314.

48 Ibid., 315.

49 Ralph J. Gleason (1968), 'Can the White Man Sing the Blues?', *Jazz and Pop* 7 (8): 28–9.

50 See Joel Rudinow (1994), 'Race, Ethnicity, Expressive Authenticity: Can White People Sing the Blues?', *Journal of Aesthetics and Art Criticism* 52 (1); and (1995), 'Reply to Taylor', *Journal of Aesthetics and Art Criticism* 53 (3).

51 James O. Young (2008), *Cultural Appropriation and the Arts* (Malden, MA: Blackwell), 5.

52 Taylor (1995), '… So Black and Blue', 313.

53 LeRoi Jones (1963), *Blues People: Negro Music in White America* (New York: William Morrow and Co.), 94. In 1967, Baraka was still publishing under his birth name of LeRoi Jones.

54   For reasons of space, I have omitted discussion of Young's category of *object appropriation*, where the possession of some tangible cultural object is taken by members of another culture, such as Lord Elgin's famous removal of the Parthenon friezes from Athens in the early nineteenth century.

55   Husain Haddaway (1990), *The Arabian Nights* (London: Norton), xiii.

56   Young (2008), *Cultural* Appropriation, 120.

57   Petti Fong, '"Degrading" B.C. Murals Removed', *Toronto Star*, 25 June 2007, https://www.thestar.com/news/2007/06/25/degrading_bc_murals_removed.html (accessed 17 March 2016), quoting Grand Chief Edward John of the First Nations Summit.

58   Young (2008), *Cultural Appropriation*, 143.

59   Ibid., 149.

60   Steve Huey (2003), 'Paul Butterfield', in *All Music Guide to the Blues: The Definitive Guide*, ed. V. Bogdanov, C. Wodstra and S. T. Erlewine, 3rd edn (San Francisco, CA: Backbeat Books), 91.

61   Jeanette Bicknell (2009), 'Reflections on "John Henry": Ethical Issues in Singing Performance', *Journal of Aesthetics and Art Criticism* 67 (2): 179–80.

62   Ibid., 179.

63   Ibid.

64   Clive Bell, whose definition of art we discussed back in Chapter 1, writes, 'I have noticed a consistency in those to whom the most beautiful thing in the world is a beautiful woman, and the next most beautiful thing a picture of one.' Clive Bell (1913/2006), *Art* (Rockville, MD: IndyPublish), 8.

65   Sherri Irvin (ed.) (2016), *Body Aesthetics* (Oxford: Oxford University Press), 1.

66   Edmund Burke (1757/1887), *A Philosophical Inquiry into the Origin of Our Ideas of the Sublime and Beautiful*, in *The Works of the Right Honourable Edmund Burke*, Vol. 1 (London: John C. Nimmo), 226–7.

67   George Yancy (2008), *Black Bodies, White Gazes: The Continuing Significance of Race* (New York: Rowman & Littlefield), xx.

68   Burke (1757/1887), *A Philosophical Inquiry*, 229.

69   Ralph Ellison (1952), *Invisible Man* (New York: Random House), 3. Notably, Ellison's protagonist, who narrates the book, goes unnamed. Wells's science fiction novel, *The Invisible Man*, was published in 1897.

70   Black personhood is further obscured by treating black characters as interchangeable – what Taylor calls the 'denial of black plurality'. Taylor (2016), *Black is Beautiful*, 62.

71   Taylor (2016), *Black is Beautiful*, 53.

72   Quoted in George Yancy, 'The Invisible Asian', *New York Times*, 8 October

2015, http://opinionator.blogs.nytimes.com/2015/10/08/the-invisible-asian/ (accessed 17 March 2016). Matters are perhaps unique for Latinas and Latinos – people of Latin America descent – some of whom are white and some of whom are not. Ofelia Schutte writes, 'To maintain this binary, where white is also hierarchized over non-white, is to reproduce the ideology that white is the norm and brown, yellow, red, black, and mixed race are the marks of difference.' Ofelia Schutte (2000), 'Negotiating Latina Identities', in *Hispanics/Latinos in the United States: Ethnicity, Race, and Rights*, ed. J. J. E. Gracia and P. De Greiff (New York: Routledge), 71.

73 Tobin Siebers (2016), 'In/Visible: Disability on the Stage', in *Body Aesthetics*, ed. S. Irvin (Oxford: Oxford University Press), 145.

74 Cited in Siebers (2016), 'In/Visible', 145.

75 Ibid., 142.

76 A. W. Eaton (2016), 'Taste in Bodies and Fat Oppression', in *Body Aesthetics*, ed. S. Irvin (Oxford: Oxford University Press), 37–8.

77 Ibid., 39, 43.

78 http://www.merriam-webster.com/dictionary/Rubenesque (accessed 17 March 2016).

79 Harry Beaumont (1752/1885), *Crito: or a Dialogue on Beauty* (Edinburgh: Edmund Goldsmid), 60.

80 Eaton (2016), 'Taste in Bodies', 53.

Chapter 8: Aesthetics Without Art

1 http://uglyanimalsoc.com (accessed 17 March 2016).

2 http://www.nmfs.noaa.gov/rss/podcasts/weirdfins/blobfish.htm (accessed 17 March 2016).

3 Trent Dalton, 'The Blobfish and Other Deep Questions', 17 January 2015, http://www.theaustralian.com.au/news/features/the-blobfish-and-other-deep-questions/story-e6frg8h6-1227184917005 (accessed 17 March 2016).

4 Aristotle (350 BCE/1989), 'Poetics', in *On Poetry and Style*, trans. G. M. A. Grube (Indianapolis, IN: Hackett), §1451a.

5 St Augustine (c. 426/1888), *City of God*, trans. Marcus Dods (Edinburgh: T&T Clark), XI.18.

6 Torquato Tasso (1587/1993), 'Discorsi dell'arte poetica', in *The Genesis of Tasso's Narrative Theory: English Translations of the Early Poetics and a Comparative Study of their Significance*, ed. and trans. Lawrence F. Rhu (Detroit, MI: Wayne State University Press), 127.

7 Giovan Pietro Bellori (1672/2005), *The Lives of the Modern Painters,*

Sculptors and Architects, trans. Alice Sedgwick Wohl, ed. Alice Sedgwick Wohl et al. (Cambridge: Cambridge University Press), 57.

8   J. C. Loudon (1835), *An Encyclopaedia of Gardening* (London: Longman, Rees, Orme, Brown, Green and Longman), 321.

9   Immanuel Kant (1790/1987), *The Critique of Judgment*, trans. Werner S. Pluhar (Indianapolis, IN: Hackett), §350.

10 G. W. F. Hegel (1886/1994), *Introductory Lectures on Aesthetics*, trans. Bernard Bosanquet (New York: Penguin).

11 Ibid., §46.

12 R. W. Hepburn (1966), 'Contemporary Aesthetics and the Neglect of Natural Beauty', in *British Analytical Philosophy*, ed. Bernard Williams and Alan Montefiore (New York: Humanities Press).

13 See, e.g., Allen Carlson (1979), 'Appreciation and the Natural Environment', *Journal of Aesthetics and Art Criticism* 37 (3).

14 John Muir (1894/1911), 'A Near View of the High Sierra', in *The Mountains of California* (New York: Century Co.).

15 Ibid., 52.

16 Carlson (1979), 'Appreciation', 271.

17 Robert Stecker (1997b), 'The Correct and the Appropriate in the Appreciation of Nature', *British Journal of Aesthetics* 37 (4).

18 Yuriko Saito (1998b), 'The Aesthetics of Unscenic Nature', *Journal of Aesthetics and Art Criticism* 56 (2): 105.

19 Emily Brady (1998), 'Imagination and the Aesthetic Appreciation of Nature', *Journal of Aesthetics and Art Criticism* 56 (2).

20 http://uglyanimalsoc.com (accessed 17 March 2016).

21 Morgan J. Trimble and Rudi J. Van Aarde (2010), 'Species Inequality in Scientific Study', *Conservation Biology* 24 (3): 886–90. See also Stephen R. Kellert (1996), *The Value of Life: Biological Diversity and Human Society* (Washington, DC: Island Press), 102; and Yuriko Saito (2007), *Everyday Aesthetics* (Oxford: Oxford University Press), 58–65.

22 Sheila Lintott (2006), 'Toward Eco-Friendly Aesthetics', *Environmental Ethics* 28 (1).

23 Yuriko Saito provides an extremely interesting counterargument to this position in her Saito (1998b), 'The Aesthetics of Unscenic Nature', expanded in Chapter 2 of Saito (2007), *Everyday Aesthetics*.

24 And many have. See, e.g., Claire Lower, 'Please Leave The Poor Blobfish Alone. Here Are Some Much Uglier Animals', *xoJane*, 23 September 2013, http://www.xojane.com/fun/please-leave-the-poor-blobfish-alone (accessed 17 March 2016).

25 Franz Lidz, 'Behold the Blobfish', *Smithsonian Magazine*, November 2015, http://www.smithsonianmag.com/science-nature/behold-the-blobfish-180956967 (accessed 17 March 2016).

26 Noël Carroll (1993b), 'On Being Moved by Nature: Between Religion and Natural History', in *Landscape, Natural Beauty and the Arts*, ed. S. Kemal and I. Gaskell (Cambridge: Cambridge University Press).

27 Brady (1998), 'Imagination and the Aesthetic Appreciation of Nature'.

28 Arnold Berleant (1992), *The Aesthetics of the Environment* (Philadelphia, PA: Temple University Press).

29 Ibid., 28.

30 Allen Carlson (2000), *Aesthetics and the Environment: The Appreciation of Nature, Art and Architecture* (London: Routledge), 133.

31 Ibid. (2001), 'On Aesthetically Appreciating Human Environments', *Philosophy and Geography* 4 (1).

32 Ibid. (2009), *Nature & Landscape: An Introduction to Environmental Aesthetics* (New York: Columbia University Press), 60.

33 Malcolm Andrews (2007), 'The View from the Road and the Picturesque', in *The Aesthetics of Human Environments*, ed. Arnold Berleant and Allen Carlson (Peterborough, ON: Broadview Press), 284.

34 Pauline von Bonsdorff (2005), 'Agriculture, Aesthetic Appreciation and the Worlds of Nature', *Contemporary Aesthetics* 3.

35 http://www.guardian.co.uk/news/datablog/2009/aug/18/percentage-population-living-cities (accessed 17 March 2016).

36 Carlson (2001), 'On Aesthetically Appreciating', 15.

37 Arnold Berleant (1986), 'Cultivating an Urban Aesthetic', *Diogenes* 34 (136).

38 Pauline von Bonsdorff (2000), 'Urban Richness and the Art of Building', *Yhteiskuntasuunnittelu* 38 (3).

39 Arnold Berleant (1997), *Living in the Landscape: Toward an Aesthetics of Environment* (Lawrence, KS: University Press of Kansas), 16.

40 Tom Leddy (1995), 'Everyday Surface Aesthetic Qualities: "Neat," "Messy," "Clean," "Dirty"', *Journal of Aesthetics and Art Criticism* 53 (3).

41 Saito (2007), *Everyday Aesthetics*, 155.

42 Kevin Melchionne (1998), 'Living in Glass Houses: Domesticity, Interior Decoration, and Environmental Aesthetics', *Journal of Aesthetics and Art Criticism* 56 (2).

43 Saito (2007), *Everyday Aesthetics*, 181.

44 Leddy (2005), 'Everyday Surface Aesthetic Qualities', 7.

45 See Immanuel Kant (1798/2006), *Anthropology from a Pragmatic Point of View*, trans. Robert B. Louden (Cambridge: Cambridge University Press).

46 Emily Brady (2005), 'Sniffing and Savoring: The Aesthetics of Smells and Tastes', in *The Aesthetics of Everyday Life*, ed. A. Light and J. M. Smith (New York: Columbia University Press), 183.

47 Linda M. Bartoshuk and Gary K. Beauchamp (1994), 'Chemical Senses', *Annual Review of Psychology* 45: 419–49.

48 Rachel S. Herz and Trygg Engen (1996), 'Odor Memory: Review and Analysis', *Psychonomic Bulletin & Review* 3 (3): 300.

49 Sherri Irvin (2008), 'Scratching an Itch', *Journal of Aesthetics and Art Criticism* 66 (1).

50 Ibid., 30.

51 Ibid., 31.

Bibliography

Adams, Laurie Schneider (2002), *Art Across Time, Second Edition. Volume II: The Fourteenth Century to the Present*. New York: McGraw-Hill.

Allston, Washington (1850/1998), 'Art', in *Art in Theory: 1815–1900*, ed. C. Harrison, P. Wood and J. Gaiger. Oxford: Blackwell, 93–6.

Anderson, James C. and Jeffrey T. Dean (1998), 'Moderate Autonomism'. *British Journal of Aesthetics* 38 (2): 150–66.

Andrews, Malcolm (2007), 'The View from the Road and the Picturesque', in *The Aesthetics of Human Environments*, ed. Arnold Berleant and Allen Carlson. Peterborough, ON: Broadview Press, 272–98.

Aquinas, St Thomas (c. 1274/1921), *Summa Theologica*, trans. Fathers of the English Dominican Province. London: Burns Oates & Washbourne Ltd.

Aristotle (c. 350 BCE /1987), 'Eudemian Ethics', trans. M. J. Woods, in *A New Aristotle Reader*, ed. J. L. Ackrill. Princeton, NJ: Princeton University Press, 479–539.

Aristotle (350 BCE/1989), 'Poetics', in *On Poetry and Style*, trans. G. M. A. Grube. Indianapolis, IN: Hackett.

Augustine, St (398/1876), *Confessions*, trans. J. G. Pilkington. Edinburgh: T.&T. Clark.

Augustine, St (c. 426/1888), *City of God*, trans. Marcus Dods. Edinburgh: T.&T. Clark.

Barthes, Roland (1967/77), 'The Death of the Author', in *Image, Music, Text*, ed. and trans. Stephen Heath. New York: Noonday, 142–8.

Barthes, Roland (1977), 'From Work to Text', in *Image, Music, Text*, ed. and trans. Stephen Heath. New York: Noonday, 155–64.

Barwell, Ismay (1986), 'How Does Art Express Emotion'. *Journal of Aesthetics and Art Criticism* 45 (2): 175–81.

Battersby, Christine (1989), *Gender and Genius: Towards a Feminist Aesthetics*. Bloomington, IN: The Women's Press.

Batteux, Charles (1746), *Les Beaux-Arts réduits à un même principe*. Paris: Durand.

Beardsley, M. C. (1958), *Aesthetics: Problems in the Philosophy of Criticism*. Indianapolis, IN: Hackett.

Beardsley, M. C. (1963), 'The Discrimination of Aesthetic Enjoyment'. *British Journal of Aesthetics* 3 (4): 291–300.

Beardsley, M. C. (1969), 'Aesthetic Experience Regained'. *Journal of Aesthetics and Art Criticism* 28 (1): 3–11.

Beardsley, M. C. (1970), 'The Aesthetic Point of View'. *Metaphilosophy* 1 (1): 39–58.

Beardsley, M. C. (1983), 'An Aesthetic Definition of Art', in *What is Art?*, ed. H. Curtler. New York: Haven Publications, 15–29.

Beardsley, Monroe C. (1982), 'Intentions and Interpretations: A Fallacy Revived', in *The Aesthetic Point of View: Selected Essays*, ed. M. J. Wreen and D. M. Callen. Ithaca, NY: Cornell University Press, 188–207.

Beaumont, Harry (1752/1885), *Crito: or a Dialogue on Beauty*. Edinburgh: Edmund Goldsmid.

Bell, Clive (1913/2006), *Art*. Rockville, MD: IndyPublish.

Bellori, Giovan Pietro (1672/2005), *The Lives of the Modern Painters, Sculptors and Architects*, trans. Alice Sedgwick Wohl, ed. Alice Sedgwick Wohl et al. Cambridge: Cambridge University Press.

Berleant, Arnold (1986), 'Cultivating an Urban Aesthetic'. *Diogenes* 34 (136): 1–18.

Berleant, Arnold (1992), *The Aesthetics of the Environment*. Philadelphia, PA: Temple University Press.

Berleant, Arnold (1997), *Living in the Landscape: Toward an Aesthetics of Environment*. Lawrence: University Press of Kansas.

Berry, Sarah (2004), 'Hollywood Exoticism: Cosmetics and Color in the 1930s', in *Stars: The Film Reader*, ed. L. Fischer and M. Landy. London: Routledge, 181–97.

Bicknell, Jeanette (2009), 'Reflections on "John Henry": Ethical Issues in Singing Performance'. *Journal of Aesthetics and Art Criticism* 67 (2): 173–80.

Bonaventure, St (1259/1956), *The Journey of the Mind to God*, trans. Philotheus Boehner. Indianapolis, IN: Hackett.

Borges, Jorge Luis (1939/62), 'Pierre Menard, Author of Don Quixote', in *Ficciones*, trans. Anthony Bonner. New York: Grove Press, 45–55.

Brady, Emily (1998), 'Imagination and the Aesthetic Appreciation of Nature'. *Journal of Aesthetics and Art Criticism* 56 (2): 139–47.

Brady, Emily (2005), 'Sniffing and Savoring: The Aesthetics of Smells and Tastes', in *The Aesthetics of Everyday Life*, ed. A. Light and J. M. Smith. New York: Columbia University Press, 177–93.

Brand, Peggy Zeglin (1998), 'Disinterestedness and Political Art', in *Aesthetics: The Big Questions*, ed. C. Korsmeyer. Oxford: Blackwell, 155–70.

Budd, Malcolm (1995), *Values of Art: Pictures, Poetry, and Music*. London: Penguin.

Burke, Edmund (1757/1887), *A Philosophical Inquiry into the Origin of Our Ideas of the Sublime and Beautiful*, in *The Works of the Right Honourable Edmund Burke*, Vol. 1. London: John C. Nimmo, 67–263.

Carlson, Allen (1979), 'Appreciation and the Natural Environment'. *Journal of Aesthetics and Art Criticism* 37 (3): 267–75.

Carlson, Allen (2000), *Aesthetics and the Environment: The Appreciation of Nature, Art and Architecture*. London: Routledge.

Carlson, Allen (2001), 'On Aesthetically Appreciating Human Environments'. *Philosophy and Geography* 4 (1): 9–24.

Carlson, Allen (2009), *Nature & Landscape: An Introduction to Environmental Aesthetics*. New York: Columbia University Press.

Carroll, Nöel (1987), 'Can Government Funding of the Arts be Justified Theoretically?' *Journal of Aesthetic Education* 21 (1): 21–35.

Carroll, Noël (1992), 'Art, Intention, and Conversation', in *Intention and Interpretation*, ed. Gary Iseminger. Philadelphia, PA: Temple University Press, 97–131

Carroll, Nöel (1993a), 'Moderate Moralism'. *British Journal of Aesthetics* 36 (3): 223–38.

Carroll, Noël (1993b), 'On Being Moved by Nature: Between Religion and Natural History', in *Landscape, Natural Beauty and the Arts*, ed. S. Kemal and I. Gaskell. Cambridge: Cambridge University Press, 244–66.

Carroll, Noël (1999), *Philosophy of Art: A Contemporary Introduction*. London: Routledge.

Carroll, Noël (2000a), *Theories of Art Today*. Madison, WI: University of Wisconsin Press.

Carroll, Noël (2000b), 'Interpretation and Intention: The Debate Between Hypothetical and Actual Intentionalism'. *Metaphilosophy* 31 (1–2): 75–95.

Cassidy, Claudia (1974), 'On The Aisle: The Devil you say'. *Chicago Tribune*, 7 April, h16.

Cicero, Marcus Tullius (45 BC/1883), *De natura deorum, Vol. II*. Cambridge: Cambridge University Press.

Cody, Gabrielle and Lee Breuer (1989), 'Lee Breuer on Interculturalism'. *Performing Arts Journal* 11 (3)/12 (1): 59–66.

Collingwood, R. G. (1938/74), *The Principles of Art*. Oxford: Oxford University Press.

Croce, Benedetto (1909/22), *Aesthetic: As Science of Expression and General Linguistic*, trans. Douglas Ainslie. New York: Noonday.

Currie, Gregory (1989), *An Ontology of Art*. New York: St. Martin's Press.

Currie, Gregory (1991), 'Work and Text'. *Mind* 100 (3): 325–40.

Danto, Arthur (1964), 'The Artworld'. *Journal of Philosophy* 61 (19): 571–84.

Danto, Arthur (1981), *The Transfiguration of the Commonplace: A Philosophy of Art*. Cambridge, MA: Harvard University Press.

Davies, David (2004), *Art as Performance*. Oxford: Blackwell.

Davies, David (2007), *Aesthetics and Literature*. London: Continuum.

Davies, David (2009), 'The Primacy of Practice in the Ontology of Art'. *Journal of Aesthetics and Art Criticism* 67 (2): 159–71.

Davies, Stephen (1991), *Definitions of Art*. Ithaca, NY: Cornell University Press.

Davies, Stephen (2001), *Musical Works and Performances: A Philosophical Exploration*. Oxford: Oxford University Press.

Delacroix, Eugène (1824/1998), 'On Romanticism' (journal entries, 1822–1824), in *Art in Theory: 1815–1900*, ed. C. Harrison, P. Wood and J. Gaiger. Oxford: Blackwell, 26–30.

Devereaux, Mary (1993), 'Protected Space: Politics, Censorship, and the Arts'. *Journal of Aesthetics and Art Criticism* 51 (2): 207–15.

Dickie, George (1974), *Art and Aesthetic*. Ithaca, NY: Cornell University Press.

Dickie, George (1984/97), *The Art Circle: A Theory of Art*. Evanston, IL: Chicago Spectrum Press.

Dodd, Julian (2000), 'Musical Works as Eternal Types'. *British Journal of Aesthetics* 40 (4): 424–40.

Dodd, Julian (2007), *Works of Music: An Essay in Ontology*. Oxford: Oxford University Press.

Du Bois, W. E. B. (1926), 'Criteria for Negro Art'. *The Crisis* 32: 290–7.

Eaton, A. W. (2008), 'Feminist Philosophy of Art'. *Philosophy Compass* 3 (5): 873–93.

Eaton, A. W. (2016), 'Taste in Bodies and Fat Oppression', in *Body Aesthetics*, ed. S. Irvin. Oxford: Oxford University Press, 37–59.

Eaton, Marcia M. (1982), 'A Strange Kind of Sadness'. *Journal of Aesthetics and Art Criticism* 41 (1): 51–63.

Eliot, T. S. (1919/1982), 'Tradition and the Individual Talent'. *Perspecta* 19: 36–42.

Ellison, Ralph (1952), *Invisible Man*. New York: Random House.

Export, Valie (1973/2003), 'Woman's Art', in *Art in Theory: 1900–2000*, trans. N. Walker, ed. C. Harrison and P. Wood. Oxford: Blackwell, 927–9.

Feagin, Susan (1983), 'The Pleasures of Tragedy'. *American Philosophical Quarterly* 20 (1): 95–104.

Feinberg, J. (1994), 'Not With My Tax Money: The Problem of Justifying Government Subsidies for the Arts'. *Public Affairs Quarterly* 8 (2): 101–23.

Fish, Stanley (1980), *Is There a Text in This Class? The Authority of Interpretive Communities*. Cambridge, MA: Harvard University Press.

Foucault, Michel (1969/77), 'What is an Author?', in *Language, Counter-Memory, Practice*, trans. Donald F. Bouchard and Sherry Simon, ed. Donald F. Bouchard. Ithaca, NY: Cornell University Press, 124–7.

Frueh, Joanna (1988), 'Towards a Feminist Theory of Art Criticism', in *Feminist Art Criticism: An Anthology*, ed. A. Raven, C. L. Langer and J. Frueh. Ann Arbor, MI: UMI Research Press, 153–65.

Gammel, Irene (2002), *Baroness Elsa: Gender, Dada, and Everyday Modernity*. Cambridge, MA: MIT Press.

Gaut, Berys (1993), 'Interpreting the Arts: The Patchwork Theory'. *Journal of Aesthetics and Art Criticism* 51 (4): 597–609

Gaut, Berys (1998), 'The Ethical Criticism of Art', in *Aesthetics and Ethics: Essays at the Intersection*, ed. Jerrold Levinson. Cambridge: Cambridge University Press, 182–203.

Gautier, Théophile (1848/1998), 'Art in 1848', in *Art in Theory: 1815–1900*, trans. Jonathan Murphy, ed. C. Harrison et al. Oxford: Blackwell, 315–20.

Gilbert, Elizabeth (2003), 'Play It Like Your Hair's on Fire', in *Da Capo Best Music Writing*, ed. Matt Groening. New York: Da Capo, 89–106.

Gleason, Ralph J. (1968), 'Can the White Man Sing the Blues?' *Jazz and Pop* 7 (8): 28–9.

Goodman, Nelson (1976), *Languages of Art: An Approach to a Theory of Symbols*, 2nd edn. Indianapolis, IN: Hackett.

Haddaway, Husain (1990), *The Arabian Nights*. London: Norton.

Hanfling, Oswald (1995), 'Art, Artifact and Function'. *Philosophical Investigations* 18 (1): 31–48.

Harari, Josuë V. (ed.) (1979), *Textual Strategies: Perspectives in Post-Structuralist Criticism*. Ithaca, NY: Cornell University Press.

Hegel, G. W. F. (1886/1994), *Introductory Lectures on Aesthetics*, trans. Bernard Bosanquet. New York: Penguin.

Hepburn, R. W. (1966), 'Contemporary Aesthetics and the Neglect of Natural Beauty', in *British Analytical Philosophy*, ed. Bernard Williams and Alan Montefiore. New York: Humanities Press, 285–310.

Higgs, John (2015), *Stranger That We Can Imagine: An Alternative History of the 20th Century*. London: Weidenfeld & Nicolson.

Hirsch, E. D., Jr (1967), *Validity in Interpretation*. New Haven, CT: Yale University Press.

Huddleston, Andrew (2012), 'In Defense of Artistic Value'. *Philosophical Quarterly* 62 (249): 705–14.

Huey, Steve (2003), 'Paul Butterfield', in *All Music Guide to the Blues: The Definitive Guide*, 3rd edn, ed. V. Bogdanov, C. Wodstra and S. T. Erlewine. San Francisco, CA: Backbeat Books, 91–2.

Hume, David (1748/1875), 'Of National Characters', in *Essays: Moral, Political, and Literary*, Vol. 1. London: Longmans, Green, and Co., 244–58.

Hume, David (1757/1987a), 'Of the Standard of Taste', in *Essays, Moral, Political, and Literary*, ed. Eugene F. Miller. Indianapolis, IN: Liberty Fund Books, 226–49.

Hume, David (1757/1987b), 'Of Tragedy', in *Essays: Moral, Political, and Literary*, ed. Eugene F. Miller. Indianapolis, IN: Liberty Fund Books, 216–25.

Hume, David (1742/1987c), 'Of the Delicacy of Taste and Passion', in *Essays,*

Moral, Political, and Literary, ed. Eugene F. Miller. Indianapolis, IN: Liberty Fund Books, 3–8.

Hutcheson, Francis (1725/2008), *An Inquiry into the Original of Our Ideas of Beauty and Virtue*, ed. Wolfgang Leidhold. Indianapolis, IN: Liberty Fund Books.

Ingarden, Roman (1979), *The Literary Work of Art: An Investigation on the Borderlines of Ontology*. Evanston, IL: Northwestern University Press.

Ingarden, Roman (1989), *Ontology of the Work of Art: The Musical Work, the Picture, the Architectural Work, the Film*. Athens, OH: Ohio University Press.

Irvin, Sherri (2006), 'Authors, Intentions and Literary Meaning'. *Philosophy Compass* 1/2: 114–28.

Irvin, Sherri (2008a), 'Scratching an Itch'. *Journal of Aesthetics and Art Criticism* 66 (1): 25–35.

Irvin, Sherri (2008b), 'The Ontological Diversity of Visual Artworks', in *New Waves in Aesthetics*, ed. K Stock and K. Thomson-Jones. New York: Palgrave Macmillan, 1–19.

Irvin, Sherri (ed.) (2016), *Body Aesthetics*. Oxford: Oxford University Press.

Iseminger, Gary (1992), *Intention and Interpretation*. Philadelphia, PA: Temple University Press.

Janko, Richard (1987), 'Introduction', in *Poetics* by Aristotle. Indianapolis, IN: Hackett, ix–xxvi.

Janson, H. W. (1969), *History of Art: A Survey of the Major Visual Arts from the Dawn of History to the Present Day*. New York: Harry N. Abrams, Inc.

Jones, LeRoi (1963), *Blues People: Negro Music in White America*. New York: William Morrow and Co.

Kant, Immanuel (1764/1960), *Observations on the Feeling of the Beautiful and Sublime*, trans. John T. Goldthwait. Berkeley, CA: University of California Press.

Kant, Immanuel (1790/1987), *The Critique of Judgment*, trans. Werner S. Pluhar. Indianapolis: Hackett.

Kant, Immanuel (1798/2006), *Anthropology from a Pragmatic Point of View*, trans. Robert B. Louden. Cambridge: Cambridge University Press.

Kermode, Mark (1998), *The Fear of God: 25 Years of 'The Exorcist'*. BBC documentary.

Kermode, Mark (2003), *The Exorcist*, rev. 2nd edn. London: British Film Institute.

Kivy, Peter (1983), 'Platonism in Music: A Kind of Defense'. *Grazer Philosophische Studien* 19: 109–29.

Kivy, Peter (1984), *Sound and Semblance*. Princeton, NJ: Princeton University Press.

Kivy, Peter (1987), 'Platonism in Music: Another Kind of Defense'. *Philosophical Quarterly* 24 (3): 245–52.

Kivy, Peter (1989), *Sound Sentiment*. Philadelphia, PA: Temple University Press.

Kleingeld, Pauline (2007), 'Kant's Second Thoughts on Race'. *Philosophical Quarterly* 57 (229): 573–92.

Korsmeyer, Carolyn (1999), *Making Sense of Taste: Food and Philosophy*. Ithaca, NY: Cornell University Press.

Krausz, Michael (1993), *Rightness and Reasons: Interpretation in Cultural Practices*. Ithaca, NY: Cornell University Press.

Leddy, Tom (1995), 'Everyday Surface Aesthetic Qualities: "Neat," "Messy," "Clean," "Dirty"'. *Journal of Aesthetics and Art Criticism* 53 (3): 259–68.

Leddy, Tom (2005), 'The Nature of Everyday Aesthetics', in *The Aesthetics of Everyday Life*, ed. A. Light and J. M. Smith. New York: Columbia University Press, 3–22.

Levinson, Jerrold (1979), 'Defining Art Historically'. *British Journal of Aesthetics* 19 (3): 232–50.

Levinson, Jerrold (1980a), 'Autographic and Allographic Art Revisited'. *Philosophical Studies* 38 (4): 367–83.

Levinson, Jerrold (1980b), 'What a Musical Work Is'. *Journal of Philosophy* 77 (1): 5–28.

Levinson, Jerrold (1990), *Music, Art, and Metaphysics*. Ithaca, NY: Cornell University Press.

Levinson, Jerrold (1992), 'Intention and Interpretation: A Last Look', in *Intention and Interpretation*, ed. Gary Iseminger. Philadelphia, PA: Temple University Press, 221–56.

Levinson, Jerrold (1996), 'Intention and Interpretation in Literature', in *The Pleasures of Aesthetics: Philosophical Essays*. Ithaca, NY: Cornell University Press, 175–-213.

Lind, Richard (1992), 'The Aesthetic Essence of Art'. *Journal of Aesthetics and Art Criticism* 50 (2): 117–29.

Lintott, Sheila (2006), 'Toward Eco-Friendly Aesthetics'. *Environmental Ethics* 28 (1): 57–76.

Margolis, Joseph (1977), 'The Ontological Peculiarity of Works of Art'. *Journal of Aesthetics and Art Criticism* 36 (1): 45–50.

Margolis, Joseph (1999), *What, After All, Is a Work of Art?* University Park, PA: Pennsylvania State University Press.

Matisse, Henri (1931/2003), 'Notes of a Painter', in *Art in Theory: 1900–2000*, ed. C. Harrison and P. Wood. Oxford: Blackwell, 69–75.

Matravers, Derek (1998), *Art and Emotion*. Oxford: Oxford University Press.

Melchionne, Kevin (1998), 'Living in Glass Houses: Domesticity, Interior

Decoration, and Environmental Aesthetics'. *Journal of Aesthetics and Art Criticism* 56 (2): 191–200.

Meskin, Aaron (2008), 'From Defining Art to Defining the Individual Arts: The Role of Theory in the Philosophies of Arts', in *New Waves in Aesthetics*, ed. K Stock and K. Thomson-Jones. New York: Palgrave Macmillan, 125–49.

Mills, C. W. (2005), 'Kant's *Untermenschen*', in *Race and Racism Philosophy*, ed. A. Valls. Ithaca, NY: Cornell University Press, 169–93.

Morreall, John (1985), 'Enjoying Negative Emotions in Fiction'. *Philosophy and Literature* 9 (1): 95–103.

Muir, John (1894/1911), 'A Near View of the High Sierra', in *The Mountains of California*. New York: Century Co., 48–73.

Mulvey, Laura (1975), 'Visual Pleasure and Narrative Cinema'. *Screen* 16 (3): 6–18.

Nathan, Daniel (1982), 'Irony and the Author's Intentions'. *British Journal of Aesthetics* 22 (3): 246–56.

Nathan, Daniel (1992), 'Irony, Metaphor, and the Problem of Intention', in *Intention and Interpretation*, ed. Gary Iseminger. Philadelphia, PA: Temple University Press, 183–202.

Nehamas, Alexander (1981), 'The Postulated Author: Critical Monism as a Regulative Ideal'. *Critical Inquiry* 8 (1): 133–49.

Nehamas, Alexander (1986), 'What an Author Is'. *Journal of Philosophy* 83 (11): 685–91.

Nietzsche, Friedrich (1872/1999), *The Birth of Tragedy*, in *The Birth of Tragedy and Other Writings*, trans. Ronald Spiers, ed. Raymond Geuss and Ronald Spiers. Cambridge: Cambridge University Press, 1–116.

Nochlin, Linda (1971), 'Why Have There Been No Great Women Artists?' *ARTnews*, January, 23–39.

Nornes, Abé Mark (2007), *Cinema Babel: Translating Global Cinema*. Minneapolis, MN: University of Minnesota Press.

Novitz, David (1980), 'Fiction, Imagination and Emotion'. *Journal of Aesthetics and Art Criticism* 38 (3): 279–88.

Page, Clarence (1974), '2 being restrained: 6 who saw "Exorcist" under care'. *Chicago Tribune*, 18 January, 1.

Pater, Walter (1873), *Studies in the History of the Renaissance*. London: Macmillan and Co.

Peirce, C. S. (1906), 'Prolegomena to an Apology for Pragmaticism'. *The Monist* 16: 492–546.

Pettit, Philip (1983), 'The Possibility of Aesthetic Realism', in *Pleasure, Preference, and Value: Studies in Philosophical Aesthetics*, ed. E. Schaper. Cambridge: Cambridge University Press, 17–38.

Plato (c. 360 BCE/1963), *Laws*, in *The Collected Dialogues of Plato*

Including the Letters, trans. A. E. Taylor, ed. Edith Hamilton and Huntington Cairns. Princeton, NJ: Princeton University Press, 1225–513.

Plato (c. 360/1963), *Republic*, in *The Collected Dialogues of Plato Including the Letters*, trans. Paul Shorey, ed. Edith Hamilton and Huntington Cairns. Princeton, NJ: Princeton University Press, 575–844.

Plato (c. 380 BCE/1963), *Ion*, in *The Collected Dialogues of Plato Including the Letters*, trans. Lane Cooper, ed. Edith Hamilton and Huntington Cairns. Princeton, NJ: Princeton University Press, 215–28.

Plato (c. 390 BCE/1963), *Greater Hippias*, in *The Collected Dialogues of Plato Including the Letters*, trans. Benjamin Jowett, ed. Edith Hamilton and Huntington Cairns. Princeton, NJ: Princeton University Press, 1534–59.

Radford, Colin (1975), 'How Can We Be Moved by the Fate of Anna Karenina?' *Proceedings of the Aristotelian Society* 49 (Supplement): 67–80.

Roelofs, Monique (2014), *The Cultural Promise of the Aesthetic*. London: Bloomsbury.

Rudinow, Joel (1994), 'Race, Ethnicity, Expressive Authenticity: Can White People Sing the Blues?' *Journal of Aesthetics and Art Criticism* 52 (1): 127–37.

Rudinow, Joel (1995), 'Reply to Taylor', *Journal of Aesthetics and Art Criticism* 53 (3): 316–18.

Saito, Yuriko (1998a), 'Appreciating Nature on Its Own Terms'. *Environmental Ethics* 20 (2): 135–49.

Saito, Yuriko (1998b), 'The Aesthetics of Unscenic Nature'. *Journal of Aesthetics and Art Criticism* 56 (2): 101–11.

Saito, Yuriko (2007), *Everyday Aesthetics*. Oxford: Oxford University Press.

Schaper, Eva (1978), 'Fiction and the Suspension of Disbelief'. *British Journal of Aesthetics* 18 (1): 31–44.

Schier, Flint (1983), 'Tragedy and the Community of Sentiment', in *Philosophy and Fiction: Essays in Literary Aesthetics*, ed. Peter Lamarque. Aberdeen: Aberdeen University Press, 73–92.

Schlesinger, George (1979), 'Aesthetic Experience and the Definition of Art'. *British Journal of Aesthetics* 19 (2): 167–76.

Schutte, Ofelia (2000), 'Negotiating Latina Identities', in *Hispanics/Latinos in the United States: Ethnicity, Race, and Rights*, ed. J. J. E. Gracia and P. De Greiff. New York: Routledge, 61–75.

Scruton, Roger (1974), *Art and Imagination: A Study in the Philosophy of Mind*. London: Methuen.

Serra, Richard (1991), 'Art and Censorship'. *Critical Inquiry* 17 (3): 574–81.

Shaftesbury, 3rd Earl of (Anthony Ashley Cooper) (1711/1999), *Characteristics of Men, Manners, Opinions, Times*, ed. Lawrence E. Klein. Cambridge: Cambridge University Press.

Shusterman, Richard (1984), 'Aesthetic Censorship: Censoring Art for Art's Sake'. *Journal of Aesthetis and Art Criticism* 43 (2): 171–80.

Sibley, Frank (1959), 'Aesthetic Concepts'. *Philosophical Review* 68 (4): 421–50.

Sibley, Frank (1974), 'Particularity, Art and Evaluation'. *Proceedings of the Aristotelian Society* 48 (Supplement): 1–21.

Siebers, Tobin (2010), *Disability Aesthetics*. Ann Arbor, MI: University of Michigan Press.

Siebers, Tobin (2016), 'In/Visible: Disability on the Stage', in *Body Aesthetics*, ed. S. Irvin. Oxford: Oxford University Press, 141–52.

Silvers, Anita (2000), 'From the Crooked Timber of Humanity, Beautiful Things Can Be Made', in *Beauty Matters*, ed. P. Z. Brand. Bloomington, IN: Indiana University Press, 197–221.

Sircello, Guy (1972), *Mind & Art: An Essay on the Varieties of Expression*. Princeton, NJ: Princeton University Press.

Siskel, Gene (1974), 'Crowds upset neighborhood: "Exorcist" also is disturbing outside theater'. *Chicago Tribune*, 10 February, 10.

Smith, S., M. Choueiti and K. Pieper (2016), *Inclusion or Invisibility? Comprehensive Annenberg Report on Diversity in Entertainment*. Los Angeles, CA: USC Annenberg School for Communication & Journalism.

Stecker, Robert (1984), 'Expression of Emotion in (Some of) the Arts'. *Journal of Aesthetics and Art Criticism* 42 (4): 409–18.

Stecker, Robert (1993), 'Art Interpretation'. *Journal of Aesthetics and Art Criticism* 52 (2): 193–206.

Stecker, Robert (1997a), 'The Constructivist's Dilemma'. *Journal of Aesthetics and Art Criticism* 55 (1): 43–52.

Stecker, Robert (1997b), 'The Correct and the Appropriate in the Appreciation of Nature'. *British Journal of Aesthetics* 37 (4): 393–402.

Stecker, Robert (1997c), *Artworks: Definition, Meaning, Value*. University Park, PA: Pennsylvania State University Press.

Stecker, Robert (2003), *Interpretation and Construction*. Oxford: Blackwell.

Stecker, Robert (2010), *Aesthetics and the Philosophy of Art: An Introduction*, 2nd edn. New York: Rowman & Littlefield.

Tasso, Torquato (1587/1993), 'Discorsi dell'arte poetica', in *The Genesis of Tasso's Narrative Theory: English Translations of the Early Poetics and a Comparative Study of their Significance*, ed. and trans. Lawrence F. Rhu. Detroit, MI: Wayne State University Press, 99–153.

Tatarkiewicz, Władysław (2005), *History of Aesthetics in Three Volumes*, Vol. 3. London: Continuum.

Taylor, Paul C. (1995), '… So Black and Blue: Response to Rudinow'. *Journal of Aesthetics and Art Criticism* 53 (3): 313–16.

Taylor, Paul C. (2016), *Black is Beautiful: A Philosophy of Black Aesthetics*. Oxford: Blackwell.

Thomasson, Amie L. (2004), 'The Ontology of Art', in *The Blackwell Guide to Aesthetics*, ed. P. Kivy. Oxford: Blackwell, 78–92.

Thomasson, Amie L. (2005), 'The Ontology of Art and Knowledge in Aesthetics'. *Journal of Aesthetics and Art Criticism* 63 (2): 221–9.

Tolhurst, William (1979), 'On What a Text Is and How It Means'. *British Journal of Aesthetics* 19 (1): 3–14.

Tolstoy, Leo (1896/99), *What Is Art?*, trans. Aylmer Maude. New York: Thomas Y. Crowell & Co.

Tompkins, Jane P. (1980), *Reader-Response Criticism: From Formalism to Post-Structuralism*. Baltimore, MD: Johns Hopkins University Press.

Tormey, Alan (1971), *The Concept of Expression: A Study in Philosophical Psychology and Aesthetics*. Princeton, NJ: Princeton University Press.

von Bonsdorff, Pauline (2000), 'Urban Richness and the Art of Building'. *Yhteiskuntasuunnittelu* 38 (3): 28–40.

von Bonsdorff, Pauline (2005), 'Agriculture, Aesthetic Appreciation and the Worlds of Nature'. *Contemporary Aesthetics* 3. Available online: http://www.contempaesthetics.org/newvolume/pages/article.php?articleID=325 (accessed 17 March 2016).

Walton, K. L. (1970), 'Categories of Art'. *Philosophical Review* 79 (3): 334–67.

Walton, K. L. (1978), 'Fearing Fictions'. *Journal of Philosophy* 75 (1): 5–27.

Walton, Kendall (1990), *Mimesis as Make-Believe: On the Foundations of the Representational Arts*. Cambridge, MA: Harvard University Press.

Weitz, M. (1956), 'The Role of Theory in Aesthetics'. *Journal of Aesthetics and Art Criticism* 15 (1): 27–35.

Wimsatt, W. K., Jr and Monroe C. Beardsley (1954), 'The Intentional Fallacy', in *The Verbal Icon: Studies in the Meaning of Poetry*, ed. W. K. Wimsatt, Jr. Lexington, KY: University of Kentucky Press, 3–18.

Wollheim, Richard (1968/71), *Art and Its Objects*. New York: Harper & Row.

Wolterstorff, Nicholas (1980), *Works and Worlds of Art*. Oxford: Clarendon Press.

Woolf, Virginia (1929), *A Room of One's Own*. New York: Harcourt, Brace and Co.

Xiao, Zhiwei (2002), 'Nationalism, Orientalism, and an Unequal Treatise of Ethnography: The Making of *The Good Earth*', in *The Chinese in America: A History from Gold Mountain to the New Millennium*, ed. S. Cassel. Walnut Creek, CA: Altamira, 274–90.

Yancy, George (2008), *Black Bodies, White Gazes: The Continuing Significance of Race*. New York: Rowman & Littlefield.

Young, James O. (2008), *Cultural Appropriation and the Arts*. Malden, MA: Blackwell.

Ziff, Paul (1953), 'The Task of Defining a Work of Art'. *Philosophical Review* 62 (1): 58–78.

Index